"Cheyenne, Cheyenne, . . ."

Our Blue-Collar Heritage

PHOTO COURTESY OF WYOMING STATE ARCHIVES, MUSEUMS AND HISTORICAL DEPARTMENT

A freight train on the new Union Pacific tracks after the turn of the century.

"Cheyenne, Cheyenne, . . ."

Our Blue-Collar Heritage

by

Gladys Powelson Jones

Published by
Gladys Powelson Jones
Cheyenne, Wyoming

Library of Congress
Catalog Card Number
83-82304

ISBN 0-9612628-0-X

Manufactured by
Frontier Printing, Inc.
— Cheyenne —

CONTENTS

LIST OF ILLUSTRATIONS

PREFACE

Working people were on the scene waiting for the engineers to make up their minds where to stake out "Crow Creek Crossing." Rumor had it that the new division point of the railroad would be "where the railroad crossed the creek." It would be a winter camp, at least, and they were ready to go to work.

They came from Julesburg, via Denver, thence north. They came west along the tracks, to the railhead, following the line of engineers' stakes to the site; and waited. The trail marked by their wagons was the forerunner of the Lincoln Highway, later to be known as US 30; now I-80. William Kuykendall claimed to have "marked the first trail north from LaPorte." He brought logs and cattle to the townsite.

"On the 19th of July, 1867, the engineers commenced staking off the town site for the city, and completed the survey on the 21st," according to E. H. Sawtiel and George Burnett, editors of the first *Cheyenne Directory*, who were also waiting, ready to go to press. "Many tents were now up giving the place the appearance of a fairground. Mr. R. E. Talpey arrived and opened an office for the sale of lots . . . A small western house (log house?) was erected by one of our oldest frontiersmen, named Wm. Lorimer, on the south side of Crow Creek. This was the first wooden house within the city limits."

The townsite was named Cheyenne by General Grenville M. Dodge. Major General C. C. Augur established Fort D. A. Russell and its supply station, Cheyenne Depot, began to serve the western troops and Indian Reservations. There was work to be done.

Colonel Elias P. Carling, popular commandant of the station, made it a habit to ride among the travelers camped for the night on this new shortcut to Oregon. He inquired as to their destinations, the health of their families and their skills. He was recruiting skilled men for the operation of the depot. In addition to teamsters, wheelwrights, harnessmakers and blacksmiths, he needed carpenters, woodsmen, butchers, cooks, clerks and laborers.

History remembers the depot as "Camp Carlin'," and descendants of the original workers proudly cite their Carlin' connection, as many of them stayed to make their homes in Cheyenne.

There were tales of another boss handed down by old timers. He dressed like a Cossack with high boots, a fur trimmed hat and coat; a style acquired while building the Czar's railroad. His crews laid as much as a mile of track a day in eastern Wyoming.

"Jack Casement, he carried a whip," they said. "And he didn't hesitate to lay it on the backs of Irishmen. It's a good job they got him out of town in time. There was going to be a mutiny." General Jack Casement, track contractor, was "elected" to represent the Territory in Washington. He could not be seated but stayed to represent the railroad as a lobbyist.

Unions were informal and independent, as were the Packers and Teamsters who met in the Arcade Saloon Club Rooms, 1623 Pioneer, according to William J. McInerney. These men moved freight from the railroad line to the reservations and upstate towns, as well as to the gold camps, until the railroads displaced them.

The Packers and Teamsters were actually a loose confederation, but due to their unity of purpose and importance to the economy, they could and did name the conditions of their service and pay. No wheel turned unless the wagons were outfitted with barrels of fresh water and food for man and beast, a wheelwright, repairs and supplies.

Capital and labor, although interdependent, were more often at odds, than not, during the first fifty-five years of Cheyenne's history. This attitude was reflected in the anti-labor, anti-union stance of the press, although its own house was not free from strife. In October 1883, "the Typographical Union called the *SUN* office a 'rat office,' professing a maudlin love for the working man;" *Cheyenne Weekly Leader.*

The skilled use of tools and fine hand-craftsmanship earned a living for the pioneer and sustained his family. "I'm a boilermaker, by trade," he says today, "or a catskinner, or an electrician." He identifies himself with his work as an extension of his personality. His clothes were made to stand the stress of the job. He wears them with pride.

In the lives of the blue-collar people we glimpse the heritage of mind and skill, of muscle and sweat; the pride of Cheyenne's unsung builders; and we remember our roots.

To them, we humbly dedicate this book;

Sing of wheel and chisel
Of hammer and tong,
Of life that is short
And art that is long.

ACKNOWLEDGEMENT

"Cheyenne, Cheyenne, . . .", Our Blue-Collar Heritage, could not have been written without the help of the family historians who graciously shared their stories of courage and inspiration. My gratitude goes out to Rosemary Belecky, Doris and John Willoughby, Carol Christensen, Cassie Cole, Miriam Hammond, Erma Shipley, Chizu Agasawara, Nettie Arias, Isador Goldhammer, Julia Huffer, Carl and Eddie Johnson, Anna Hess, Anna McBee, Henrietta Mecomber, Ernest Viner and Murriel Woods as well as to church historians Violet Breisch, Edvina Weiderspahn, Rev. Sam Hayes and Rose Ramirez.

For encouragement, proofreading and helpful criticism I am indebted to Jean Brainerd, Dr. Wilson O. Clough, Joan Clark, Ellen Crowley, Peggy Simpson Curry, Ruth Gowdy, Katherine Halvorsen, Byron and Virginia Hirst, Mag Jiacolletti, Jessie L. Johnson, Mr. LeClercq Jones, Cherry Reed, Wavis Twyford, Virginia Trenholm, Janet Whitehead and Patricia Wunnicke.

U.S. Government officials and staffers who provided valuable assistance were: Olivia Haag and Dee Rodekohr, Senator Alan Simpson's office; Kirby Cavett and Gus Meier, Department of Agricultural Statistics; Lowell Burns and Dorothy Hogan, Department of Commerce; Don Heine and Dr. Ade Stevenson, Soil Conservation Service; Marvin A. Crist, United States Geological Survey; Ellen Stockdale, Office of the Comptroller of the Currency and S.Sgt. Edwin A. Tarbell, Francis E. Warren Air Force Base.

State Treasurer Shirley Wittler and State Examiner Dwight Bonham shared their insights and concerns. Charles Porter, Director, Solid Waste Division, Department of Environmental Quality, and his staff provided technical information as did staffers of the Land and Water Quality offices and Dick Stockdale, Andrew Bieber and Phillip Velez, of the State Engineer's office.

Dr. George C. Frison, Head of the Department of Anthropology, University of Wyoming supplied pictures and information on the Lummis Pre-Historic site. Wyoming Archeological Society members, Craig Casner, Paula Durnford and Lou Steege contributed first hand accounts of the dig. Ralph D. Cline contributed anecdotes of the 1929 flood.

John E. Witherbee, Research Specialist, Union Pacific Railroad, Omaha, graciously aided in this research.

For the last two years, State Archives, Museums and Historical Department people have given their support and assistance in this project. Special thanks to Bill Barton, Jean Brainerd, Jim Laird, Phil Roberts, Dan Siglin, Paula West, Ida Wozney and the entire staff. Thanks also to Gwen Rice, Wyoming State Library; Emmett Chisum, Western Research Center, as well as the Colorado Historical Society for assistance and to Bea Grams, Laramie County Library who aided in the family histories.

Cheyenne City Water Department Director Herman Noe, Board Consultant Ray Sherard and Jack Young furnished historical and technical information. Floydine Gay, Secretary of the South Cheyenne Water and Sewer District shared valuable data. Thanks too, to Diana De Aguero, Cheyenne City Clerk.

I am grateful for the unfailing courtesy, efficiency and assistance of the staffers in the offices of County Assessor, County Clerk and Clerk of the District Court.

Cheyenne-Laramie County Regional Planning Office Director Tom Bonds, Planners Jon Arason, Maury Plambeck and Will Sanchez provided research assistance as did staff members Connie Brown and Linda Hostetter.

Special research materials came from Marilyn Tammany and Kirk Knox, Cheyenne Newspapers, Inc., Keith Henning, AFL-CIO and Jim Christensen and Lois Santini of the Cheyenne Abstract and Title Company.

Finally, my children Patricia and Lee and my husband Raymond sustained me with their understanding, encouragement and patience.

BACKGROUND

"CHEYENNE, CHEYENNE, . . ."

"Cheyenne, Cheyenne, hop on my pony
There's room here for two dear . . ."

We sang it endlessly, my little sisters and I, and we didn't know all of the words. It was hot and dusty on the train coming down from Billings, early August, 1921. Little brother Charles, we called him "Buddy," was cutting a tooth. Mama had a headache. The hard worn seats of the old Burlington coach did nothing for our father's disposition, either. The car did not compare with the gold velour elegance of the Great Northern coach with its swaying amber and brass chandeliers on which we had left North Dakota.

The uncertainties of the move to Cheyenne in anticipation of a building boom with nothing more to go on than the eternal optimism of a generation nourished on free land and boom psychology, added to the tension.

No one was more optimistic than I. At twelve, I would be in the seventh grade in a school with just one grade to the room. There would be special teachers for art, music, penmanship and physical training. I had read Grandma's letter over and over.

"Sing something else, Dear, or read to the children."

"I have already read all of the stories in *Old Mother West Wind's Children*."

We tried "Row, row, row your boat," but little sisters, Margaret Eunice, Lanore Yvonne, and Ethel Mae, kept getting it all mixed up. On purpose, I think. We recited all of the poems we knew, or parts of poems, riddles and nursery rhymes for the little ones, and even the alphabets in English, Norwegian and French.

Then it was time for the box lunches. "Eeks, Egrek, Zed," laughed Ethel, sprinkling three shakes of salt on her sandwich, just like Papa.

"That means 'x, y, z;' not 'one, two, three,' Mama, she threw salt on me."

Lunch over, I told them a made-up story.

"It is all so exciting! We are going to live in a real city in the wild west, like in the movies. There will be handsome cowboys, and thousands of cattle, and they will drive them right through the streets, riding their prancing horses. We will see them on our way to concerts, and the library and church, every Sunday."

They laughed and clapped their hands and started singing the song again.

"Children, children, please, less noise."

I lowered my voice to a whisper. "And Mama will sing again in church before hundreds of people, and wear beautiful gowns and hats and Papa will build big, beautiful houses, and one for us, and we will be rich and have after-dinner mints and ladies will come to tea." I dreamed and curled my pinky, just so.

The train rounded a long curve. We could see the engine and tender, followed by a few oil cars, some empty coal cars and half a dozen cattle cars. Papa said we were now in Wyoming. "Wyoming, W-Y-O-M-I-N-G, Wyoming," I spelled.

The train stopped on a siding at a stockyard filled with bawling cattle. Papa and some of the men passengers got off the train to stretch their legs and watch the loading. Men on horseback moved nervously about, yelling and waving their hats. The cattle moved up the chute onto the cars. The air was thick with dust and the smell of crushed sagebrush.

Papa looked worried when he came back and the train started to move with much jerking and bumping, gathering speed on the downgrade.

"I was talking to the fellow with the cattle. He said it has been so dry that they have to sell the cattle early. They didn't look too good, either. If it is like this all over, we might better have stayed in North Dakota."

He took out a little book and started to figure in it and talked to Mama in a low voice about the economy. I pulled her sleeve. "How do you spell economy?" I had guessed its meaning. "Economy, E-C-O-N-O-M-Y, Economy."

I wanted to ask him how much taller he was now that he had stretched his legs, but I had a feeling that this was no time for jokes.

"It's hot. Papa, may we have a window open?" He opened it a few inches. The car smelled of lunches, oranges, pickles, and the baby who had been sick. The sharp scent of sage came in on the hot wind.

The cowboy who had got on after loading the cattle had been talking with the conductor. Now he came down the aisle and sat across from us. Soon he was dozing with his hat over his eyes. His feet in worn, shabby boots were propped on the opposite seat with his rolled up chaps, his saddle and battered suitcase. He didn't look like the cowboys in the movies. He looked older than Papa who was thirty-seven.

Mama said, "It isn't nice to stare."

As evening came on, I seemed to be the only one awake. Cinders and dust blew in on Lanore's damp red curls. I tried to close the window. While I considered trying to wake Papa, the cowboy got up and closed the window easily.

"Thank you," I said.

"You're welcome ma'am." He touched his hat.

"Ma'am," he called me "Ma'am!" Then like a grown-up sister, I wiped the dirt and cinders from Lanore's face without waking her.

I watched the moonlit landscape go by, listening to the crossing whistles and the hollow sound of bridges as we crossed the shining little streams, and dreamily followed a silver river into a dark canyon, and a darker tunnel, the metallic meter of the miles lulling me finally to sleep.

Papa tapped me on the shoulder once, "Look Sis. It is a refinery where they make gasoline out of oil. I didn't want you to miss it."

A forest of towered, twinkling lights and billowing steam lighted the night sky, mingled with the stars and floated on the river.

We were awakened by a jolting, jerking and clanking, followed by the sensation of riding backwards. Suddenly we were awake, "We're here!"

"Look Sis, the Capitol Building. See the gold dome!" Papa always saw to my education.

The sun was just coming up, horizontally lighting the streets with momentary gold. Alleys and mean sheds, warehouses and trash cans were luminously outlined in gold. Prisms of fractured light shattered and fell from the silhouetted trees, the marvelous big trees! The gold dome of the Capitol, presiding serenely over this city of light, welcomed us.

The cool air of this oasis rushed in the door and somewhere in those alleys a rooster crowed. The train backed to the station, ringing its bell all the way.

I fell in love with Cheyenne in the rising sun. This was to be my city for better or worse!

There was Grandma waving her handkerchief beside the huge, dark red brick Burlington Depot. Beside her on the wide, brick sidewalk was Mr. R. S. Collins, her new husband, after twenty-three years of widowhood. The top of his hat was about even with her shoulder. He had a large pointed nose, several chins and no neck.

There was a lot of hugging and kissing and introductions by Grandma. Mr. Collins took his cigar out of his mouth and wanted to kiss the children. I hid behind Mama. He smelled like an old spittoon.

"She is very shy," said Mama.

We piled into the open Studebaker touring car. Papa, holding Buddy, sat up in front with Mr. Collins. "We live over the viaduct," said Grandma. "Mama, how do you spell viaduct?" "Viaduct, V-I-A-D-U-C-T, Viaduct." Up there we seemed so close to the tall Union Pacific tower with its clock. It was still only 5:30 A.M., a clear, sunny morning, August 15, 1921.

"Housing is tight," Mr. Collins was saying above the clatter of the planks as we passed over them. "We still haven't been able to locate anything for people with children. You will have to bunk in with us for a little while. We'll keep looking. As for ourselves, we have been too busy to build what we want. Putting it all back into the business, you know."

As we swooshed down the south end of the viaduct to Tenth Street and around the block where he pulled up in front of 1013 Warren Avenue, I had a feeling that he did not welcome our presence.

By the time we had freshened up, Grandma had a big breakfast ready which we children enjoyed while grownups talked, and talked and talked.

Finally, Mr. Collins suggested that Papa come and see the houses he was building.

That first week we were busy getting acquainted with Cheyenne. There were evening drives to see the town or to inspect the houses being built in Pershing Heights, Paul Moore Real Estate Company's new subdivision. Grandma took us around the neighborhood, proudly introducing us to the Bonsers on their porch swing. The Bonsers owned all of the houses on the block. None were vacant.

There was Mrs. Minnie McIver who lived in the cement block house on the southeast corner of Tenth Street and Warren Avenue. It was said that she had built that house with her own hands. The neighbors also said that if her husband was unable to go out on a plumbing job, Minnie would go. Some preferred to have Minnie. She had beautiful lace curtains. She and Grandma talked about lace. We children enjoyed her soft ginger cookies.

Mrs. Mary Doak, widow of David, came by with her granddaughter, Edith. She was on her way to O'Connell's Market on the corner of Eleventh Street and Warren. She left Edith to play with us. Returning, Mrs. Doak reported that Mr. O'Connell did not know of any houses for rent anywhere in town.

Clearly, Grandma was enjoying her role of grandma and housewife. Her full name was Dena Gunhilde Christophersen-Skude Helgesen Collins. She explained that when he was homesteading in Wisconsin, her father Anders Christophersen had so many neighbors with the same last name that he added "Skude," the name of his family grange in Norway, to distinguish him from the other Scandinavian settlers. People just took to calling him "Skude." Eventually the family dropped the long name using it only for legal papers.

Grandma, born June 2, 1866, was the first child born after her father returned from the Civil War. He served with Company B, 6th Wisconsin Volunteers. In 1888 Grandma Dena married Nicholai Helgesen, a native of Bergen, Norway. He died when Mama was nine years old.

Dena apprenticed herself to her sister Annie, a milliner and dressmaker in Chippewa Falls, Wisconsin, to learn the business. Later, she went with her younger sister Hanna and cousin Amanda Brunstad to Chicago. In Chicago they worked as trimmers for Gage, a famous maker of ladies' hats. They roomed together and took work home "to get ahead" and to save enough to go into business for themselves.

Grandma left Mama Nora with her parents while she was working to get established in the millinery-dressmaking business. Mama adored her grandparents but felt abandoned, first by her father and then by her mother. She resolved to have a large family.

When Mama was sixteen, Grandma sent for her but Mama was not interested in the dressmaking business. She worked in a general store and sang in the choir. Then she and Grandma took up a homestead. They drove back and forth to the homestead with a rented horse and buggy. When the claim was "proved up," they turned it into cash.

It was there in Ryder, North Dakota, that Mama met Charles Howard Powelson, a homesteader and grain buyer from Moscow Mills, Missouri, who was to be our father.

For the most part, Grandma's investments in land and stocks had been modestly successful. She was thrifty and cautious, never liking to put money into anything that she "could not get her hands on." She said that she had every intention of going back into the millinery business again but was content to "play the real estate game for awhile." She always knew the price of wheat.

She had found it profitable to go where the latest "boom town" was flourishing. She had a millinery shop in Casper when the oil boom was on. She had met Collins there at church. She was a Christian Scientist, having tried several religions. Collins had a nice baritone voice and seemed to be quite religious. He admitted to being a "fallen away Catholic" and a former altar boy. He always said the prayer before meals.

Paul Moore, the real estate man with whom Collins was building the new houses, was a dinner guest that first Sunday in Cheyenne. Grandma said that if she had had a son, she would want him to be just like Paul. Mama and Papa gave each other "looks." It took some getting used to, hearing Grandma called "Dena-my-dear," as if it were one word, the way Collins said it. "Dena-my-dear, please pass the potatoes."

It was a special occasion, the celebration of Papa's and Ethel's birthdays, the eleventh and thirteenth of August, which had somehow gotten lost in the moving. Paul was a charming dinner guest, regaling us with stories. He said he had come to Cheyenne "with ninety dollars in his pocket, a double-barreled shotgun and a German Shepherd dog," all of which he had won at poker.

Papa went with Mr. Collins for a couple of days as he made his rounds of suppliers and the houses he had under construction. He accepted an offer to work for Collins as an assistant with the option of doing some subcontracting after he had "learned the ropes" locally.

Papa had managed lumberyards for a chain in North Dakota. His architectural advice on homes and barns had made his yard a popular business. He had designed some beautiful barns and had built a "prairie style" house for us. The house had burned during a terrible blizzard in February 1917. The asbestos we needed for covering the furnace and cold air return had been on a snow bound train. On a Sunday morning he had stoked up the furnace and had gone back to bed. He nearly lost his life fighting the fire and we lost most of our belongings. We dated many events in our family history as "before" or "after" the fire.

I sensed that he was uncomfortable and unhappy in his new job. Then the third evening, he drove up to the door in a secondhand Model T Ford. He was all smiles. I overheard him tell Mama that now he could get around on his own and not be "beholden." He was "in charge" again!

After supper we all scrambled into the "Lizzy" and went for a spin.

"She's not as fancy as the old Paige, but she sure goes!"

She was light and bouncy and she surely did go. The gravel flew out from behind her wheels with a satisfying swish as we dashed down the Tenth Street hill, bumping over the bridge across Crow Creek, around the curve at Stanfield's Cottage Grove Camp Ground with its tall cottonwoods, headed south, up the Denver Highway, past the smouldering City Dump polluting the atmosphere.

There was a map pinned up in Grandma's kitchen showing this high section overlooking the city to be "Interior Heights." Papa turned the car around up there on the hill, facing the city. The gold dome of the Capitol caught the evening light beyond the elegant Union Pacific tower. A few tall buildings stood out above the tree canopy. A steam engine puffed idly, sending up a golden cloud.

SCHOOL DAYS

We set out to buy school shoes one morning, just Mama and me. The little ones had gotten new shoes before the trip to Wyoming. A tree-shaded block west on Eleventh Street brought us to the foot of the old wooden viaduct.

Crossing it on foot for the first time was a bit scary. It was so high and so far. The worn, knotty planks of the old structure rattled and shook when cars passed. The pedestrian walk was separated from the roadway by a wrought iron fence and great steel panels. Stairways at Twelfth Street and at the depot exit had iron stairs. At the far end, halfway between Fifteenth and Sixteenth Streets, east and west ramps led down to the street level.

It seemed to be a special time and place as we stood at the corner of Sixteenth and Capitol, beside the Burlington depot. There was the Union Pacific Depot at one end of Capitol Avenue and the Capitol Building at the other.

"Am I too old to play 'Let's be two ladies?' " I asked.

"No, Miss Powelson. I'd say you are just the right age to be a lady on a shopping trip with her friend." We were always very formal, consulting each other on pattern and print for our dresses.

Mama spotted J. F. Jenkins Shoe Store in the middle of the next block on the north side of the street, next to the Washington Market.

"There used to be a Jenkins Shoe Store at home. Shall we try there, Miss Powelson?" We waited for the street car to go clanging by.

Mr. James Flood Jenkins, himself, came to wait upon us. While I was being fitted with brown school oxfords, Mama told him that she had grown up in a town with a Jenkins Shoe Store. "In fact, the Jenkins family lived right next door to us in Chippewa Falls, Wisconsin," she said.

"It's a small world," said Mr. Jenkins. "I have brothers in the shoe business in Chippewa Falls. I came out to Camp Carlin' in 1876. This is my son Horace." Horace came over and welcomed us to Cheyenne.

We did all of our shopping around the two hundred block between Sixteenth and Seventeenth Streets. There seemed to be more people about as we came out of the store. We looked into shop windows, noted the theatres, the Atlas across the street, the Amuse and the Lyric around the corner on Carey Avenue and the beautiful Princess, across the street. All closed at this time of day.

F. W. Woolworth's Emporium wrapped itself around several stores on the corner of Seventeenth and Carey. One could enter on Carey and emerge on Seventeenth. We made a tour of it, buying some peppermints for Grandma, gumdrops for the children and our school supplies. Then, even before lunch, we stopped at Ellis' Confectionery for our favorite treat from the days of our shopping trips to Minot, North Dakota, by train, a scrumptious maple-nut sundae. Ellis' hand-dipped chocolates were tempting but far too expensive for our budget.

Next at the Golden Rule Store, later renamed the J. C. Penney Store, we met Mr. Fred C. Hultquist, proprietor. Here we bought gingham for school dresses, matching thread, and stockings for all.

Turning the corner at Capitol Avenue we passed the small Cheyenne State Bank and Trust and its shiny brass grilles; a little bakery and lunch room, Mr. Paul Moore's office and a barber shop. The imposing Hynds Building housed the American National Bank and a book and stationery store. On the opposite corner was the First National Bank. We crossed here and returned to our starting point at the Burlington Depot.

Retracing our steps over the viaduct, we stopped at O'Connell's market for some rice, some tea and two ten-cent loaves of bread. O'Connell had a city wide clientele. Clerks scurried to wait on customers or to take their orders over the telephone and deliver, free, anywhere in town.

Across the street, kitty-corner, there seemed to be a lot of activity at the fire house. Carved in a stone arch over the door was the name "J. T. Clark Volunteer Hose." It was now officially a part of the city fire department but once had been a fiercely competitive volunteer company. A poster advertised a Labor Day Dance sponsored by the South Side Improvement Association, to be held upstairs at the Fire House. There seemed to be something going on there almost every evening, such as a band practice or a meeting.

Grandma's house was two doors south of the fire house. As we approached, Mama asked me to be extra helpful to Grandma and entertain the children.

"Much as she loves us, it is uncomfortably crowded. I hope we find something soon."

"I understand," I said, still in my role of Miss Powelson.

The small house, situated on the alley, had no front yard. Built of vertical board and batten siding, it was painted an olive green. There had originally been three bedrooms. The small one had been converted into a bathroom. There was a combination kitchen-dining room and a small living room. We children slept on a sofa bed called a "Davenport" in the living room, unless there was company, then we were put to bed in our parents' room.

There was a small drying yard behind the house enclosed by a high board fence, a coal and wood shed and a tool shed, which had once been a privy. Most of the houses on the block had privies. A few had vines or hollyhocks as a screen. High board fences around the back yards were common, as were smelly, smoking ash pits.

"Good news," cried Grandma as we walked in. "My friend Georgette called. There is an apartment being vacated in the Nettford Apartments on Eighteenth. No children allowed, so Mr. Collins and I will take it and you can have this."

PHOTO COURTESY OF FLOYD ARTIST

Dutch and Roxy, the J. T. Clark Volunteer Hose Company horses, being driven by "Monk" Artist, Driver. The fire house was located at Eleventh and Warren.

It had been a happy day.

The next few days were filled with the bustle of moving. Grandma said that she had lived out of a trunk for so long that she could make a home anywhere, whether it be a furnished room at the parsonage or the backroom of the millinery shop. "All it takes is a little imagination," she said.

Grandma cooked with creativity and served food with a flair. When she laid a table with her beautifully embroidered linens, china and a "suitable" centerpiece to "set the tone," it made an everyday meal a celebration. Her pearl handled service was for everyday. She called it her "Sheffield." It was always washed and dried before anything else, and put away in a blue kid case.

As often as Grandma had moved to a new land rush town on the prairie or an oil boomtown, she had found it uneconomical to move furniture. One place had bird's eye maple. Here, she had found some nice mahogany pieces. It would go with the dark mahogany woodwork at the Nettford. Her trunks and chests held her real homemaking treasures, fine linen and china, a few paintings by members of the family, her pots and pans. Special trunks held her velvets, feathers and materials for hats, and gowns, suits and coats for her clientele.

We brought in our boxes and barrels and unpacked our household furnishings. We had no piano so our music was not unpacked. We missed the piano. We had sold some of our furniture in North Dakota but it had added little to the family coffer.

While Mama was busy sewing, it was my job to mind the children. There were no parks on the South Side. We went to the school yard to the swings and teeters. Often others were there who would not share.

We heard the talk about the Labor Day holiday. It must be something like the Fourth of July, I thought. Over at O'Connell's, people were laughing about last year's Labor Day. "That was a real toad strangler! It took the town a week to dry out," they said. "The celebration was a washout."

Some said they were going fishing instead of listening to a lot of hot air. Since the average family did not have a car, it was assumed that there would be a pretty good crowd at the Labor Day festivities, if it did not rain.

The four block City Park near the Capitol was to be the scene of a patriotic program with speeches, games, foot and sack races, potato races for young and old, plus free ice cream!

Papa read the headline: "Trinidad, September 6, Five Colorado mines again working." He tucked the newspaper into the picnic basket and we went to absorb this new cultural event. We parked the car across the street from the Capitol and found a choice spot under the canopy of the big cottonwood trees which all leaned toward the southeast.

I got myself into a three-legged sack race by being a spectator and standing too close. A girl with one leg in a sack grabbed me around the waist and said, "Put your foot in here." I did. The gun went off and we hopped and

EDDIE JOHNSON COLLECTION

First grade, Johnson School, 1915. Miss Kellogg, teacher.

EDDIE JOHNSON COLLECTION

Same children, Seventh grade, 1922. Last class to complete the curriculum at Johnson.

ran somehow. Some fell. We won theater tickets. Amazing and fun! The band played, we all sang "The Star Spangled Banner." There was a scattered, polite applause for the speakers. When someone read the President's message, there was a bit more applause, and it was over.

That night there was a big dance in the upstairs of the firehouse. We sat outside to listen to the music. We children were allowed to walk to the corner but could see nothing of the activity. People had to have a ticket to get in. The firemen sat at the door as usual, ready for anything.

The crowd converging on the firehouse seemed to be a happy group. Ladies wafted by with a rustle of taffeta skirts, trailing perfume. Their high heels clicked on the sidewalk.

Mrs. Bonser observed that Mr. Geary would be doing a "land office" business tonight. Mr. Geary was alleged to sell the best "moonshine" in town. Some boys were tossing firecrackers into the street, making the dogs bark. We went to sleep with the sound of music coming in the window.

Finally the great day came. We dressed in our new clothes and went off to enroll in Johnson School. Mama, Ethel and Buddy went along to supervise. Lanore's first grade was in the annex, a small wooden building, on the northeast corner of the block. Margaret and I had our North Dakota report cards. We hugged our Big Chief tablets and pencils for security.

Mama took Lanore to the annex, while I escorted Margaret to the fourth grade room. Then I climbed the noisy wooden stairs and crossed the cavernous hall to the seventh grade room. There I followed others to the pencil sharpener although Papa had whittled sharp points on all of our pencils.

By looking obliquely out through the west windows, I could see the small yellow houses of the railroad section workers inside the nine foot tall red fence. Twelfth Street ran along the fence north of the school yard. The school stood on the north half of the block, bordered by House and Evans with Eleventh Street on the south, the main entrance of the school. There was a line of young trees along the front sidewalk and the playground was covered with gravel and cinders.

The engines switched constantly back and forth, their staccato whistles and metallic percussion part of the daily opera for this neighborhood. I returned to my seat. Somehow this was not the city of glamour that I had expected.

Suddenly a loud bell rang. I jumped. Everyone dashed for seats.

Miss Lavinia A. Cole entered. She was grey eyed, fair skinned and slightly plump.

"Good morning, boys and girls."

"Good morning, Miss Cole," was the loud response.

She took a pencil out of the flat roll in her brown hair and began to take the attendance. A brother and sister were transfers from Converse School.

I was the only outsider. I presented my North Dakota report card and vital statistics.

Books were distributed. Miss Cole was to be our Arithmetic teacher, the first class of the day. We were told that we could take our books home to study but would have to pay for them if they were lost. Fines would be levied if they were damaged or defaced in any way. I was apprehensive about Arithmetic. It was my hardest subject. Would I be able to learn it?

Papa had said, "Arithmetic is arithmetic anywhere in the world."

The tall sad faced girl across the aisle was named Billie. I had never known a girl named Billie.

As we filed out for recess, Miss Cole asked, "How is your Mother, Billie?"

"Mama died in July, Ma'am," Miss Cole murmured her sympathy.

I was fascinated by this girl. She stood off by herself. I invited her to come home with me after school. "I can't," she said. "I have chores to do."

"Where do you live, on a farm?"

"No, you can see it from here," pointing down Evans, south and east. "Down by the creek." There were a few houses and fewer trees.

I could see a small dark red house, some sheds and animals. "There is something on the roof!"

"That's Blackie, my pet goat." She had a nice smile.

We could see a green strip in the brown meadow. I asked about it.

"There is a little spring. It has been so dry, we were afraid it would dry up. The grass stays green and the animals like it. The cow is named Bonnie."

A boy came by and said, "Hi, Billie Goat."

"Shut up. Cracker," she hissed.

Then the bell rang.

At lunchtime, we ran home. There was so much to tell. "Don't talk with your mouths full. There will be plenty of time to talk," Mama said.

We returned to school early and stood watching some girls jumping rope.

I had never seen such fancy rope jumping. "Come on, run in," called a Dutch-bobbed girl named Betty. I jumped straight counts but soon missed, being out of practice.

"Can you do 'Hot Pepper'?" called Kate, turning the rope.

"No, it's too fast."

They did "Hot Pepper," "High Water," and the amazing "Double Dutch," rhymes and stunts I had never heard of. Due to my lack of skill, I spent most of my time turning the rope.

The bell rang. We lined up, quieted down and marched to our rooms.

A girl named Helen spoke in a low, hoarse whisper, "Don't play with Kate. Her father is a scab."

I didn't know what a "scab" was but it had a fearful sound.

Mama tried to explain about strikes and that there was a strike going on at the railroad. "Scab" was one of the bad names the Union workers called the people who worked instead of striking. There was much bad feeling amongst neighbors and even between members of families over the issue.

"It is often best to listen and try to understand the different points of view," she said. "Always try to have an understanding heart."

I thought it must be like the Civil War with families divided.

OLIVE WILLS

She walked into our seventh grade room at old Johnson School carrying a wild sunflower in a glass of water. In her other hand she balanced a box of pencils on a sheaf of drawing paper.

"Hello, boys and girls." Her smile included us all in its glow.

"Hello, Miss Wills," chorused the loud and friendly response.

I was a new kid, from a small town in North Dakota, thrilled by the big school, with its many teachers, yet timid and afraid to show my ignorance. I was filled with excitement and anticipation of an "ART" class. Remembering my father's advice, "Just keep your eyes and ears open and learn everything you can." It was an indelible experience.

The afternoon sun deposited a diamond in the bottom of the glass, which she placed on a small table in the front of the room. She added a couple of books from the principal's desk to the arrangement. Shards of light danced and sparkled across the books and up the wall.

"Shall I pull the blinds?" asked Miss Cole.

"No, thank you," said Miss Wills. "See how lovely the light is on the flower and the glass! Now, boys and girls, let me see how much you remember from last year." She seemed full of excitement, too, as materials were passed.

I did not know what they had learned last year but I had been drawing and painting since before I had started to school. I sketched quickly. The two teachers talked quietly in the doorway, then Miss Cole went away. Miss Wills began to walk around the room, pausing now and then to ask a question, or to bend over and talk softly with a student. She stopped beside me for a moment, said nothing, then moved on. I felt let down but kept on drawing.

Vaguely, I was aware that other children were reaching or pointing but I was too busy to try to figure out what they were doing. Finally, this tiny woman came back to my desk and sat down beside me. Her shoulder was only a little higher than mine.

"You are doing nicely," she said. "Did you measure first?"

"Measure?" My glass looked too fat but a diamond sparkled in the bottom.

Taking my pencil she instructed me quietly in the art of "measuring," or observing proportions. She did not ridicule me or scold.

She addressed the class, reminding them of the many ways of seeing. She recited the poem about the blind men who went to see the elephant. We laughed together.

We would now see that the children on the left side of the room had a somewhat different view of the arrangement from those in the center and those on the right. A few selected examples of each viewpoint were placed on the chalktray on the blackboard. No comparisons of ability or perfection were made.

The work and materials were gathered. Too soon, it was over.

"Next time, boys and girls, we will see if this method will work for drawing people. Until we meet again, practice seeing and measuring the proportions of things in your home, buildings, trees and everything around you, and drawing, drawing, drawing, just for the fun of it!"

I couldn't wait for next time.

As I grew up, Miss Wills became my treasured friend and remained so throughout her life.

THE FIRST WINTER

The first six weeks of school passed quickly. One day we came home from school and Papa was home, figuring at the dining room table. I could tell that Mama was upset about something.

"Children, go and change your school clothes."

While we were doing this, Grandma arrived. She had walked over the viaduct she said, "to try to reason with Charlie."

Papa was angry. He said that Collins was a crook and Grandma should not be surprised if she is "flim-flammed" out of her eye teeth! He had quit R. S. Collins after being "shorted" on their contract for the house in Pershing Heights.

Grandma told Papa "to come to his senses." She would not stay to have supper with us and Papa drove her back to the Nettford. Papa and Grandma often did not "see eye to eye."

Papa wasn't out of work long. He lined up several remodeling jobs for Mr. W. O. Benner. Benner had a house which had been moved to the outskirts of Cheyenne. It was on the south side of Happy Jack Road. There were no other houses nearby. It was not liveable due to a fire or explosion in the basement which served as a garage for the hillside house. It needed glass in the windows and refinishing. The well was not working. We could live in it for a year as part payment for work on the other jobs and repairing this house. Papa fixed it and we moved in. "It isn't much, but it beats paying rent," he said.

As it turned out the well-drillers had trouble with the rig. They quit the drilling business and went to work for the railroad as strikebreakers.

We hauled our water from the flowing artesian well in Bresnahan's pasture all winter. Trying to stand up on the icebergs around the water tank gave me sympathy for the polar explorers. (Little America Motel was to be built near the well some forty years later.)

There was no seventh grade at Corlett, the nearest school, so Mama went to Mr. A. S. Jessup, the Superintendent of Schools, who gave his permission for all three of us to go to Churchill School together. At that time there was no bus transportation for the schools.

In contrast to Johnson, this school was relatively new, having been built in 1919. Mrs. Liston, the principal, was the most stern and terrifying teacher I had ever known. She taught arithmetic. Her electric blue eyes seemed to see into the poor addled percentages inside my brain. The kids said that she could read your mind and tell if you were lying, and then you would get it. You had better not forget to say, "Yes Ma'am and No Ma'am."

It was true. I forgot one day. We didn't have to say it in North Dakota. She slapped me on the face hard and said, "Didn't they teach you manners where you come from?"

It was a long walk from Happy Jack Road to Churchill School. Papa took us in the car in bad weather and in good weather, if he didn't have to go to work too early. We often had a long wait before the building opened when he took us.

Most of the time we enjoyed the walk, we saw Cheyenne close up, we chose circuitous routes to vary the scene. We would cut across the corner of the military reservation, carrying our books and dinner pail. The best way to go through the reservation fence was to lie down and roll under, then brush each other off.

We would cross the Burlington, Colorado and Southern tracks at the Hynds Boulevard crossing, then cut through the Cole's brickyard. Sometimes, when the kilns were going, we walked through a warm place in the winter. Edna Cole, an eighth grader, lived there. She joined us often for the remaining ten blocks of our walk. She would lift the little ones over the mud puddles.

One day a train was stopped on the crossing. We waited and waited. The train was idly puffing, but we didn't know anything about trains. The engineer and fireman laughed and shouted something but we could not hear or understand. I began to panic. We would be late. We looked under a freight car. It seemed too risky. To get around in front of the engine we had to go up a steep, short bank. We hurried. With the two little sisters in front of me, we made it safely across. Then my foot rolled on the gravel and cinders. I went down, tearing my stockings and skinning my knee. We ran all the way and arrived dry-mouthed and breathless.

Sure enough, we were late. I was met at the head of the stairs by Mrs. Liston and her blazing blue eyes. Then she saw my knee. She took me into the office and cleaned the wound, bandaged me gently and heard my story. I cried more from relief than pain.

"I think she is more scared than hurt," she told the teacher who came in.

As at Johnson, the pencil sharpener was located at the window sill, a good place to observe the city. There were few buildings close to the school on the north. Papa was building a house for the Orville Weavers at 3117 O'Neil, across the street from the red brick home of the Belecky kids, Albert, Frank and Marie. I could watch its progress. Later, Papa would help to fill those empty blocks with houses.

One day Mama came to school and I was called out into the hall to speak with her. She told me that Grandma had been in an accident and that I was to go to the Nettford after school and stay with her for a week or two. They would bring in my clothes and would pick up Margaret and Lanore, "so don't worry about them."

Mama was by then noticeably pregnant. At recess, the girls asked me, "When is she due?" Suddenly, the white flannel on the sewing machine, the little crocheted sacque, the whispered conversations with Grandma, were clear to me. Why couldn't she have told me, her friend, Miss Powelson?

"How did the accident happen?" I asked Grandma when I entered the apartment.

"You might as well know, Mr. Collins has taken to drinking, more and more. He is running with a pretty fast crowd. He never used to drink." She started to cry. (I remember Mama describing Collins' nose as a "rum blossom.")

"We were out riding in Paul's Pierce Arrow. R. S. is thinking of buying a big car. He was driving, Martha and Paul were in the back seat. They are going to be married, you know. I was in the front seat." She wiped her eyes.

"You know the corner of Seymour and Pershing, by the cemetery? The gravel is very deep. It piles up in furrows. He turned the corner too fast and out I went. I just went rolling. There are no doors in the front of the Pierce, you know." She wiped her eyes and blew her nose.

"Not that doors would have stopped me. He was driving like a wild man and drinking, right out of the bottle." She showed me her skinned forehead under her bangs. She had put up her wrist to shield her face. Her wrist was bandaged, her glasses broken. Her right ankle was in a cast.

I had never seen Grandma cry before. I put my arms around her and cried, too. I wanted to make her better and I didn't know how to help her.

"He was very mad. He said he wished he had tossed me into the cemetery and finished me." She maneuvered herself onto her crutches with some inexpert help from me and we went into the kitchenette. She showed me how to light the gas. We had some tea and a light supper.

I slept on the sofa. We didn't see much of Collins. He came in only a few times to see if we needed anything. Groceries were delivered by O'Connells' Grocery. I washed the dishes, ran the carpet sweeper, did some simple cooking and kept up my home work. I stayed for two weeks.

She treated me like a grown-up and we had some wonderful visits. She answered my questions about having babies and we discussed religion. She had tried several of them, including spiritualism. She was often psychic. I wondered why she hadn't been able to tell that Mr. Collins was not a good man.

Grandma had a theory that, since all people understand music and music is the universal language, why shouldn't we have a universal speech? She reasoned that universal speech would eliminate wars. To this end she had studied Esperanto. She had me bring the Esperanto book. It did not seem simple to me. I resolved to learn more than one language, for someday I would be a world traveler. My armchair knows no international boundaries.

Over the years, I learned from her about fabrics, the craft and culture that created them, their names and history. If she did not tell me all, she whetted my curiosity so that I had to find out more about it. She taught me about art. She could paint and draw and insisted that I do these things as a part of my education. All of her family was creative. Two of her brothers, Gus and Charlie Skude, were good artists in oil and water color. She said that "it is our business to make the world beautiful. The principle ingredient is within ourselves."

She also had some valuable rules about business, which we discussed while I was studying percentages. "Never spend your reserves. Always make a little profit, a lot is better," she laughed. "Don't trust banks too much. Shop for the best interest on your money. They don't pay enough for using your money. They loan it out at higher rates. Save and invest in a growing business."

I wondered if she still trusted Collins and his growing business?

Much as I enjoyed being with Grandma, I was glad when she no longer needed me and I could be with my family. The kids missed me.

The weather was consistently cold, windy and dry. We spent a lot of time at the library after school reading and waiting for Papa to pick us up. Sometimes he couldn't make it before closing time. Miss La Fontaine, the children's librarian, would wait so we could be warm. Her superior fussed, but she waited anyway.

Sometimes, we were joined on the walk from school to the library by Catherine Colley. Her father was a military officer who had an office in the Capitol Building. Her mother worked downtown. Catherine gave us a tour of the Capitol Building. We learned a lot about Wyoming history from the displays on the third floor.

One time, by ourselves, killing time, we rode the old brass birdcage elevator and it stuck between floors. The offices had closed. We yelled and yelled, "Help, help!" The echoes bounded back and forth in the spacious empty building. Finally the janitor came. After that we took the stairs.

All went well until about Thanksgiving. Margaret came down with a fever and aching joints. Her legs were swollen. She missed a couple of weeks of school. Papa was building a house on West Twenty-Seventh Street; we would wait there for a ride home. We gathered the wood scraps to take home for kindling. Times were hard, money was going out for materials and nothing was coming in. What little help Papa hired had to be paid.

At Christmas, we children each had a dollar to spend. We walked downtown after school and had a glorious time at Woolworth's Five and Ten Cent Store. Pooling our money for little gifts, with much plotting and whispered consultations, we bought something for everyone.

Margaret was sick again after Christmas. It hurt her to move her swollen legs. Although Mama was a Christian Scientist, this time we had a doctor come to the house. He said that Margaret's heart was enlarged and that she had rheumatism. (Nowadays, they call it rheumatic fever.)

"Keep her in bed," he said. "She will get over this, but there will be other spells."

Margaret finally went back to school. There was no more walking. The teacher did not make her go out for recess. They made her drink milk. Margaret did not like milk. She was a quiet obedient child and never complained. A month later she was sick again.

Margaret's class had been making Mother's Day cards. Miss Patterson, her teacher, gave me her cards and drawings to take home when we went back to school after the funeral,

Margaret Eunice, carved in stone,
Pillowed, lying here alone,
In your Springtime,
Forever.
May 11, 1911 to April 16, 1922.

THE BOTTOMS

Mama could not stay in the Happy Jack house after Margaret died, even though we had not used the agreed upon rent. Papa found a little house in the "bottoms" on the South Side, south of Crow Creek.

It was an old neighborhood with small neat houses, shady lawns and big sunny gardens. There were great old cottonwoods and willow trees. The creek flowed in a wide lazy S curve through green meadows around the north and east sides of it.

The creek reflected the sky, sparkled in all of the right places, meandered around hummocks and rocks or moved briskly in narrowed banks with its spring snow-melt tide. A creek by any definition, bona fide, alive, yet dying, as it carried along the burden of Cheyenne's untreated sewage, April 1922.

We all walked down to the Tenth Street bridge that first evening to inspect it. Sadly, we knew that this was not like the creeks of North Dakota; here no fishing, no fun. Alas, poor creek!

"When the water goes down and the weather gets warm, the creek will begin to smell bad. We'll be out of here before then. You children stay away from the creek. Understood?"

He looked at each of us directly, with his big brown eyes.

We understood. We knew better than to disobey. Nothing physical, just his disapproval was enough to keep us on the straight and narrow path of respect and obedience.

"It's a downright disgrace," he said. "When we get situated, I mean to speak up about this."

There were just two main rooms in the little yellow-painted brick house plus a lean-to kitchen and pantry. Like most of the houses in the bottoms, it had a privy. It was no different from any small rural town in America. The house was fairly clean and its roof did not leak.

"It will have to do for now," Mama said. " We are just camping here but it will have to be spic and span."

There was something for everyone to do. We all got dressed up for the job with towels pinned around our heads, and aprons. My job was to go over the windows, inside and out, with ammonia and water, then polish them shining with finely crumpled newspapers. I had to stand on a chair to do the top sash. Windows can be boring and I had to have frequent inspections to keep up my courage. There was liberal praise for everyone.

Mama cleaned walls and ceilings with a towel over the business end of a broom. Lanore got to sweep the porch and back stoop. Her job was quickly finished and she spent the afternoon pushing Buddy on his little wooden "kiddie car." Ethel happily washed the clothespins and rinsed and rinsed and rinsed them, getting herself very wet.

"I'll help you Sister," she said, "when I get through with my work."

Papa added to the prestige of housecleaning by insisting on an apron. He scrubbed the floors with a broom and warned, mimicking Mama, "Don't anybody track up my floor."

Lanore, Ethel and I slept in the sofa bed. Buddy's crib stood in the corner of the living room. The curtains were up and the little house was as clean as we could make it. We all felt that we had done something important. We were loved and cherished. If this is poverty, we should share the wealth.

I was glad to go back to school after that last weekend in April. The new neighborhood was interesting in the assortment of people who lived there. We were still getting settled when Mama discovered a mouse-nest in an old chest. She swept it up in a newspaper and took it to the ash pit.

Looking up she saw a white haired lady coming down the alley. "Welcome to the bottoms," she said. "I am Mary Benson. I live at 610 West Tenth, keeping house for my father, he's ninety, and my brother Tom, he's sixty-five. I'm a mid-wife, I've birthed half the babies in this town. I see ye'll be needin' my services. When are you due?" She hardly stopped for a breath.

Mama loved her on sight. So did we all.

"Tom, the old pennypincher, won't have a telephone. Do ye mind if I call my son, John? He's butcher at Olsen's grocery." She vigorously cranked the wall telephone, gave the number to the operator and after a bit of banter, gave the grocery order to her son.

Then she asked if she could give the number to Dr. Henneberry, with whom she worked on maternity cases. "So many women are having their babies at the hospital these days. Some of the doctors are refusing to deliver at home."

"Of course," Mama said, "there are always plenty of willing feet to run errands at this house."

The Glovers lived next door, on the corner. They had big trees and a lawn but the two little boys preferred to dig in the dirt outside of the fence. There were no sidewalks, only worn paths outside of the fences.

Mrs. Glover came over to introduce herself and to "borrow" the telephone, telling the operator, "36, please." Her husband was the ticket agent at the Burlington depot.

"Honey, this is Mae. Honey, please bring home some bread and lunch meat. And don't forget my magazine." She had red hair and fair freckled skin. She phoned her grocery list almost every day.

The Liotas lived next door west of Grandma Benson, as everyone called her. Mrs. Liota was English. Mr. Liota, a Sicilian, had lived in England waiting for the quota to allow him to immigrate to the United States. They kept a cow and had a very productive garden. Already, in early spring, they had greens from their hot beds.

West of the Liotas lived the Horns, a black family. We seldom saw then except for Mrs. Horn's two pretty little girls by a former marriage. The children went to Johnson school. Their mother did part-time house work, we heard, and Mr. Charles Horn was a cook at the Union Pacific.

All of them lived on the Tenth Street side of the block. There was no street on the west side of the block, just a grassy place between the fences, where Victor Jam, the French painter who lived at 700 West Tenth, picketed his goats. He was the only resident of the seven hundred block.

Crow Creek took the place of a street on the north side of the block.

Our house, 1010 O'Neil was the only house facing the east side of the block.

The three northwest lots in the block belonged to Mary Burk, who was the mother of Charles Horn, we learned later. (In the city directory of 1922, this place was listed as "rear of 1010 O'Neil.") She lived in a small low gabled house. It was much later that we learned that Mary had inherited the property from a lady whose laundress she had been for many years.

Papa was already in the "flivver" one morning waiting impatiently to take us to school when we saw her coming down the alley, the only access to her place. She was accompanied by her great giant of a husband and pushing a wobbly-wheeled, discarded hand-cart, branded "UP" on the side.

She stopped at our gate. She read our curiosity and found no prejudice.

"Mornin' y'all. I'm Mary Burk, and this here's my man, George. 'Kid Fox' they called him. He were a prize fighter," she said proudly. The huge old man touched his derby and made a rumbling noise, deep in his throat. He was the blackest man I had ever seen and he wore that remarkable brown derby at a jaunty angle. It was covered with a mesh of crocheted black yarn, which probably held it together. Mary wore a man's felt hat and suit coat over layers of skirts and sweaters.

"We goin' to town to get scraps for my little dowgs." There were about twenty dogs, all sizes and colors, chained or tied to their hutches, whining and yelping, on the other side of the fence.

"Don't woik too hard, now. Be easy. Be easy fo' you baby." They moved on toward town. It was dark when they returned, singing. I could not make out words or tune. It had a kind of spiritual sound, like "vox humana" on an organ. The dogs set up a joyful yelping.

Grandma Benson had suggested that we might be able to get milk from the Robataille family. She said that there used to be a lot of small dairies in the neighborhood, her brother John's being the best. He had quit the business and moved away in 1915.

Mama called the Robatailles. They said that they no longer sold milk but we could get it as long as they had a surplus. We were to bring our own containers and the price was ten cents a quart. We started that evening. It was my pleasure to go and fetch the milk in mason jars. Several times a week they gave us a gallon of skim milk which I carried in a Karo syrup pail.

The Robataille compound consisted of the entire nine hundred block on O'Neil. A French-Canadian, Antoine Robataille had built his home in the middle of the block, giving a house and lot to each of his children, the neighbors said. Some of them had sold or rented theirs. Daughter Emma still lived at home. Behind the house, the dairy barn and outbuildings were connected by raised board walks. Everything had a well-scrubbed look.

One day I saw Mr. Robataille sprinkling something on his lawn. I asked what he put on it that made it so green? He laughed and said he was just putting some seed on the bare spots. I could not see any bare spots.

The story in the neighborhood was that as a young man Robataille had quarrelled with his sweetheart. He had married someone else and eventually brought his family to the United States. Many years later, after his wife had died, he returned for a visit and found that Stephanie had not married. It was so romantic.

Now they sat on the front porch on warm days, in their rocking chairs, the picture of sedate vieillesse. M'sieur in patriarchal black with a broad brimmed hat; Madame, also in black with a white apron, lacy white cap and a dainty white shawl.

We did not have much time to get acquainted. Lanore and I were still attending Churchill School, kept busy with chores and home work. Year end exams were coming up and my parents were ignoring my worries. I was teaching the Irish Reel to my sisters. The Churchill girls were performing it for the May Fete scheduled for the last Saturday in May in City Park. School would be out the first week in June.

The fifteenth of May, Papa was waiting for us to get out of school. Usually we waited for him.

"Come on, hurry up, get in," he seemed impatient. He drove faster than usual, down Snyder, through the underpass, east on Tenth Street to O'Neil.

"Change your clothes and help your Mama, she isn't feeling well."

Mrs. Benson was there, having tea. Mama had baked bread. Again we were urged to hurry and change. "Wash and you can have some hot bread and butter."

"Mmm, my favorite. It smells so good." Then, "Outside, on the porch to eat your bread and butter. Off with you!"

Mrs. Benson went home to give her men their supper. Grandma called a couple of times. Mama assured her that everything was all right. Mama rested on the sofa. Papa dished up supper, right off the stove!

Something was going on and I wasn't in on it. Mrs. Benson came back and she and Mama went into the bedroom. I dawdled, washing the dishes. I found excuses to go in and see how she was feeling. This must be the time for the baby but still no one was telling me anything. I felt let down and angry with my parents.

After a final roundup and scrubbing of the little ones, we were told to take our nighties and go home with Mrs. Benson. She put us to bed in her high wooden bed. Her Bible was on the night stand. I wanted to read a little but she put out the light and said, "When you wake up there will be a new baby at your house."

We said our prayers and I comforted myself with the "scientific statement of being," from *Science and Health with Key to the Scriptures* by Mary Baker Eddy, and a few favorite psalms. Life was mysterious enough but I still resented not sharing the confidence of my parents.

True to her word, Mrs. Benson woke us with a cheerful, "Time to rise and shine. You have a new baby brother at your house."

"A brother? We're s'posed to get a sister to take Margaret's place," complained Lanore.

"Nobody could take Margaret's place," I said angrily. "Hurry or I'll leave you here." We struggled into our clothes and dashed down the alley to be first to see the new baby. He was incredibly small and dark, the only child to have dark hair like Papa.

Grandma was there and allowed us to take turns holding the baby.

No matter what was happening, we had to go to school as usual.

That evening, Mr. Liota brought over a bottle of his home-made cherry wine, to congratulate Papa on having a son. I had a jealous feeling that Papa thought that sons were better than daughters. The wine "went to his head" and he recited the Powelson "begats." He knew all of it from pre-revolutionary times. It has taken me years to trace it down because the fire took our old Bible, where it had been written by many hands.

The discussion about naming the baby went on for days. Papa had made up his mind to name him Joseph, after his brother Joseph Walker Powelson. Mama did not hold with naming children in an ancestral naming pattern. Papa admired Josephus Daniels, Secretary of the Navy under President Wilson. He had named Charles Woodrow for the "Peace President." Lanore thought Papa said "Donald." She like the name Donald. We all voted for Donald. He was finally named Joseph Donald Powelson, born May 16, 1922.

It was a beautiful day for the May Fete. There was a Maypole in each of the four blocks of old City Park. The park was an animated garden of crepe paper flowers with children in them. This cultural event was poorly reported by the press. It was an unforgettable sight. I do not know if it had ever happened before but never again after that day.

The new High School with its combination gymnasium and stage was the scene of similar events and presented less risk of nervous breakdown on the part of parents and teachers due to weather.

Lanore and I both passed. Summer arrived and we played in the neighborhood, explored and visited the library once a week. Occasionally we were sent to the grocery stores at Eleventh Street and Central Avenue, the hub of the South Side. Everywhere there were new, interesting people.

The discovery of Clear Creek, a clean, intermittent little stream that we could step across delighted us. It ran out of Van Tassell's pasture into Crow Creek between where Sixth and Seventh Streets would be, if there had been streets. It ran through the meadow where Cole School now stands. There the first yellow sweet peas (Linaria) grew. Patches of creeping white phlox lay like melting snow and as June came on, the wild rose thicket gave us countless bouquets.

Across the street, on the corner of Tenth and O'Neil was a square old tan and brown house with gingerbread spool trim on the porch, a big willow on the west side of the house and cottonwoods in front. An old boxelder leaned over the east fence. Lanore and Ethel had discovered new playmates in Dody and Bubba Hough who lived there.

In June, the Hough grandparents came from New York to visit. They drove a large sedan and stayed at the Plains Hotel. One day Lanore came running home. "Dody's grampa wants to take us to the park." Mama called to verify. "Yes," said Dody's mother, "we would like to take the children with us." The little ones had a wonderful time, "pink ice cream and everything." That evening at supper Lanore said that Dody was moving away.

Grandma Benson came over and confirmed the news. The Houghs had given her a lift on Tenth Street. She was "Nana" to the children. She said that the Houghs were trying to get the young people to come back to New York to take their "rightful" place in the family business of textile manufacturing and importing. The family had apparently patched up their differences.

Mrs. Benson told them that she knew a family that might be interested in their property. She hastened to tell Papa. A week later we were moving again.

The former Hughes dairy occupied the entire five hundred block on West Tenth Street. Although it had not been a dairy for some years, other residents had kept cows and chickens. The north half of the block was still in pasture, bounded by Crow Creek. City water was piped to its water trough. The south half of the block was woven wire fenced with turned posts every twelve feet, topped by a two by four railing.

Behind the house was the wood and coal shed, and an eight foot counterweighted gate that moved at a child's touch. The barns, all in good condition, were wrapped in an L shape around the back yard. There were two places in the carriage shed; one had been for the family buggy and the other for the horse-drawn milk wagon that once delivered milk to the city. The white-washed "dairy" where the milk was processed stood in the middle of the yard. The open mangers of the feed lot ran the length of the block outside of the house yard on Tenth Street. Behind it, a six foot board shelter fence ran from the barns to the bunk house on the east end of the block.

Most of the houses in the bottoms dated from the early 1880s, some were much older. If they had indoor toilets, they had to have cesspools. The first thing Papa did was to have Bill Talbot install a new bathroom upstairs and a more modern septic tank with an extensive drain field. At that time there was no sanitary sewer in the southwest part of Cheyenne.

Downstairs there were four big rooms, two large bedroom closets, one under the stairs, and a big pantry with shelves to the ceiling. The upstairs had probably been a bedroom, too. There was a double-hung window in the east gable and a small casement window in the south gable — with a trunk under it, that became my favorite place to read. This was the most room we had had since coming to Cheyenne.

One of my jobs was to bring down piles of old newspapers that had accumulated there. They went back to World War I. Maybe someone was saving them for their historic value. They all had to go. "Too much of a fire hazard," Papa said. I began to read. They had to call me back to 1922. I managed to save a few for future reading.

After what we had been through as a family, 522 West Tenth Street seemed like heaven. Before the summer was over, the house had been scraped and repainted. There were new cabinets in the kitchen. All of the wallpaper had been steamed off with a patent steamer from J. Rosenblum's Paint Company and the whole house had been repapered.

Much of our furniture was secondhand from the stores on West Sixteenth Street. The round extension table and the big icebox were oak. There was a good Wilton rug in a Persian pattern on the living room floor. A Victorian walnut bedroom set with burl inlays and marble tops graced our parents' bedroom. They found an oval mirrored dressing table and maple chest for the girls' room and new friends in the Waxes, the Komisars and the Bregmans. Our parents were genuinely as interested in people and their backgrounds as in the treasures they found.

In all of the activity of getting settled, the younger children forgot the warning not to play near the wide, shallow creek. Someone had placed stepping stones on the north side of the Tenth Street bridge. The Kite boys, Leo and Floyd, who lived across the street were showing the younger kids how to cross on the stones. Lanore, our tomboy, made it safely. Ethel was not so lucky. The next to last step was too long and she fell in. She waded out muddy and dripping, and stood spitting and blowing. The kids ran yelling for Mama, and she came running.

Wiping Ethel's face with her apron, Mama demanded to know if Ethel had gotten any water in her mouth? Ethel was marched home, stripped, scrubbed, shampooed, purged and put to bed to contemplate the error of her ways. We all watched to see if she would come down with some dread malady from the sewage in the creek. She apparently suffered no ill effects.

We had discovered the blessing of twenty pounds of wet wash for a dollar, delivered, by the Cheyenne Steam Laundry; flat work ironed. It was a great time saver for our busy family. I had become the family ironing girl. It was a tedious chore, even with the new electric iron and instructions in the art of pressing from Grandma.

Papa was busy with several houses but took time to take us to the Frontier Days parade, and the rodeo on Saturday. We sat in the old wooden grandstand.

On Sundays we children went to Sunday School. Mama and Grandma usually went to Wednesday evening meeting at the Christian Science Church at Twenty-Sixth and Randall. Papa didn't hold much with organized religion but enjoyed our evening reading of the lesson and the singing of the hymns. If anyone said anything about his not attending church, he reminded us that Jesus had said, "Wherever two or three are gathered in My name, there will I be also, even in the midst of them." He knew the Bible from long acquaintance but had seen too much of families quarrelling over religion. He included the entire human family in that statement. He believed that more wars had been fought in the name of religion than for any other reason. He practiced the Golden Rule and expected us to do the same.

The willow tree was my ivory tower. When not looking after my brothers and sisters, washing dishes and ironing, I grabbed a book and climbed to the crotch of the tree to catch up on my reading.

All of our hard work was rewarded when Mama gave in and let us take a picnic to Initial Cliff. In addition to sandwiches and buttermilk doughnuts we carried lemonade in a gallon syrup pail. The neighbors had assured Mama that Initial Cliff was safe enough for children. They didn't tell her we had to cross the creek on stones and planks.

The Kite kids, the Brady kids and the four of us trooped across the Tenth Street bridge and more or less followed an extinct irrigation ditch that once carried water to the packing house pond. The Galloway twins, Gerald and Geraldine, saw this little army heading for their playground and caught up. They recognized Lanore and Leo as friendly invaders. We offered to share our lunch.

Buddy got tired and kept asking if it was time to eat? We negotiated the crossing, making several trips to carry the little ones across. There we were, at the foot of this sandstone cliff, which rose above the trees.

Hand and toe holds had been carved in the soft rock and sure enough, there was the "Devil's Slide," for down traffic only. The Galloway kids scrambled up to demonstrate, then, grabbing their ankles, slid down on their shoe soles. Buddy clamored for the picnic.

We enjoyed the picnic but I was apprehensive about my athletic ability. Up was fine. Down was a disaster. I bravely went up again. This time I stayed to look at the world from this high place.

At the top of the cliff the prairie sloped away to the south and east, unbroken except for a few fields of corn and wheat and a small cluster of houses in the distance. Down the creek ranch buildings could be seen. Northeast the smoking stacks of the packing house rose beside the railroad tracks.

One of the kids pointed east, downstream, indicating the ranch buildings and said, "That's Perry Organ," the name of an early owner of the ranch. I thought she said "prairie organ." How poetic! I was moved to recite. Standing there on top of Denver Hill, I recited all thirteen stanzas of "The Brook," by Tennyson. There were really only twelve stanzas but I always threw in an extra:

> "I chatter, chatter, as I flow
> To join the brimming river
> For men may come and men may go,
> But I go on forever."

As usual, they wanted me to go on forever, but it was time to go home.

The crowning touch of our first summer came on August eighth, our parents' fourteenth wedding anniversary when the new, secondhand piano arrived. The music had not been unpacked since we had left North Dakota almost a year ago.

Hesitantly, at first, Mama played the old favorites. Home at last! There were happy tears.

"Jingle bells, jingle bells," cried little Charles. We all sang joyful "Jingle Bells," in August, "laughing all the way."

"Bells!" That reminded us of one of our favorites, "Bells of Seville." "Please, Mama, sing it." Grandma was there, urging her on. She had not wanted Mama to give up the promise of a career for marriage. Now her own marriage was in trouble.

I overheard Mama telling Papa that Collins was behaving badly again and that they were "having trouble."

"In gay Seville, long, long ago/ When folks and friends were always bright/
My happy home, I loved so well/ Ah happy, happy was the sight/
The orange grove shed sweet perfume/ The bells rang out their merry lay/"

The melody lingers on . . . How could I forget the words?

Grandma had baked an impressive cake for the anniversary dinner. She brought candles and flowers. Unfortunately, Mr. Collins had a business meeting, she said, and apologized for him.

It was a festive meal, we had so much to be thankful for. They began to reminisce. Grandma had brought some old pictures taken by her photographer brother, Gus. Mama's pictures had all burned in the fire.

Grandma, our mother, Nora Corneda Helgesen and Charles Howard Powelson had gone to Wisconsin for the wedding at the Skude grandparents' home. Relatives came from near and far. It was a garden wedding and her many cousins outdid themselves with decorations and Norwegian delicacies, August 8, 1908.

Their wedding trip was by Mississippi riverboat to visit the Powelson kin in Moscow Mills, Lincoln County, Missouri.

The summer sped by and Mama was sewing school clothes again. John Eckhart had come to work for Papa, making cabinets and millwork in the former dairy barn. Papa had bought a secondhand Chevrolet sedan with silver flower vases in the corners. There were jump seats for our always extra passengers. Papa called it our "limousine." He also had a Ford truck for hauling materials to the jobs, although he still used the flivver as a run-about.

Mama was learning to drive. Papa was an impatient teacher. They would drive around on the prairie and come back with Mama "upset" and Papa still telling her what she did wrong.

One weekend Papa and our plumber, Bill Talbot, were going to the hills fishing. Bill used to ride for the Two Bar and knew all the best places, "like the palm of his hand."

They loaded a tent, army cots purchased from the Army Surplus store, bedrolls and "enough food for an army," Mama said. She had put in plenty of corned beef, in case the fish weren't biting.

After they had gone, Mama asked Mr. Blanchard if he and Mrs. Blanchard would take a little ride in the sedan. She said that she would appreciate it if Mr. Blanchard would drive out of town a little way, then let her drive and instruct her in the proper technique. The young Blanchards understood and went along with the plan. (The Blanchards had bought one of the first little houses Papa had built on the former feed lot.)

We children, Baby Joe, Mrs. Blanchard and little Bobby, all crowded into the back seats. We started out on the Hereford road. Mr. Blanchard explained very slowly "how to shift," several times, demonstrating. Then Mama took the wheel. After she had made several attempts, grinding the gears a little, I could not resist remarking that "it doesn't make that noise when Papa drives." She turned right around on that washboard road and drove home.

Pulling up in front of the Blanchard house, she said, "Thank you very much Mr. Blanchard. I think I have the hang of it now." They disembarked. She drove on to our house and stopped in front. "Gladys, you may give the children each a doughnut and a glass of milk. I'll see you later."

She drove around for about an hour, came home and put the car in the carriage shed. She didn't quite have the confidence to put the car in the garage, (formerly a barn).

After that, she drove whenever she wanted to. We didn't hear the gears when she started and although we begged to go along, it was some time before she would take us. Papa wisely refrained from comment.

Finally, one day she drove me to the dentist. Before we started, she said, "Do you think that you can avoid making rude remarks about a person's driving?" She drove bravely over the rickety wooden viaduct, the planks "gallumping" loudly as we passed over them.

I vowed that someday I would drive like that!

On our return I was not hurting too badly to remember to thank her.

OLD CENTRAL SCHOOL

On the first day of school in 1922, I wondered if any of the kids from Johnson School would remember me. We had been busy all summer and there were no children my age in our immediate neighborhood. I had not renewed acquaintance. For the first time, sister Lanore and I would be separated.

When the day came, Mama got out the "limousine" and took Lanore and the little ones and our neighbor Mrs. Kite and her boys to Johnson School. I preferred to walk over the viaduct to Central School. I felt almost grown-up, yet apprehensive at the prospect of the new school.

As I reached the top of the hill at Central Avenue, where the sidewalk began, I recognized Irene Buckley, Evelyn Faulk and Helen Galloway coming together for the walk over the bridge. We said, "Hi!"

Helen said, "Where do you live now?" I told her. Nobody said much.

We crossed Eleventh and started up the viaduct.

Some boys came up the Twelfth Street stairs and ran past us.

About halfway over, Agnes Berkley caught up. "Hi, Aggie. Do you know Gladys?" asked Helen. We looked at each other and said, "Hi," without breaking stride. We turned right, down the Warren Avenue ramp, crossed the Burlington tracks and hurried up the street.

Aggie was a pretty girl with brown hair and a sprinking of freckles on her turned-up nose. She was animated and friendly. She left us at the Central playground to continue on toward the turreted old high school on Twenty-Second street. We just stood around waiting for the bell to ring, watching the little kids at play.

The park-like front schoolyard, with its dark spruces and great cottonwoods, took up the south half of the block. It was alive with activity. Teeters and swings were going full tilt. Little girls were jumping ropes, playing jacks or hop-scotching through the chalked mazes on the quarried stone sidewalks. Boys were knuckled down playing marbles in the dirt.

At the first sound of the bell, children began to stream toward the three sets of double doors in the old red brick buiding. Miss Lulu McCormick, herself, pulled the bell rope, saying "Good morning, good morning," and calling some by name. The bell boomed overhead sending a glissando of shivers down my spine.

Inside, a pair of stairs led (boys to the left, girls to the right) around the supply room, up to the cloakroom and office, and there, straight ahead was the big square eighth grade room. Windows wrapped around the north third of the room.

We could see the roof of the Central gymnasium over its arched windows. The gymnasium was used by all of the schools. The downstairs housed the offices of the Superintendent of Schools, Mr. A. S. Jessup, and the art, music and physical education teachers, in addition to the school nurse.

After the usual enrollment formalities and the Pledge of Allegiance, Miss McCormick said, "We are required to have prayer in the schools. If you object, you may step out into the hall or sit quietly in your seats." None left.

Then she prayed, "Heavenly Father, help us to learn, this day and throughout the year. Amen." We responded with a loud "Amen," and some relief on my part.

I remembered prayer in the schools of North Dakota. The battle raged for the last year I was in school there. Children were drilled in dogmatic prayers by their parents and the churches. Like little preachers, they lectured us at the beginning of each day, and we had to listen, whether we had our own convictions or not. I wondered if others were as embarrassed as I, at the invasion of privacy? Do they pray to improve themselves or to convert a captive audience? If they felt the need to pray, why couldn't they do it any time, anywhere, silently, I wondered?

The issue seemed to have died a peaceful death as I do not recall it going on for any length of time. I simply recited the Lord's Prayer when it was my turn. (Article 7 of the Wyoming State Constitution protects us from sectarian instruction in the public schools.)

The busy schedule began at once. Teachers came in for History, English, Geography. Math, Hygiene and Literature were the province of the principal. She felt it her duty to prepare us for citizenship. She told us anecdotes of early Cheyenne history and prepared us for social change the best she could.

Our old school, Cheyenne's first permanent school building, was built in 1871. The middle portion, with the bell tower, had been built in 1876 and the west wing was added in 1879-80, Miss McCormick said. The school would soon be going the way of the houses across the street. It would make way for a new Junior High School. Ours would very likely be the last class to graduate from the eighth grade. Next year we would go to the new senior high school at Twenty-Eighth Street and House Avenue.

At my first opportunity I went to the pencil sharpener on the windowsill, near the principal's desk. The telephone shared the sill. The window overlooked the east playground where we would play ball. An old pump without a handle, a relic of a by-gone day, stood on a platform near the back door of the east wing of the old school.

The pencil sharpener on the west windowsill, however, presented a more dramatic entertainment break from study; the traffic of Capitol Avenue, the houses across the street coming down one by one, Judge Thompson's wife, shaking her rugs.

The north windows looked down on the restroom addition which had replaced the row of privies, and the coal bin. An unexpected symphony of coal being shoveled by hand to staccato and tympani down the metal slide into the bin would remind me of the "Halls of the Mountain King," a favorite of our music appreciation class.

A corps of Girl Reserves, the Young Women's Christian Association program for grade school girls, was organized. We had meetings on Friday afternoons in the first grade room, directly under ours. We would spend the last half of the afternoon meeting "learning to dance." Miss McCormick said that we must be prepared for the high school dances. Dances! I wondered what my parents would say?

One Saturday morning I walked into the kitchen to find Grandma Benson there. She and Mama were talking in hushed tones. They turned and looked at me.

Old Territorial Central School, 1923.

PHOTO COURTESY OF WYOMING STATE ARCHIVES, MUSEUMS AND HISTORICAL DEPARTMENT

"The oldest girl was just your age. Now she will have to raise all those children," Mrs. Benson said, shaking her head sadly.

"Who died?" I asked.

Grandma Benson was shaken by her experience of the night before and repeated the story for me, although Mama tried to interrupt her or stop her. It seems that someone had sent a car for her "to come quick!" When she arrived at the house she found a woman had "knitting needle disease." She could do nothing to stop the bleeding. The doctor came and he could not correct the situation. Finally, they rushed the woman to the hospital where they said, "It is too late." She left six children.

Mama sent me to round up the children and get them washed for lunch.

Although it was never mentioned, I learned much later which one of my classmates it was, whose mother had tried to bring about an abortion. She missed a lot of school, having to stay home with the children when they were sick.

The trip over the viaduct was probably good for our lungs and legs. As the windy winter came on it was sometimes hard to keep from being blown off my feet. Eighty-seven pounds is not a lot of ballast.

Coming from North Dakota with its tornadoes, my parents kept me home one day, fearing the worst when the winds were so strong. How the kids laughed when they heard my excuse! North Dakota had wind, too, but this was to be a windy winter even for Wyoming.

One afternoon, on our way home over the viaduct, we met a tall gaunt man in black, with coattails flapping, holding tightly to his hat. (I thought he would make a perfect Ichabod Crane.)

"Hello boys," he said. We giggled.

"Hello Father," answered Helen. Her elbow jabbed my ribs. "You're supposed to call him 'Father'," she said.

"He's a long way from his church," said Charlotte.

"His name is Bishop Patrick A. McGovern," continued Helen Galloway. "He visits the sick and the old folks who can't go to church, my mother says. He walks all over town in all kinds of weather to see after folks."

I was surprised by her apparent defense of the man. "Are you Catholic?" I asked. "No, but my mother says there aren't many who put themselves out to look after the old and sick, except the Salvation Army and a few preachers."

I met him one day, near the Tenth Street bridge. I remembered to say, "Hello Father." I guessed that he had been to see Mrs. Jordan and probably the Robatailles. Mrs. Mary Jordan, our Irish neighbor, was from the old country and I imagined that he too was from Ireland. I was disappointed to learn that he had been born in Omaha, Nebraska.

I smelled the cardamon scented doughnuts before I got into the house.

Mama said, "Here take a plate of doughnuts over to Mrs. Jordan, poor soul. The priest has been to see her; she has been sick."

I was supposed to hurry back but I lingered to admire her tea pot with the shamrocks and the pretty lace cloth.

I told Mrs. Jordan that I had met her visitor.

"He's a good man. He hears me confession," Mrs. Jordan said.

At home I told Mama, "Helen says he's a bishop. Imagine! A bishop. That's supposed to be like a prince of the Church! And he walks all over town!"

From the pencil sharpener at school we could see the steel being erected for the Wyoming Consistory buiding on Capitol Avenue, across the street. Huge blocks of grey stone were being lifted by a steam crane. Something was always happening.

Miss McCormick knew all about the pencil sharpener syndrome. One day she called us to the window. We talked about the principle of the steam crane, and its power to lift the stones. The boys explained it. Then she said, "Now let's see if we can get some work done."

When the building was demolished in the late sixties, I wondered why such a lot of beautiful stone should be wasted.

The legislature met in January, 1923. Our principal took us to observe. We had been studying about how an idea becomes a law. Representative Thomas Hunter introduced us, and the legislature applauded! I had a great report for my family at supper that night.

Soon after that Miss McCormick called us to the window to watch the University of Wyoming students marching through the mud of Capitol Avenue to lobby for the Library at the University. They had come over from Laramie by train. They waved at us! One of them, Olga Moore Arnold, later wrote about the trek from the depot to the Capitol in her book, *I'll Meet You In the Lobby.*

History and literature came alive under the tutelage of our great and dedicated teacher. She sent all of us out to interview an "old timer," or an older relative who had lived in Cheyenne a long time. She, herself, had been teaching at Central since 1886. She told us about the flood of 1904. When we were studying hygiene she told us about the many deaths from typhoid, due to contaminated water wells. We were horrified to learn that the source of contamination was human excreta entering the water supply.

I made an appointment with Theresa Jenkins, a friend of our family. Mrs. Jenkins had been a prominent suffragist working for the vote and equal rights. She had made the oration on behalf of women on the occasion of the official celebration of Wyoming statehood, July 23, 1890. She regretted that women were not taking enough advantage of equality in the business world.

She talked about life in old Cheyenne. Going shopping meant wearing a long, heavy dark skirt that swept the ground. One had to put it on the clothesline and beat it on returning home. Or let the mud dry and beat it later. Sanitation on every front was a problem. Water was a problem.

Betty Law lived next door to Mrs. Tom Durbin, whose husband had been a driver for the Deadwood Stage. We called on Mrs. Durbin together. She told us about the famous incident, when she hid the bank's money in the baby's diaper bag so the holdup men did not get it.

Betty had also interviewed her grandfather, Hudson P. Norcross. As a child he had arrived on the first train from Julesburg with his parents. His father had built some of the first houses in Cheyenne. He too, became a builder.

Once during a history discussion, I said, "My Papa says, . . ."the kids laughed. That evening I called my father, "Dad," at supper, for the first time.

He gave me a sharp, surprised look.

Mama drew in a big breath and said, "Young lady, mind how you address your father."

"I meant no disrespect, Papa," I said. "Today, the kids laughed when I said 'My Papa says'."

"Well, as long as you are not meaning to be rude," he said. "Down home, in Missouri, we always called our father 'Pap.' We meant no disrespect."

To myself, I thought, "I'll bet that plenty of those kids call their fathers 'Papa,' especially if 'Papa' is foreign-born."

To keep us on our toes, Miss McCormick would call on us at random for current events. One morning at breakfast, I suddenly remembered that I did not have a current event for the day.

Papa said sharply, "Didn't you read the paper last night?"

"Yes Papa, but I don't remember anything important."

"Why don't you give the item about Carrie Chapman Catt?" Papa was an admirer of the great leader of the woman suffrage movement. At that moment I had no idea of the influence she was to have on my life.

I recited the news item in the *Tribune* that Mrs. Catt had "called the second convention of the League of Women Voters to meet jointly with the Pan-American Conference of Women in Chicago." The League of Women Voters had been formed at the last convention of the National American Woman's Suffrage Association. They would embark on a never-ending commitment to improve the status of women.

In the discussion that followed, I reported that my grandmother had marched in a suffrage parade in Wisconsin. The marchers sang a song to the tune of "Onward Christian Soldiers," and people threw eggs at them. Grandma said that it was hard to maintain your dignity with egg running down the front of your blouse. An egg hit cousin Amanda but she kept on singing at the top of her voice, tears streaming down her face. Grandma still believed that women would be equal when they learned to use the vote.

Several boys reported the latest rumors about the strike settlement. Their manner was matter-of-fact, strangely as though it were happening in Outer Mongolia; their account of an issue so wrapped in the emotional involvement of a generation, like true Stoics, betrayed no personal feelings.

"The National Railroad Board had given eight hours as the working period. The minimum wage was to be seventy-five cents. Union request for an increase was not granted."

The headlines reflected the anti-labor sentiment of the press. "Punitive Overtime Ordered for Sundays and Legal Holidays." "Labor Legislation Rough Sledding; No Repair Sheds Over Rip Tracks by Action of Law."

The animosities between the families of strikers and non-strikers were not lost on me. One did not ask personal questions about such things.

Learning to interview had given me a new appreciation of the people in our neighborhood. Some had been in Cheyenne since its early days. However, some of the newcomers were equally interesting.

The Sam Beaumonts were new, since 1921. Sam had been a traveling salesman, now considered too old. He worked as a night clerk in the Normandie Hotel. They were down on their luck, as he put it, when they rented our little bunk house.

In England, Mrs. Beaumont had married a young man of good family who turned out to be a drunkard and a gambler. She placed him in a private institution. Then divorce and disgrace being synonymous in that day, she immigrated to Canada.

There she met Sam. They were married and lived in Washington and New York. Then came Chicago, which she hated, except for the library, museums and concerts. I guessed that she was too refined to comment on Cheyenne.

Although she was very nearsighted, she continued to read a shopping bag full of books every week. She and Sam had a little grey Italian poodle, they called "Scotty." The three of them walked everywhere together.

We did not know her first name. It was not polite to ask an older person's first name, Mama explained. Mrs. Beaumont played sonatas from memory, although it had been years since she had owned a piano. When she read music, her nose was inches from the page. Her glasses were the thickest I had ever seen.

Afternoon tea was a well-earned break for my hard working mother. Some of the neighbors would drop in to just visit or to use the telephone. They were there when I burst in from school with the news that I was to play Queen Isabella for history class. I had to have a long dress, "a very long dress."

"Maybe Grandma has something we can use. We will improvise something," said Mama.

"I have the very thing," cried Mrs. Beaumont, dumping Scotty unceremoniously off her lap. "I shall return presently." She cut through the backyard and returned, out of breath. Scotty yapped excitedly. She carried a large suit-box tied with yellow ribbons. With trembling fingers, she undid the knots and we saw a silk and lace dream of a dress shake out of the folds. It smelled of lavender. She held it up to me.

"Slip it on, dear, slip it on."

The tiny waist would be too small, even if I held my breath.

"Oh, no," Mama said, "It's much too precious!"

The bodice was made with small vertical pleats sewn onto a deep yoke of handmade lace, "Suisse de Soie," she said. The skirt glowed softly in graduated bands of old ivory Bengal silk, faggotted together over a heavy satin underskirt. It buttoned up the back with tiny lace covered buttons. Every stitch was hand made. We knew it had been a valuable gown in its day. It was a priceless antique now.

They gathered around and buttoned me into it. "Stand up straight," Mama commanded. The skirt lay around me on the floor. I sagged with the weight of it. Mama rushed to the bedroom for safety pins.

"It is so beautiful, but I can't let you," said Mama.

"I insist. It is my pleasure," Mrs. Beaumont replied. They embraced.

Mrs. Beaumont was so elated that she sat down and played a Sonata all the way through. I wondered what memories caused the tears that dampened her cheek.

Grandma came over to inspect the marvel and to mend a raveled seam.

"See how the warp thread is wrapped tightly with twisted silk, then wefted with a lighter twist of silk to give that heavy corded look? Bengaline is the name generally given to any heavy corded material, this is the real thing. True Bengali silk, the finest I have ever seen." Grandma wanted us to appreciate fine craftsmanship.

I wondered how many silkworms had given their lives for that dress?

Betty Law liked theatricals, too. She and I had written the play together. She had made a sword and a crown of cardboard covered with gold paper from her father's drug store. She was to be lady-in-waiting and hand me the jewels to give to Christopher Columbus, played by Herbert Harris, after I had tapped him on the shoulder with the gold sword. The play was just for class. There were no auditoriums in the schools.

When the day came, Mama drove me to school. She fretted about the dress. The wooden floors were oiled and swept with an oily compound to keep down the dust. "Keep the dress up off the floor," she warned.

I had told the class about the dress being Mrs. Beaumont's wedding dress, made for her at the Paris Exposition in 1889. She had also given me a lacquered box of beads, brooches and bracelets to use on the big day. I wore some of them myself. The gown stole the show.

Miss Sullivan, Miss McCormick and Betty helped me dress. Other teachers came in to see the dress. I held my shoulders as high as I could, but still a brown streak marked the bottom of the skirt. Miss Sullivan muttered that it would serve us right if the mark would not come out. It was outrageous to let a child wear such a gown. Fortunately, some of Grandma's dry cleaning compound dissolved in naptha removed it.

Mr. Beaumont found a job as a bookkeeper for a machinery company and they moved into Elee Robataille's little three room house on Tenth and O'Neil, kitty-corner from us. Later they bought a new little house on East Lincolnway.

After Sam died, friends got Mrs. Beaumont into the Pioneer Home at Thermopolis. She was nearly blind. I have often wondered what became of that dress.

The day of the play, as usual, after school, I had to change from school clothes and bring in arm-loads of wood for kindling the fires; a scuttle of lump coal for the range and a scuttle of chunks for the heater.

I had been queen for a day!

One morning I was almost late, and I would have been, except that Miss McCormick had three seventh grade boys in the office. They were big boys, all from the South Side. They found their courage in unity. However, they were visibly moved by her caring. Hanging up my wraps, I could see them. She could not see me. She pleaded with them not to leave school for apprenticeship at the shops.

I slipped into my seat and tried to look busy.

We heard them clatter away down the boy's stairs. She came into the room and forgetting the preliminaries, lectured us about staying in school to prepare for a better way of life. One of the boys told her that he had applied for apprenticeship but was turned down because he was "too small." It was not long before he, too, left to be a "call boy." "Call boys" were the bicycle messengers who were sent to notify the trainmen that they were needed for a run. Not many people had telephones in those days.

Although the south and west sides of town had no monopoly on "blue-collar" workers, the people who lived in these areas were, for the most part, in the labor force. The fact that there had been no eighth grades in either the south or west schools for many years, if ever, seems to indicate that there was a concentrated effort to force these children into the labor market early.

We frequently saw a girl that I remembered from seventh grade crossing the viaduct. She wore a white uniform and worked in a laundry. She always seemed to be cross and sometimes would not return our greeting. She had had to work or starve, she said. Her father was out on strike. Her brother was a "call boy." Four other children were in school and they had to keep food on the table.

When I reported these events at home, my parents repeated the lecture about getting a good education to help me to have a better quality of life.

Most parents perceived an education to be the road out of a life of poverty and hard, long hours of labor.

THE CLASS OF '27

Ours was the first freshman class to register at the new high school in 1923 at Twenty-Eighth and House Avenue. When the new school was ready, the previous class and the teachers, en masse, had walked to the new school carrying their books and gear, through the falling leaves of the beautiful old City Park where the Barrett Building now stands.

The old Victorian building then served as a junior high school for eighth grade only, until McCormick Junior High School was built on the grounds of old Territorial Central School. Home economics and shop classes were taught in the basement of Central gymnasium for this first junior high school.

Of the South Side kids, only Evelyn Faulk, Frances Junge and I registered for College Preparatory. Most of our colleagues opted for commercial and mechanical courses. "Learn something to make a living," our parents urged. I loved it all but Math and Home Economics, which was required of all girls at that time.

For the first time in my life I experienced discrimination because of the location of my home. On our walks to school, up Warren Avenue, girls from both east and west fell in with the girls from the south. They seemed to have a lot of social activities. I guess I envied them.

PHOTO COURTESY OF SCHOOL DISTRICT NO. 1

CHEYENNE HIGH SCHOOL, Twenty-Eighth and House Avenue. Erected 1922.

One time I heard them planning a party. One of the South Side girls was going, call her Susan. I was not invited. They were planning to start at one home and go on to a country dance hall called Pine Grove.

About three o'clock in the morning Susan's mother called our house.

"Do you know where your daughter is?" Susan's mother asked.

"Yes, she is asleep in her bed," Mama said.

"Well, those kids are in jail. There was a raid on Pine Grove."

"What kids?"

"Didn't she go to the party?"

"What party?"

Mama came in and woke me. "Your friends are in jail," she said. "Your friend Susan told her mother that she would be spending the night here."

The story was all over school Monday. Just because we walked to school together, I was supposed to be one of the bunch. Susan came to school to check out. Her folks were sending her to live with relatives in another state. She finished school there and grew to respectable citizenship despite being involved in a so-called wild party. She was the only South Side girl I ever knew who was supposed to have done anything unconventional.

After that I was never allowed to go to a dance. Even my parents' friends thought they were being too old-fashioned. I could go to games, play practices, other evening events, but never dances; not even the proms! It was hard to believe that my parents had my "best interests at heart."

In the summer of my sophomore year, 1925, *The Wyoming Eagle* was being launched by Tracy S. McCraken. There was a subscription contest. I thought that I could get a lot of subscriptions on the South Side. I walked and walked and knocked on many doors.

The winner of the contest, Claudia Hopka, won the Chevrolet. Claudia was the time keeper at the Union Pacific. She got to the subscribers before I did.

My twenty-five dollar fourth prize was the most money I had ever had. I bought my first "store-bought" coat at J. C. Penney's with the money. Mama was a bit hurt, I think. She was an excellent seamstress. She considered "ready-mades" to be poorly constructed. At 1925 prices, she figured, that I could have had a dress and shoes, plus a coat in my choice of color and fabric.

Although there was more precipitation and livestock prices were better in 1926 through 1928, the building business continued to decline. My parents were urging me to take Normal Training in my senior year. I would be able to earn college money while teaching in a country school. It would delay my plans to study art but it made sense. Mama's cousins had all been teachers. I would also take correspondence courses in my spare time.

Papa was building a new cream colored brick house for us at Twentieth and Morrie Avenue. He had been working very hard and had a summer cold.

It turned into pneumonia. The doctor came every day. Papa was unconscious. Then finally, they said, the crisis had passed.

Mama had to go uptown and take care of some business. There were a dozen "stick-built" houses under construction. We had a good foreman in Jake Weber, but there were many things to be attended to. Mama said that the children should be kept quiet and outside. "Don't let anyone in to see him." I promised. People were calling every day. The bell rang and there was Mr. R. on the porch. He thrust a huge bouquet of flowers at me. "Here, Honey, put these in some water, I just want to see good old Charlie for a minute."

I said, "Papa is asleep. He can't be disturbed."

Papa heard, "What is it, Sis?"

Mr. R. rushed past me. I took the flowers to the kitchen and put them into a pitcher. I hurried back. Papa lay on his pillows, so white and drawn. Mr. R. was putting some papers back into his breast pocket. He left in a hurry. I just knew I had done something bad.

Later there was litigation with Mr. R.'s firm, several of the houses under construction were for these people. They were afraid Papa was going to die. Our attorney questioned me closely. He told me I might have to take the stand. I didn't. They settled out of court.

The depression had started early in Cheyenne, our profit margin was very small and it was hard to stay ahead of the game. We are never immune to crooks.

Much as I had resisted the idea of being a teacher, I found the subject fascinating. Miss Virgil Payne was an inspiring teacher. She also taught us psychology. I did my practice teaching under the guidance of Miss McCormick. All of the teachers were my friends. They did all they could to help me.

That year a new class for handicapped children and those with learning disabilities, was being tried at Central. It was called, "Special Education." I marveled at the innovative methods of the teacher. We visited the class as a group. The teacher, Mrs. Kvenvolden, urged us to specialize in this new field.

I threw myself into my art work, trying to absorb as much as possible from my friend and teacher, Miss Wills, while there was still time. My family encouraged me. I was invited to join the all-adult Cheyenne Art Club.

Mama's uncles Gus and Charlie Skude, were good artists in oil, water color and photography, but worked as house painters to make a living. Art gave them satisfaction and a lift above the mundane, some acclaim and a little money. I decided to take my cue from them.

We moved into our new house in February of 1927. The whole family had helped with the sanding of the back banded woodwork, hand selected by our father. After the sanding, we were given a piece of glass and taught to "glass finish." The woodwork glowed satin smooth. The dining room was my work.

Victor Jam, our painter for several years, stippled the walls over aluminum paint giving them an iridescent, polychrome look. A native of Lisle, France, he had been our neighbor on the South Side. I used to try out my school French on him.

My parents once invited him, a bachelor, far from home, to share a traditional American Thanksgiving dinner. He created a social crisis by bringing a bottle of his home-made wine. Mama was a "teetotaler" but she brought out the best glasses for him and Papa. Victor laughed and said, "In France even the children take wine with meals." The next day he brought a gift of his home-made goat cheese. It was delicious.

Money was very tight, there was little building. It took several more years to finish the house. Papa did all of the work on the upstairs, himself. He floored it with the maple from the recently demolished Central gymnasium, refinishing it to gleaming perfection. During the depression of the thirties he created several apartments which brought in a little income.

Leaving high school, the safe cocoon of home, the comfort of friends, generated mixed emotions for me as for most teen-agers. Life would never again be so predictable. The next day after graduation, June 10, 1927, I would be eighteen. I was eager to get on with it.

As we waited in the library for the signal to go down to graduation on the combination stage-gymnasium, Mr. McIntosh, our principal, told us that the aviators, Levin and Chamberlain, had landed in Paris. (This was the team that had followed Lindberg's historic flight.) They had flown first to Germany, landing June 4, 1927, then on to Paris. A cheer went up, breaking the tension. We had entered the air age!

Frances Junge, a South Side girl, was salutatorian. She gave us a serious view of the world and our responsibilities in it. My parents commented that it was a sobering thought to contemplate the world their children were facing.

Arnold Ridderstadt, the South Side boy who went through high school on crutches, was given a standing ovation as he went to get his diploma. For four years, Arnold would wait at the foot of the stairs until the rush had passed. Then he would pull himself up, using the stair rail and his crutches under one arm. He had been sending us an subconscious message, "If I can do this, think what you can do."

THE PEOPLE

GRANDMA BENSON

Among the fondest memories for many a child in a blue-collar family, was the comfort of being rocked in Grandma Benson's aproned lap, as she "teld thee wee toes; this little piggy went to market," or softly sang a universally understood lullaby in her strange, unintelligible Welsh.

She was a baby-sitter, midwife and neighborhood granny. She knew all of the news about the blue-collar people as well as the backgrounds and pedigrees of the well-to-do. She told her stories without malice, but with great tolerance for the foibles of humanity.

She had washed and laid out the dead in Wales and in Cheyenne. She cried as she told of going with a neighbor to help her identify the charred and dismembered body of the woman's husband, killed in an explosion and fire in the coal chutes, which she called the "colliery." The bodies had been laid out on tables in the "beanery." Although her own life had been hard, she taught us to care about the sufferings of others. We remember her tears.

Born Mary Ann Hughes in Moynton, Wales, in 1855, she had married John Benson and had seven children when she came to the United States in the 1890s. Coming down the gangplank, upon their arrival in the United States, Mary Ann heard someone say, "Look at all the foreigners."

She turned to John and said, "Jack, did you hear that? They called us foreigners. Are you going to stand for that?"

It was a long trip with so many restless children. Somewhere west of Chicago, a lady asked, "How far are you going?"

"Shinny, Wyoming, wherever in the world that is," she replied.

When the family arrived in Cheyenne, they lived in the little brick house at 1010 O'Neil. The house, built before 1877, is still in use.

Her parents, John and Elizabeth, brothers Tom and John and sister Jenny, had all come to Cheyenne about 1880. The elder Hughes worked as a sander, when sand for braking the locomotives had to be carried up by hand. Tom, unmarried, was a pipefitter. John operated a dairy at 610 West Tenth Street, the family home. He later moved to 522 West Tenth Street. He built his new barns and feed yard on this block. In 1915 he sold this business and moved to Oregon.

Sister Jenny married Harry Cole and lived at the corner of Tenth and O'Neil, in the midst of the family group.

Times were little better in the United States, however, with low pay, strikes and many mouths to feed. Benson was a finish painter of railroad cars with their many coats of varnish, decorated with fancy curlicues and lettering. In the British tradition of class, even in the trades, he would not take a job "beneath himself" when that work ended.

Disillusioned, Benson returned to the old country. Mary Ann refused to go with him. He found conditions even worse in England and returned after several years. Mary Ann refused to take him back.

At the time of our directory, 1922, Mary Ann and her children, John, Frank, and Jim, butchers; Tom, a grocer; George and Albert, who were working for the Union Pacific, all lived on the South Side.

Daugther Rose Roberts had moved to California. Soon Tom and George left for California also. Then Benson went to live with his daughter.

Mary Ann supported herself as a midwife, and boarded railroad workers. She did their laundry, which she washed on a board, scrubbing with a brush and lye soap. After her mother died, she moved to her father's house and took care of him for the rest of his life. For this, she received the little house at Seventh and Capitol, income property when she was not living there.

The Hughes family had for generations followed the butcher's trade. Mary Ann's son, John, learned it from the Nimmo brothers and taught his brothers. They worked in the local markets.

Jim Benson worked as meat cutter at O'Connell's Market. O'Connell had supported the strike. Many a striker would not have been able to feed his family, if it had not been for credit at O'Connell's. The big-hearted Irishman had grown up on the South Side, and though he now lived "up-town," he was one of our own.

After the store failed, Jim Benson and his cousin, Donald Pierce bought it and tried to carry on. It was not a good year to start a business in 1924. Later, Jim worked in the Post Office until his retirement at age seventy. He and his wife, Carrie, had three daughters, Barbara, Virginia, and Romona.

Agnes Benson remained single and worked for a local insurance company for many years.

Murriel Woods recalls the tragedy of John and Ida Benson's family. Four of their children died of diphtheria within a few days of each other. Paul, Eugene and Hughes survived. Paul, at eighteen, came down with appendicitis at National Guard Camp in California. Invalided home, he lived a few months after the operation. The birth of daughter Beth in 1920 was considered a blessing, she brought joy to the family. They moved to Lander in 1923.

Polly (Mary) Benson married Paul Milatzo, a shoemaker. He was appointed Italian Consul for Wyoming and served as an interpreter for the

Union Pacific. From a yellowed clipping, we have the following account which appeared in the June 5, 1924 issue of the *Wyoming State Tribune*:

FIVE GENERATIONS
OF FAMILY
ALL RESIDENTS OF CHEYENNE

Mrs. Paul Milatzo, a 46 year old grandmother brought the record of the Hughes family, all residents of this city are as follows:

John Hughes, age 92 years, 610 W. 10th, great-grandfather.

Mrs. John W. Benson, 69, resides with her father, great-grandmother.

Mrs. Paul Milatzo, 46, 3029 Snyder Ave., grandmother.

Mrs. Clifford A. Long, 22, 923 Richardson Ct., mother.

Paul Clifford Long, 22 months, and Violet Marie, 4, children of Mrs. Long.

Al and Myrtle Benson raised four children, Dorothy, James, Robert and John.

Frank and Naomi and their children, Bill and Rosemary, moved to Rawlins. After high school, Rosemary returned to the old neighborhood and attended the Cheyenne Business College. She met and married John Belecky, who had come to this country from Vienna, Austria, in 1921.

The Belecky family operated a confectionery shop in the middle of the 700 block on Central Avenue, close to Johnson School, as well as a filling station on the corner. This family enclave was one of the casualties of the I-180 Connector demolition in the early seventies.

The schoolkids' favorite place in the neighborhood was presided over by Rosemary, known to everyone as "Babe." The kids were usually well behaved for they knew that Babe would tell their parents if they got out of line. She did not allow them to smoke in her shop.

The home-neighborhood business was just a block away from Babe's grandmother Mary Ann's house. The little Belecky boys had the good fortune of knowing this wonderful lady, their great-grandmother.

The boys, John and Robert, graduated from the University of Wyoming. John is in hospital adminstration at Gillette. He and his wife, Georgia, have two children, Craig and Teri. Craig graduated from Casper College and Teri is studying at the University of Wyoming.

Robert is Manager of Construction for the Public Service Company of Colorado. He and his wife, Jo Queta Shadley Belecky, live in Denver.

In 1961, the Beleckys built a home on an acreage on Terry Road. When John retired after forty-two years with the Cheyenne Light Fuel and Power Company, they decided that they had had enough of suburbia. They now live the condo life in east Cheyenne.

BERKLEY - WILLOUGHBY

Great-uncle Junius Berkley set up his law practice in Boulder in the gold rush days. He was soon joined by his father Grenville Berkley, and his younger brother, Grenville II. Grenville Berkley, Sr., did not plan to stay; however, he too set up a law practice and became a judge in the Boulder-Clear Creek District. (He carried a little gold-scale for weighing out the payment for his services in gold dust.)

Grenville Berkley II married Clarissa Cordelia White and operated a freighting business, hauling supplies and machinery for the gold camps from the railroad at Cheyenne. He also had an ice business, storing ice from the lake to be delivered in the summer.

Frank Berkley, son of Grenville II, married Minnie Katrine Jensen, who had come to Colorado, via Kansas, from Aalberg, Denmark. They homesteaded near Magnolia, Colorado.

In 1902, after the panic of 1897, they moved to Cheyenne with their children Roland, Benjamin, McKenzie and Madeline. Five more children were born in Cheyenne: Adeline, Grenville III (Bob), Agnes, Doris and Clarence.

Frank went to work in the Union Pacific shops as a machinist. As the boys grew up, they became apprentices and eventually, machinists, too. Madeline (Madge) and Adeline were secretaries for the State of Wyoming.

A favorite story of the Berkley family concerns Aggie and Sank, their St. Bernard. Sank was a homebody, rarely leaving the yard. One day Aggie was sent to mail a letter at the mailbox on the corner of Ninth and Central. Sank followed. He wore a little silver heart on his collar but no license tag.

On the way home Aggie picked up a broken shovel that her little brother had left while playing at the neighbors'. Just then the dog catcher leaped out of the alley and grabbed poor Sank. As he bent over to tie the rope around the dog's neck, Aggie whacked him on the behind with the shovel, knocking him flat.

"Home, Sank," yelled Aggie and they ran for dear life. Sank stayed out of sight at home thereafter. Fifty years later, Doris treasures his little silver heart.

Aggie grew up to be Agnes, and helped her husband Maurice Wilson through medical school. They moved to Georgia.

After finishing high school, Doris taught in a rural school. She married John C. Willoughby, a UP machinist, and continued to live in the South Side neighborhood except for pre-war years when John worked on the Panama Railroad.

A memorable day for Minnie Berkley was on November 20, 1903, when she was uptown shopping with her small children. There were crowds of people and an air of excitement. She was profoundly shocked to learn that it was the day of the hanging of Tom Horn. She considered it "uncivilized."

Life in America was harsh, with its strikes and hard times. Minnie taught her children the values of thrift, hard work and the pride of home ownership. Many of her descendants still live and work for a better quality of life in the old neighborhood.

John C. Willoughby was born in Cheyenne, May 22, 1910 in old St. John's hospital, the son of William C. Willoughby and Hilda Mark Willoughby. Her father, John Mark, was a pioneer clerical worker for the railroad in Cheyenne, Hanna and Rock Springs.

John's father, William C. Willoughby, was a member of the J. T. Clark Volunteer Hose Company, stationed at Eleventh and Warren (South Side). He became the city's first paid fire department employee. In 1909, he was made the first captain of the newly mechanized city fire department.

Doris and John Willoughby celebrated their fiftieth anniversary with a reception in the Parish Hall of St. Christopher's Episcopal Church in Cheyenne, September 7, 1980. The affair was hosted by their children, Mrs. Milford (Joan) Clark, Mrs. Henry (Jacqueline) Krening, Mrs. Lloyd (Janet) Osborn, Robert and Sandra Willoughby.

A homemaker, while her children grew up, Doris was active in local and state Parent-Teachers' Associations and was instrumental in creating the first public school kindergarten in Wyoming at Johnson grade school in 1935.

She organized a Girl Reserve unit of the Young Women's Christian Association for Johnson School girls and actively participated in Girl Scouts, Future Homemakers of America and Boy Scouts.

When she was president of the Johnson School Parent-Teachers' Association, she worked to establish the first branch of the county library in the basement of the Johnson School. She was a charter member of the League of Women Voters and the Friends of the Laramie County Library.

Doris contributed her organization skills to the founding of the South Side Community League and served as treasurer. When that group sponsored the first public open-membership for Blue Cross, she was the collection agent, serving without pay until the plan was proven viable. She worked diligently for additional schools and better educational opportunities for South Side children.

She has been a member of the Cheyenne Woman's Club, Minnehaha Extension Club and St. Elizabeth's Guild. Currently, she is a member of the Ladies' Auxiliary to the Veterans of Foreign Wars, Post 1881, and is a fifty-year member of Mispah Chapter of the Order of Eastern Star.

Doris and John both attended old Johnson grade school. Their first teacher was Alice Marven Hebard. When John was seven, the Willoughby family moved to the Panama Canal Zone where Willoughby worked for the Panama Railroad. John returned to Cheyenne to begin an apprentice program in the machinist's trade with the Union Pacific Railroad.

He retired after forty-two years of service, which was interrupted by his three-year period of service with the Panama Railroad Company in the early forties. After retirement, he joined Doris in real estate, associated with Marchick Realty.

John was a charter member of the original chapter of the Order of DeMolay founded by Marshall Reynolds, and served as a master counselor in 1929. He was active in Boy Scouts, serving as a leader for many years. He belongs to the Acacia Lodge No. 11, Masonic Order, and Blue Lodge, as well as the International Association of Machinists and Aerospace Workers, Local 89.

The Willoughbys are charter members of St. Christopher's Episcopal Church, where John served many years as treasurer, vestryman and as junior warden. Both Willoughbys have served as church school teachers for a number of years. Together they actively participated in the Democratic Party, serving as precinct committee persons.

Since retirement, they have enjoyed traveling in their motor home and the hobby of collecting and restoring antiques. They have taken a very active part in supporting STRIDE Learning Center.

More recently, they were supportive of the movement to organize Neighborhood Housing Services, Inc., which selected the Johnson-Hebard area of the South Side as the focus in "a program to preserve the neighborhood and to conserve the housing stock."

Their children graduated from Johnson Junior High School and Cheyenne High School and all have continued to make their homes in Cheyenne. The couple has thirteen grandchildren and seven great-grandchildren. Their fiftieth anniversary fell on National Grandparents Day.

Their daughter, Joan Clark, was elected to the Cheyenne City Council in 1982.

The Willoughbys consider themselves to be a typical "blue-collar" family.

GERTRUDE CLEMENTS

Gertrude Clements lived at 112 East Sixth Street from 1923 until the land was required for the I-180 Connector, which consumed six blocks of homes and businesses.

Gertrude was born October 27, 1895 in Louisville, Kentucky, the daughter of Charles and Etta Ferguson.

Married to George Schneider in 1920, the couple adopted sisters, Laura Lavern and Miriam, aged five and nine respectively. George died in 1938. A woman from the agency told the children that they would have to return to the State Children's Home, as their mother would be unable to care for them, financially.

One of the daughters said, "She literally worked day and night, but we were kept!"

She had a deep compassion for those less fortunate than herself. During the Depression, many people stopped at her door for food. She always shared with them. During the Holy Days, when the Jewish family who operated the store across the street could not serve people, they sent them to Gertrude.

Her sensitivity had developed early. She recalled that, as a girl of twelve, she saw a pregnant eighteen year old girl being drummed out of the church because of her sin. She thought that Jesus would not have been so cruel.

Gertrude had no more than an eighth grade education but she read anything and everything and cultivated her fine memory. She strove for excellence in all she did. She taught herself to weave and in turn, taught weaving to the blind. She taught herself to raise orchids and supplied Cheyenne florists for many years. Her cooking skills were well known. The cinnamon rolls at the Owl Inn are still being made from her recipe.

In 1969, she and Mary Harmon, her neighbor and friend since 1923, started a senior citizen's center in the old Galloway house on East Sixth Street. It was a place where those who needed companionship could go for a time of friendship, activity and food.

The neighborhood children, who were fortunate enough to be invited into her greenhouse, learned about the care of this bountiful beauty of orchids and violets and the exotic geography of their origins. At one time she had 10,000 African violets. Her daughter Miriam Hammond rescued her roses from the demolition. The roses included the rare Damascenes, which descended from Biblical times. Her granddaughters, Sherri, Karen and Trudy carry on her interest in orchids and violets.

WALTER CHRISTENSEN

Walter Christensen, a member of old Johnson's last seventh grade, also had Miss Alice Hebard for his first grade teacher. He grew up to become chief clerk to the Representative of the Union Pacific Railroad in Cheyenne. He was given leave of absence from this position to serve in the office of the State Treasurer. He was also the administrator of the Eventide Nursing Home for eight years.

His father, Louis Christensen, was born in Laramie of Danish parents. His mother, Mathilde (Tillie) Carlsdotter, came from Dalsland, Sweden. After retirement, Walter and his wife, the former Carol Beck, visited these Scandinavian homelands.

The Walter Christensens had two daughters, Mrs. William S. (Janice) Wilfong and Mrs. John (Joanne) Steele, both of Longmont, Colorado and three Wilfong grandchildren, Michael, Stephen and Amy Wilfong.

Walter died September 2, 1981.

THE WILLIAM COLE FAMILY

"Papa shot prairie chickens from the front porch of our house at 320 East Ninth Street. When I was a little girl, there was nothing between our house and the creek," said Cassie Cole of her old home on the South Side.

Father William Cole was from Partic County, near Glasgow, Scotland, and Mother Katherine Colton Cole was from Monehan, Ireland. Both came to the United States in their early teens in sailing ships that took from three weeks to a month to cross the Atlantic Ocean.

Cassie's mother came to Grand Island, Nebraska Territory, in 1867, when she was fifteen years old. She lived with an aunt and uncle who were with the crews building the Union Pacific Railroad. Later she returned to Cleveland where she married in 1873. The Cole family lived there until the call of the West brought them to Denver, then Laramie and in 1883 to Cheyenne.

Except for John, born in Cleveland, and William, born in Denver, followed by James, born in Laramie, all of the other Cole children were born in this Cheyenne home.

Grandma McSweeney served as the midwife for all of the Cole children, born in Cheyenne, beginning with Arthur, born in 1884. He was followed by Charles, George, Emmet, Lavinia and Cassie.

William was a city councilman. He worked for the Union Pacific as a boilermaker until the strike of 1922. After that, he had his own little "boiler shop," as he called his blacksmith shop at 306 East Fifth Street.

The sons also worked for the railroad, except for Charles, who became a rancher. The daughters became schoolteachers. Lavinia taught at Johnson and Cassie taught at Converse, later at McCormick. Lavinia became principal of Johnson and had a school named for her.

Growing up on the South Side was like growing up in a small town. Everyone knew everyone else. Kids went skating on Packing House pond, played in the forbidden creek and scuffed their shoes climbing Initial Cliff.

There were many wonderful parties and dances in the homes. Houses were, for the most part, small. It was expected that the men would carry out the stove and roll up the rugs for dancing. Larry Britton played the fiddle for the dancing.

Good friends were Eileen Milward and Winnie Jessen; Gladys, Harry and Olive Cole, no relation; John and Julia McSweeney; Mort and Mary McSweeney.

If it happened to be a birthday party, there was a cake, of course. The ladies prepared a midnight lunch or carried in food for the party.

Cassie remembers most of the people in our directory and noted that two former mayors, L. R. Bresnahan and William McInerney had lived nearby during earlier years.

LAVINIA A. COLE

Lavinia A. Cole was born in Cheyenne, Wyoming Territory, October 14, 1885. Except for eight months of teaching near Pine Bluffs, she lived here all of her life.

Lavinia received her first seven years of schooling at old Johnson School at Eleventh and Evans Avenue. She attended the eighth grade at old Central School where Miss Lulu McCormick was her teacher. The original Cheyenne High School was the scene for her next four years. She then attended Colorado State Teacher's College for two years and received her Bachelor of Arts degree from the University of Wyoming.

Her entire career of teaching was spent in Wyoming. Her first school was the Rutledge, a rural school near Pine Bluffs. She taught all eight grades, receiving fifty dollars a month for eight months. She paid fifteen dollars a month for board and managed to save enough to buy materials to enlarge her parents' home.

Her second year of teaching was at her own neighborhood school she had attended, Johnson Elementary. Her beginning salary in Cheyenne was sixty-five dollars a month. She received the same salary for eleven years. After that she was promoted to principal at a salary of seventy-five dollars. About this time the salary was on a yearly basis.

Since World War I, the salary gradually increased until her last year of teaching, 1947-48, she received $3,600 for the year.

Johnson School became a junior high school in 1950 although sixth grade still occupied the building. The first four grades moved to the new Hebard School in 1948.

In 1950, the Lavinia A. Cole Elementary School was dedicated, honoring her for forty-four years of service to education in Cheyenne. The school is located at Eighth Street and O'Neil Avenue in the earliest settlement of the original city of Cheyenne.

After retirement, Lavinia and her sister Cassie traveled extensively. She had long been a vacation traveler but now she went farther afield. She had visited every state in the United States and both eastern and western Canada. On a motor trip to Mexico, she rode a mule up the new volcanic mountain. Europe, Australia, New Zealand and South America were on her itinerary.

Lavinia A. Cole died September 13, 1971.

"THE GERMANS FROM RUSSIA"

ERMA'S STORY

Cheyenne has many families of "Germans from Russia" origin. I asked Erma Lebsack Shipley to tell me about the history of these people who seem to have such a strong cultural bond. She is a former president of the American Society of Germans From Russia.

She said that after the Seven Year's War in Germany, people were literally starving. Catherine, daughter of Prince Anhalt-Zerbst was born in Settin, in 1729. At sixteen, she was married to Czar Peter III.

It was said that she became lonely for the sound of the German language and her people. There were vast unpopulated lands in Russia. Peter indulged her by inviting German farmers to come and colonize. They were excellent farmers, raising much food for Russian markets. They prospered. They had their own schools and churches in their own villages. Peter promised them a hundred years free from taxation.

She eventually became the Czarina and ruled with great success, becoming known as Catherine the Great.

After her passing, the next Czar disregarded the promise. He drafted the eldest sons and levied heavy taxes. The Russian people did not conceal their jealousy of the prosperous Germans.

Erma's father, Fred John Lebsack, served four years in the Czar's army. When he mustered out, he said, "We are leaving." He married Anna Marie Eisenach and they came to the United States in 1913. His first job was as a section hand on the railroad in Nebraska at ten cents an hour. Living conditions were primitive.

Meanwhile, Anna Marie's parents had emigrated and settled in the Scottsbluff, Nebraska area. They were farmers, so they found working in the beet fields more to their liking. They also worked in the sugar factory. The Lebsacks needed little urging to join them. Erma was born in Gering, Nebraska, in 1918.

In 1921, recruiters came to Nebraska to persuade workers to come to Cheyenne during the strike. Not knowing the pros and cons of the strike, they accepted the opportunity to make more money.

In Cheyenne they lived at 811 East Twelfth Street. They later moved to Tenth and Central, after the Milatzos moved out. The first house was in the path of the 1923 demolition for the expansion of the Union Pacific trackage, and the second was in the path of the I-180 Connector.

Mama, Anna Marie, had eight children. Two died in infancy, another died of influenza in 1921. When sister Mollie died leaving three children, the whole family helped to raise them.

Papa was a carman. Emil, the eldest, was a carman. Fred was a pipefitter. One day in 1942, Papa presented Erma to the foreman, applying for a job in the store department.

"I suppose you want your whole family to work for the Union Pacific?" said the foreman.

"When I farm, my whole family farms, when I railroad, my family railroads," Papa said.

Emma, who married Herman Dienes, worked at Fort Francis E. Warren, however, and Jake, the youngest, earned a Ph.D and became an Air Force psychologist, now retired and living in Denver.

Erma married Carl Shipley, who was in the Air Force. After World War II, they lived in England; Tripoli, Libya; and Harmon Air Force Base, Newfoundland. After the war, women who worked in the shops and store departments were laid off, permanently, it was said. They were union members and it took the union three weeks to get them reinstated. They had earned their equal rights.

Erma's father was one of the seven men who built the first Zion Congregational Church at Seventh and Maxwell. Later the congregation built the present brick edifice. Recently it merged with the United Church of Christ. The carillon strikes the hour and plays hymns on Sundays.

In addition to church and civic work, Erma and Carl's hobbies in retirement are their greenhouse and their pets.

THE ECKHARTS

John H. Eckhart was a very fine cabinetmaker. He learned the trade of carpentry as an apprentice under a system that would horrify American craftsmen. His German ancestors lived in Russia for many generations.

The apprentices were indentured to a master-craftsman for four years, leaving their homes. The boys received no pay except board and room and one outfit of clothing per year. In exchange for the opportunity to learn a trade, they worked like slaves for masters who could and did beat them if they were lazy or careless or made mistakes, or if the master had just "gotten up on the wrong side of the bed."

John married Marie Katrine Frank and as soon as they could, they immigrated to the United States. John H. Jr., the oldest, was born in Russia. He says that he didn't know a word of English when he enrolled in old Johnson School. His brothers and sisters were all born in the United States.

Clara died and Ray was killed in an accident. The others, Ann, Esther, Freda and Clarence live in Cheyenne. John is a retired postman and lives at 305 East Seventh Street.

THE MOHRLANGS

Although little was generally known about the Germans from Russia outside of their own community, until recent years, there is considerable literature about them available in the Genealogy Department of the Laramie County Library. They proved to be thrifty, hard-working, law-abiding citizens, serving in the armed forces and maintaining a quiet pride in their heritage.

In her Christmas letter, Rosa Mohrlang Meyer writes that her parents,

Christian Mohrlang and Katherine Heberline were both born in Saratov Province, Russia. Their village was called "Walter Kuhter." Their first child, Alex, was born three days before they embarked for America at the Port of Lebou, on the Baltic Sea, in 1903.

Rosa was a volunteer in the South Branch Library, active in the Friends of the Library and worked as a librarian after moving to Colorado. She is a member of the American Society of Germans from Russia.

Other Mohrlangs living in Laramie County are Emma Specht, Chris, Dan, Gladys Ferguson and Genevieve Peters.

THE FUTA FAMILY

When Masaki, "Mac" Futa arrived in the United States, he knew not a word of English. His father and grandfather were Sumo wrestling promotors who had not fared well, so he had no cushion of wealth to fall back on. He immigrated to Hawaii with his bride Miyo. Here he worked on a sugar plantation. He had never had to work so incredibly hard in his life.

When some other workers were going to the United States, he joined them. They were met on the docks by recruiters for the Union Pacific.

"You want job?"

"Sign here, you're hired."

They were put on the train for Wyoming, Colorado and Nebraska. Masaki went to work at a cement factory at Red Buttes, Albany County, Wyoming. Every night he had to dig the hard cement out of his nostrils. From there he went to railroad work, housed in cabooses and old freight cars along the railroad tracks. They had little opportunity to learn English.

One morning a gang of workers were taken out to the tracks and began to repair the tracks. A beautiful little black and white animal came ambling along. It showed no fear. They thought to take him for a pet. The foreman yelled a warning. Too late!

Next, they were rolling on the ground, in pain, rubbing their eyes, as a result of a close encounter with an American skunk equipped for chemical warfare. Their clothes had to be buried.

Eventually Futa was located in Cheyenne, where he became known as "Mac." His family lived close to work at 121 West Twelfth Street in 1922. He became the only Japanese man who was rated as a "number one machinist." For a long time he was a "helper," keeping his eyes open, quick to learn, but unable to read English.

He saw that the issued tools were sometimes not designed for their specific tasks, so he made his own tools. At a time when many Union Pacific tools were disappearing, an order went out that homes would be searched. Mac had no cause to worry. He had his own unique tools. As he moved up to better pay, he still had problems, being unable to read English.

He would receive a big sheaf of work orders, and would have to ask someone to read them to him. He relied on his superb memory. Daughter Chizu tells that sometimes he brought home the work orders for her to read to him. There were often as many as eighty to one hundred of them. Chizu worried that he would not be able to remember them.

"Pop, were you able to do many of the orders?" she asked the next day.

"I did them all," he proudly replied.

One time there was a problem with a piston that had to go in, in a certain way. The piston could not be made to work. They even had a man come from Omaha. He couldn't do it. "Isn't there someone here who can do it?" he asked.

Someone said, "Try him," indicating Futa. In one-half hour the piston was going up and down, up and down, the way it was supposed to go. Mac had used his own tools and know-how.

The Futas were a very close and loving family. After the 1923 demolition, the family moved to Seventh and Central Avenue, where the parents lived out their lives.

The older Futa children attended OLD Johnson School. George graduated from high school in 1928 and Chizu in 1930. George retired from the W. A. Corson Company, where he was considered to be an expert in the automotive parts field. He now lives near his daughter in Ridgeway, Colorado. Chizu, Taru, Tom and Fred still live in Cheyenne.

Chizu married Sam Ogasawara, during the depression. They heard that things were better in California. "You could buy a bucket of oranges for ten cents," they said. They found this not to be true. They worked in the Stockton area. Life was difficult, and a trip to the doctor with the children was expensive.

The Ogasawara parents-in-law returned to Japan, taking the two older girls with them. In the hysteria of World War II, Chizu and her family were rounded up and moved to an internment camp in Arkansas, for the duration.

At the beginning of the war, all Japanese workers were fired from the Union Pacific. As Taru says, "A good thing, too. If anything had happened, they would have blamed us." The entire Japanese community signed a loyalty oath. Copies were sent to public officials and the newspapers and radio station. Still they endured covert and open discrimination for many years.

The Ogasawara daughters, Joyce and Shirley, were held in Japan until 1949. They remembered little English when they returned, but they had the help of a reunited family. They attended Johnson Junior High School and graduated from Cheyenne High School, as a result, they are fluent in both languages. This is a great asset in their careers. Shirley is in the importing business and Joyce operates a Japanese restaurant on the West Coast.

The Wyoming Eagle — Cheyenne, December 11, 1941

CHEYENNE JAPANESE ARE LOYAL

WHEREAS, a condition of armed conflict now exists between the United States and the Japanese Empire which calls for the fullest cooperation on the part of every true and loyal American, irrespective of race or creed, who cherishes the principles of Liberty and Freedom upon which this great nation is founded, and

WHEREAS, by every instinct of Humanity, love of Freedom, Justice and Equality, the residents and citizens of Japanese ancestry in the City of Cheyenne are whole-heartedly and without any mental reservations whatsoever, in support of the action of the President of the United States, and

WHEREAS, the residents in Cheyenne of Japanese ancestry are fully cognizant and deeply appreciative of the manifold blessings and privileges which have been accorded them in this great nation, and particularly in the City of Cheyenne, and

WHEREAS, the older residents have shown their true Americanism and loyalty to the country of their adoption by fully concurring with the action of their children in their respective decisions to volunteer under the Selective Service Act of the National Defense program, and

WHEREAS, the individual selectees from the Cheyenne Japanese group in every instance, have offered their lives and their services in support of the Common Defense by voluntary enlistment, and

WHEREAS, the undersigned residents and citizens of Cheyenne are willing and eager to offer their full-hearted cooperation and support in any measure which may be undertaken by the authorities to advance the Common Defense,

NOW BE IT RESOLVED that these matters be brought to public attention through the medium of this resolution and an affirmation of the loyalty of this group and its faith in the future of this country be made a matter of public record and that an original copy of this resolution be presented to the following for their information and government:

The Honorable Nels H. Smith, Governor
The Honorable Ed Warren, Mayor
Captain Wm. R. Bradley, State Highway Patrol
Sheriff George J. Carroll, Laramie County Sheriff's Office
Chief Harvey Jackson, Cheyenne City Police
Mr. John Charles Thompson, Editor, *Wyoming State Tribune*
Mr. Tracy S. McCraken, Editor, *Wyoming Eagle*
Radio Station KFBC

IN WITNESS WHEREOF, the undersigned residents of Cheyenne have hereto set their hands this 8th day of December, 1941, in the City of Cheyenne, Laramie County, State of Wyoming.

The Ogasawaras have four other children, Richard, Lawrence, Kent and Arlene. In spite of unforgettable hardships, Chizu has fond memories of growing up on the South Side.

Chizu says that she was the tomboy of the family, tagging along after her brother George at play. One time, George, Walter Christensen, Chris and Alex Mohrlang went over Mrs. Edgar's fence to swipe some apples.

Chizu struggled hard to get over the four-foot board fence. When she did, she made a noise. Mrs. Charlotte Edgar came to the screen door. Chizu knew she could not get out easily, so she crouched down behind a bush where Mrs. Edgar found her.

"Come now, Chizu, you don't want those old green apples. They would make you sick. When they are ripe, come and I will give you all you want."

Chizu was very tenderhearted and cried when animals were hurt. One time she saw a team of horses fall through the rotten boards of a cesspool cover in a neighbor's yard. Although they were screaming, struggling and hurt, the people were able to get them out safely.

Today Chizu specializes in chrysanthemums. The Ogasawaras have a miniature Japanese garden in their back yard.

GARCIA-ARIAS

An inspiring story of courage was told to me by Nettie Garcia Arias, about her mother, Concepcion Silva, and her influence on the lives of her children.

Concepcion, a native of Zacatecas, capital of Zacatecas, Mexico, married Juan Silva of the same place. When they had three children and a fourth on the way, her husband had to seek work elsewhere.

Communications were disrupted, due to the insurrection of Pancho Villa and his followers. Villa was regarded as a "Robin Hood" by the poor. Others called him "bandit."

Concepcion had not heard from her husband for some time. She decided to go and find him. She started out with very little money, by train, taking only Adelaide, leaving Estafina and John with her mother-in-law. She carried her most prized possession, a beautiful, stiff, white embroidered petticoat, carefully in her satchel.

Their train came to a halt in the desert where the rebels had blown up a bridge. They could go no further until the bridge was repaired. There was food for the Federales but none for the passengers. Concepcion used a little money to bribe the cook to sell her some self-rising flour.

On the desert she found a bottle and a piece of sheet metal which she scoured with sand and water from the stream. She carefully scooped out a depression in the sand, took her precious petticoat and lined the depression.

Mixing the flour and water in her improvised bowl, she made a dough and formed it into cakes, rolling them with the bottle on the sheet metal. She made a fireplace with some rocks, laid the tin over it, and baked the cakes.

The camp followers of the soldiers were hungry, too, and begged for some. She hid them, saying, "These are for my little one."

The reunited family came to Cheyenne where Silva found work in the Union Pacific yards. Eulogio was born in Cheyenne. He grew up in Cheyenne and became an electrician in Fremont, California. Unfortunately, Silva was run over by a switch engine and lost a leg. "There was no interpreter. Mama couldn't understand the doctor or the lawyer. When he died she signed the paper but received no compensation," according to her daughter Nettie.

Later, Concepcion married Pablo Garcia. Although Pablo was an orphan, he was a good father to the Silva children and fathered four of his own. Nettie was born in Cheyenne in 1919, followed by Anne Marie, 1922, Dolores Camargo, 1924 and Paul in 1929.

Pablo always provided for his large family. When the strike was on, he worked in the beet fields in Nebraska. Pablo was so anxious for his children to have a good education that he took Nettie to school when she was only four.

The teacher said, "She seems awfully young but we will try it for a few days."

Nettie had to go home and wait until she was ready.

She loved school and was a good student. She graduated in the Class of '36. As with many South Side children, she did not feel any discrimination until she reached high school.

The teacher told her that it was "impossible" for a Mexican to learn shorthand. She changed her schedule, then she learned that her friend had taken the course successfully. Next year she took shorthand. It was a challenge.

She was determined that the teacher could not fault her in any way. Except for one time, when her grandmother died, she was absent four days. The teacher gave her a II. Others who had missed more, were not so penalized.

John, who had come from Mexico as a little boy with his family, finally received his citizenship, while serving in Deauville, France, during World War II.

People with Spanish surnames face daily discrimination in the work place. Nettie's father, Pablo, had an adequate command of English. He was expecting to be made foreman of the crew. Instead, a Greek, newly arrived in this country, without skill and without knowing a word of English, was given the job because he "looked" white.

Nettie serves on the election board. She has been a nutrition aide at the Family Living Center. She especially liked working as a bi-lingual aide in the program at the Administration Building of the School District.

Upon the death of Concepcion, the Arias family took sister Adelaide to live with them. They built a ramp to accommodate her wheelchair. Papa Garcia retired in 1963. He lived in the family home at 705 East Eighth Street until he, too, went to live with daughter Nettie and her family. He died in March, 1981.

Grandchildren in this family hear the stories of another generation and inherit the pride in their family values.

THE GOLDHAMMERS

We first knew Max and Bertha Goldhammer when they bought the old Archer schoolhouse and moved it into our neighborhood, near the Tenth Street bridge. The Denver Highway turned south at this point.

The Goldhammers lived in an adjoining apartment at the store until after the flood of June 2, 1929. They moved to Fourth and Central, where they built the "Lone Eagle" tourist camp as such facilities were called in those days. Max's brother, Morris, had built his store and tourist camp at Seventh and Central.

The new Denver Highway was to go straight south on Central, across the creek on a new bridge, and up "Denver Hill." The new Riner viaduct was being built and "prosperity was just around the corner."

The parents of Max and Morris Goldhammer came from Rumania to homestead in the Ft. Laramie area. The parents of Bertha and Becky Ellnoy came from Kiev, Russia. They homesteaded near Wheatland.

Max and Bertha's children are Isador and Ann. Isador still lives in Cheyenne with his wife Marian. Their daughter, Nancy, lives in Connecticut.

Morris and Becky's children are Annette, Harry and Phil, all presently living in California. All the children attended Johnson School.

The Goldhammers were good South Side neighbors and their businesses prospered through the economic ups and downs. Before the I-180 Connector swept out all of the businesses and homes for six blocks on South Central Avenue, the family built a new tourist facility on the west side of the street and called it Bungalow Court. It was later sold and is now called the Lariat Motel.

THE GREGORY CLAN

Charleton Madison Gregory, Sr., and Julia Suprise Gregory and their five sons, Charleton L., Myron S., Frank W., Albert E., and Lewis A., homesteaded in the Centennial Valley. They were accompanied by Grandpa Albert and Grandma Julia Suprise. Charleton Sr. had forfeited his homestead rights in an incompleted try in the Dakotas. They filed in the name of their son, Charleton L. Gregory. It was to be his obligation to prove up on the homestead, an obligation which he fulfilled. Then he relinquished it to his father. By that time the law had changed, making unproductive land filing no barrier to refiling. The elder Gregorys had their home.

Charleton M. Gregory, Sr., was a politician and a high-ranking Mason. He served in the Third Wyoming Legislature, representing Albany County in 1895 and again in 1903 in the Seventh Wyoming Legislature. There were also ventures into gold mining in the Snowy Range, when it was called La Plata and at Towner Lake, when it was called Lake Julia. The old mine cabin there was the headquarters of the North American Mining Company.

Grandma Julia Suprise Gregory was upper New York State French. Her training as a nurse was much in demand throughout the valley. She practiced all of the arts of homesteading, which included running a trap-line, tanning and making garments from fur. Grandpa Gregory died in 1917 and Julia spent the winter of her life with various children, or in Laramie, returning with the spring to her Centennial homestead.

Charleton L. Gregory worked on the Laramie, Hahns Peak and North Park Railroad. He married Laura Sprague in Laramie in 1895.

Laura was a pioneer, herself, having come to the Territory in 1875 when she was three weeks old. Her father was the telegrapher at Tie Siding. She was sent to Fort Collins to be educated. She met Charleton while teaching at Centennial.

Charleton L. and Laura moved to Minneapolis for better pay but returned to Centennial every six months to fulfill the requirement for residence on the homestead. Gwendola Lynn (Goldie) was born in Minneapolis. When the homestead obligation was finally completed, they settled for a time in Laramie, where Charleton M. Gregory III was born. In 1901 they moved to Cheyenne where they made their home at 115 East Ninth Street, for the next fifty years. Two daughters, Gertrude Ellen and Julia Mildred were born there.

Charleton L. Gregory worked as a brakeman for the Union Pacific. He carried the union card issued to him in Chicago in 1891. At his retirement he had completed fifty years and nine months in railroad service on several lines.

Laura was an organizer and the first president of the Parent-Teachers' Association at old Johnson School. It was the first organization of its kind in the state. She was president of the Ladies Auxiliary of the Order of Railway Conductors, a Daughter of the American Revolution, an Eastern Star, a Wyoma Rebecca, a Royal Neighbor and a lifelong Baptist. She believed in insurance and was an active agent among railroad families. She died in her ninety-ninth year.

Daughter Goldie married George Warner, Gertrude Ellen married Marshall Chambers of Lander and Julia Mildred married Simon J. Huffer. Charleton M. Gregory III died in 1923 after a long illness but Charleton L. and Laura left a flourishing clan of fourteen grandchildren and twelve great-grandchildren to carry on.

Their daughter Julia Huffer recalls that when old Johnson School had only one teacher for fifth and sixth grades, "Mama and Mrs. Parker went door to door taking a census to prove to the school board that there were enough children in school to warrant a teacher for each grade.

Laura Gregory was a leader and a legend in her time. In a day when the school board viewed such a thing as a Parent-Teacher affiliation as a revolutionary challenge to their authority, these demands from working class families were firmly resisted. The ladies, however, went right ahead and held pie suppers to raise funds for the school; working for free textbooks and providing incentives for excellence. They even thought that they could stamp out the common cold by providing handkerchiefs, made from old sheets.

One night, at a fund-raising event at the school, a prankster stuffed long johns into the toilets.

Julia Huffer reports that Mama and her cohorts called on the board and assured them that "none of the P-T-A members wore that kind of garment."

The parents and teachers continued their association for the benefit of education for many years. They made Johnson School the heart and center of the South Side community.

EDDIE JOHNSON'S FAMILY

The parents of Eddie Johnson met quite by accident in the Union Pacific Depot in the winter of 1889. The young lady was carrying two sacks of apples when one broke, sending apples rolling in all directions. Her Swedish exclamation caught his ear and August Johnson helped her pick them up. Sympathy in Swedish must have been music to her ears, too.

Anna Brundin had come to Leadville, Colorado, from her birthplace in Sollentuna, Uppland, Sweden. After working there a while, she decided to visit her aunt, Ida Matson, in Nebraska. She presented a hundred dollar bill to pay for her ticket. The ticket agent was afraid that the bill might be a counterfeit. She suggested that he put a tag on her and she would pay at her destination, Cheyenne. In Cheyenne, they accepted her bill without question.

Being hungry, she crossed the street to a store where the Albany now stands. She saw a pile of lovely apples. Knowing little English, she put down a dollar bill and indicated the apples. They filled two sacks in exchange for the dollar. Country markets stocked few such luxuries. She had no idea how delighted her relatives would be with her gift of those apples.

August Johnson, a widower with an eight-year-old son, Godfrey, was born in Vastergotland, Sweden, March 24, 1853. He was an engineer for the Union Pacific. He and Anna corresponded and were married in 1890. They raised four children, Elmer Alban Vincent, Carl August, Edna Marie Elida, and Eddie. They made their home at 920 House Avenue, where his namesake, Carl August, still lives.

Godfrey went to live with his aunt, Minnie McIver, who was childless.

Elmer lived in Laramie, as did his sister Edna. Edna was valedictorian of her class, became a school teacher and married S. J. Siren of Laramie.

Carl August Johnson was born August 27, 1903. He graduated from high school in 1921. He received his Bachelor of Commercial Science degree in 1926 from the University of Wyoming.

Some of the appointments he held were: auditor, Price Waterhouse and Company, San Francisco, 1928-29; accountant, Land Realty Company, San Francisco, 1929-30; analyst, Marchant Calculating Machine Company, Oakland, 1930-35; auditor, Wyoming Sales Tax Department, Cheyenne, Wyoming, 1935-39. During World War II he served as a Code and Cipher Analyst, with the U.S. Signal Corps, Arlington, Virginia.

Carl Johnson has published many innovative ballot and calendar systems based on precise mathematical calculations, which have gained scientific recognition. He holds several copyrights, and many honorary awards for his work.

Eddie began to sell the *Denver Post* on the corner of Seventeenth and Capitol Avenue when he was four years old. That was "his corner." Five editions of the *Post* came up on the trains from Denver every day. There was more money to be made as a newsboy than as a route carrier. It was a good corner with banks and businesses and forty-eight saloons around a twelve-block area of downtown Cheyenne.

All of the Johnson children started school at Johnson Elementary, where Alice Marven Hebard was their first grade teacher. Eddie still treasures a copy of *The Art and Life Primer*, inscribed, "For being in school from August 31, 1915 to June 9, 1916." It is in near mint condition. This first grade class was the last class to complete all seven grades offered in the old Territorial E. P. Johnson school building.

Eddie's teachers were Miss Hebard, Wilhelmina Miller, Genesta Clark, Georgia Sullivan, Margaret Weaver, Lulu Lebhart and Lavinia A. Cole, principal.

He was a good student. He still has all of his report cards from Johnson, old Central and high school to his graduation in 1927.

The Johnson children attended the Congregational Mission Sunday School, although the family became members of St. Paul's Lutheran Church.

After high school, Eddie became a sheet metal worker at the Union Pacific shops. When there were layoffs in the shops, he worked at construction or anything he could get. His mother had instilled habits of thrift in her children. She, herself, worked hard and kept a jersey cow picketed on the Crow Creek meadows when the children were young. She also worked as a hotel maid when the children were in school.

In 1942, Eddie married Mary Fochtman, a teacher in the Cheyenne schools. After retirement, Mary worked at her water color painting and Eddie at his photography. They went on a world tour and made several trips abroad. Eddie and Mary met Helen Bjorn Morris in England. Mary and Helen corresponded until Mary's death in 1975. Eddie kept up the correspondence and eventually he and Helen were married.

The Johnsons live at 414 East Fifth Street. The abstract of their property is a veritable history of South Cheyenne. It begins with a copy of the charter from Congress to the Union Pacific Railroad; to the town plat; to F. E. Warren, land speculator, politician, Territorial Governor, and Senator; to several other eastern speculators; to James Hammond and his packing company, noting the right-of-way of the Crow Creek Ditch and Reservoir Company. The historical document also notes the financial ups and downs of the packing company (which survived until 1926).

The abstract also includes the legal proceedings of the "vacation" of "No Name Ditch," although it was identical with the right-of-way of the Crow Creek Ditch and Reservoir Company right-of-way. The ditch conveyed water to Packing House Pond under the 1888 adjudicated water right number 34.

Although most old-timers on the South Side fondly remember the pond as a "great place to skate," Eddie, a local history authority, pointed out the ironies of Cheyenne's development in relation to the waters of Crow Creek.

The story of the Johnson family is entwined in the roots of Cheyenne.

LEO MANTEY

Leo Mantey's uncle Gus Mantey was the telegrapher at Cheyenne before the rails of the Union Pacific arrived in 1867. He later established a school of telegraphy in Denver. The importance of the telegraph was utmost. It was the glamour profession of the day.

The Mantey family homesteaded in Weld County on the Ft. Collins road near the "Natural Fort," which is now a designated point of interest on I-25. The children attended high school at the Academy of the Holy Child in Cheyenne.

Leo came to Cheyenne in 1918 to work for the Union Pacific. He was a tinner and a carpenter. He also taught himself photography, which became a lifetime hobby. He sometimes used a cave at the ranch for a darkroom.

His sister Anna, Mrs. Eugene Hess, who lives in Cheyenne, also attended Holy Child Academy. In 1916, their mother died, leaving Anna to raise the younger children.

A bachelor, Leo Mantey died in 1976, survived by four sisters, three brothers and numerous nieces and nephews.

ANNA EKSTROM McBEE

Walk into the Equality State Bank. On the facing wall, glowing softly in the north light, is a mahogany bas-relief mural in four three-by-four-foot panels. It depicts four periods of American history and the coins in use during these periods. The work is typical of the firm hand of Cheyenne's best known sculptor, Anna McBee.

As a child Anna was taught to whittle by her father Carl. Her art teacher at McCormick Junior High School, Lillian Harms, encouraged her. Anna had the determination to create her art from whatever materials came to hand. Her art matured as her horizons broadened. While on station in the Caribbean, she sculpted in exotic woods. In Japan, she was accepted by a famous teacher, the only foreigner so favored, and more unusual, exhibited there.

Anna has explored various techniques in stone and bronze, although wood sculpture is her favorite. Each wood sculpture is unique. The wood itself often dictates the subject and treatment.

The daughter of Carl G. Ekstrom and Louise Minchew Ekstrom, Anna was born in Cheyenne. Her family lived first on East Tenth Street and in 1927, bought the house at 221 East Ninth Street. She attended Johnson Elementary School, old McCormick Junior High, downtown, and graduated from Cheyenne High School in 1936.

She enrolled at the University of Wyoming but soon left to marry Marshell G. (Mac) McBee, who had just been made a sergeant in the First Infantry. Mac served thirty-three years in the Army, retiring with the rank of Colonel. The McBees have two daughters, Polly Hutchison, who lives in Hawaii and Kathy, married to Richard Juel, M.D., of El Paso, Texas. They have one grandson.

Upon retirement, Mac too, was able to indulge his interest in whittling and woodworking. They plan and work together. Their first project upon retirement was to remodel the Ekstrom's 1881 home, making an easy-care apartment for the parents, and an apartment for themselves. Then they tore down the family barn, where driving horses, a buggy and a cow had been kept.

They built a new "Old Barn" to house the woodworking tools, paint, and project materials that an artist is always collecting; and the studio Anna had always dreamed about, with plenty of room to display her finished works.

At ninety-one, Mr. Ekstrom was in poor health when the McBees returned to Cheyenne. Anna taught him to hook the colorful rugs she designed. His interest in life returned. His health improved. He was once more a participant in the busy scene at Two Twenty-One. The family truly believes that being involved gave him a few more happy years.

The remodeling preserved the integrity of the historic house, modernized for efficient heating. The setting was enhanced by the McBees' own originally designed landscaping. Preservation of the appearance of the old neighborhood was their goal.

Next they restored the house across the street at Two Twenty-Two East Ninth, which they subsequently sold. Finally, they applied all of their expertise in renovating and beautifying the house next door, west of the Ekstrom house, for their own residence. To this one, they added a sunroom which provides passive solar heat.

In spite of the restoration work, Anna has the discipline to spend an allotted amount of time on her art work, keeping up a steady flow of work to the galleries and working on commissions. Her work can be found in private collections throughout the United States.

Her public service has included positions in the Cheyenne Artists' Guild, the Wyoming Artists' Association and service with the Cheyenne Housing Authority. She supports efforts of home owners to preserve their own neighborhoods.

HENRIETTA KALBER MECOMBER

Almost everyone who was an adult in 1941 remembers something about Pearl Harbor Day, Sunday, December 7. In Cheyenne, it was a clear, cold day. The next morning the town awoke to pea soup fog. In the railroad yards, smoke and steam from the trains made visibility zero.

The *Wyoming Eagle* reported, December 8, 1941:

"Trainman Seriously Hurt As Engines Collide Here"

"Henry Kalber of 315 E. 9th Street, an engineer for the Union Pacific, was reported to be seriously scalded about the legs and body Wednesday noon, when the switch engine he was piloting collided with a road engine in the yards near the U.P. freight house."

Kalber, age fifty-seven, died at Memorial Hospital of his injuries. Services were held Sunday at the First Congregational Church. He was survived by his widow, Christine, a daughter, Henrietta Mecomber, two sons, Robert S. Kalber, and Arthur W. Kalber, all of Cheyenne.

Henry Kalber, son of Jacob and Minnie Kalber, came to Cheyenne when he was seven years old. His father died at thirty-eight, leaving Minnie to raise ten children.

Christine Kalber was the daughter of Hans and Anna Mumm. She played a leadership role in community and Parent-Teachers' Association activities. She is remembered as a beautiful lady with a crown of wavy white hair in her later years.

Her daughter, Henrietta, remembers her maternal grandparents with great fondness. They celebrated their fiftieth anniversary in 1932. The bridesmaid, Margaret Busch and the best man, Fred Voorhees, were still living and joined in the celebration at the German Lutheran Church on East Twentieth Street at Warren Avenue.

Grandfather Mumm was a cousin to Kaiser Wilhelm. In Cheyenne, "Germans had enough trouble without letting that out." Grandfather was a shipbuilder and master carpenter. He designed the mill in the Union Pacific yards. His blueprints were in use by the railroad for many years. He built a home for his family on East Fifth Street. It was later moved to 500 East Tenth Street.

The Mumms also raised ten children. Aunt Amelia was in the first graduating class of nurses at St. John's Hospital.

Henrietta, herself, was a well-known caterer, active in Republican politics and civic work. Her husband, Sheldon Mecomber, was employed as a warehouseman with Asher-Wyoming Wholesale and later for Francis E. Warren Air Force Base. He passed away in 1978.

The Mecomber children are James, with the Union Pacific at North Platte, Nebraska; Marlene, who works for the State of Wyoming at Cheyenne; and Walter, employed at Lowry Air Force Base, Denver.

THE VINERS

Ernest Leroy Viner was born at his parents' home across the street from O'Connell's store, December 2, 1909. His parents had come to Cheyenne as children. His mother, Ruth Millerman was born in Leola, South Dakota, December 22, 1889. His father, Raymond Viner, was born in Harrisburg, Nebraska, August 9, 1890.

Granddad Millerman came to Cheyenne with his wife and four dauthers, heading for Oregon. They camped for the night and someone stole his mules. He had four dollars in his pocket. Fortunately he found work and eventually became foreman of the Union Pacific wheel shop.

Growing up in Cheyenne, Ruth Millerman and Raymond Viner often crossed paths but did not know each other as children. Both remember the day Tom Horn was hanged, November 20, 1903. Ruth slipped out of school with a friend but hurried back when she saw her father go into the courthouse. Viner and a friend tried to climb on a fence to watch but the area was closed.

The Viners were married in 1912 and recently celebrated their seventieth anniversary. Their six children were: Ernest, Ray, Gay Houchen, Ruth Lacey and the late Kenneth Viner, all of Cheyenne, and Virgil Viner of Portland, Oregon.

One indelible memory of their son, Ernest, of growing up in Cheyenne was of being awakened by his father in the night on December, 1916, when the Inter-Ocean Hotel burned. The Union Pacific paint shop also burned. There was a great wind. Burning debris, even burning boards were flying through the air.

People were busy putting out sparks. Viner observed that it was a good thing that there was so much open space around old Johnson School. It probably saved many houses from burning downwind of the fire. The Viners lived across the street from the school at that time.

Of the 1923 demolition of the blocks between Tenth and Twelfth Streets, Mr. Viner recalls that the house which was situated on the corner of Tenth and House, now stands on the southwest corner of Twenty-Third and Seymour. At the time of the expansion, most of this area was new construction, having been built by Paul H. Moore and his partner, contractor Robert S. Collins.

A house could be bought for $250 up to $2,000 and moved anywhere. The cost of moving the house and hooking up utilities could run to $1,500. Houses were moved freely back and forth between the north and south sides over the Russell Avenue crossing.

Ernest L. Viner, a member of the Typographical Union worked for Cheyenne Newspapers. In his retirement he has taken up the study of genealogy and has contributed several volumes of his work to the collections of the Genealogical Society housed in the Laramie County Library.

JONES-WOODS

Murriel Jones was writing a column of South Side News in the *Tribune-Leader* in 1919, while attending the turreted old High School at Twenty-Second Street and Central Avenue.

When asked if she remembered the strikes, she said, "The only strike I remember was the one at High School, when Francis Brammar and Glenn Swain put the Junior Class flag on the very top of the tower. It was quite an athletic feat. The principal expelled the two young men and the whole class and some of the seniors walked out."

Even the fire department, using their longest ladder, could not get the flag down. Finally they managed to lasso it and pull if off, breaking the staff, leaving the wire attached to the finial of the tower to weather off.

The school finally relented and took the boys back, but all who walked out were penalized by having to take the finals.

Delmer and Ada Jones lived at 603 East Tenth Street. Sam and Bertha Woods lived around the block at 615 East Ninth Street. Bertha's father was an early comer to Cheyenne by the name of Marshall O'Bennett. In the 1880s, Marshall and Susan O'Bennett operated a soda-pop factory on the South Side.

The lives of those two families centered around work, church, school and neighborhood. The Jones women were supporters of the Congregational Church Mission at Twelfth and Evans when Miss Annette Belcher, Cheyenne's first woman pastor, presided. Fred Babcock was the Sunday School Superintendent and Ada Jones played the piano.

This mission was the only church on the South Side until the twenties. However, many people who attended and supported it were committed to other denominations. Bertha Woods was a Methodist.

It was no surprise when Murriel Jones married James Orville Woods and they made their home in the neighborhood. They had two boys, James Orville II and Delmer S. Woods, a Cheyenne chiropractor and former City Councilman.

Mrs. Jones and Mrs. Woods were among the leaders in the Parent-Teachers' Movement, as well as organizers of the Anna Gordon Chapter of the Women's Christian Temperance Union. Coors' Tavern located at Eleventh and Central, directly across from the main gate of the Union Pacific yards, at the foot of the old viaduct, attracted far too many wage-earners and paychecks for the well-being of the blue-collar families, in the opinion of the Womens' Christian Temperance Union members.

The organization was quite effective in its crusade.

The 1923 demolition had taken all of the houses on the north side of East Tenth Street, leaving the Jones' house across the street from the scene of devastation.

This author became acquainted with Murriel Woods during the 1949 legislative campaign to get the ten cent tax off margarine. (We had wanted to get yellow margarine legalized, too, but were advised that it would be politically unfeasible. We did it in the following legislature but that is another story.)

Mrs. Woods was always there observing the front and quietly lobbying for temperance issues. We learned our ABC's of lobbying from her. If we came in late for a session, she would tell us what was happening to our bill and any news that might help. She would suggest people we should contact.

Murriel Woods is still actively participating in community life. She works five days a week in a child care center in addition to teaching a Sunday School class.

She continues to live in her old home on the South Side.

THE OLD SOUTH SIDE CHURCHES

The South Church, which began as a mission of the First Congregational Church, was organized in 1885 with nine members. Herbert Phillips served as the first pastor of this Railroad Chapel, as it was sometimes called. It was situated opposite "the new Johnson School," at Twelfth and Evans.

Reverend Phillips painted a small water color of the Cheyenne scene, showing the church, the school and a few scattered houses with Montana House, a large brick hotel, on Twelfth Street. A single set of railroad tracks and the telegraph line bisects the town on the bare prairie. (The painting may be seen in the library of the First Congregational Church at 3501 Forest Drive.)

The pastor still best remembered was the Reverend Annette Belcher. Hers was a lively congregation with many workers and a large Sunday School.

Mrs. Mary Doak taught Sunday School here. One day she brought a Mason jar full of whiskey to class. She broke an egg into it to show the boys what whiskey would do to their stomachs. One now venerable man, who remembered the demonstration said, "I never took a drink of whiskey in my life, because of that."

The little church building was moved away and turned into a residence after the Union Pacific expansion of 1923.

FAITH UNITED METHODIST

Violet Breisch, historian for the church, sent this brief summary of a half century of service by a church, once known as the Community Church.

A group of neighbors organized a Bible class in a home on the South Side. In 1923 it became known as the South Side Sunday School. The same year a lot was purchased where a basement church was built. The Sunday School soon outgrew this structure.

The lot where the present Faith United Church now stands at Sixth Street and Maxwell Avenue was purchased. A small house was donated by the School District and moved onto the lot. It was too small. In 1925, the basement and sanctuary of the present church was built and called the Community Church. The bell for the steeple was purchased from the School District for fifteen dollars when old Johnson School was demolished. (More about the bell appears in the Lavinia Cole manuscript, page 78.)

The "Penny Suppers" prepared and served by the women of the congregation were used as fund raisers during the depression of the thirties. The fame of the good cooks and excellent food spread over the city. On March 25, 1930, the name was changed to the United Brethren Church. Later that year, a parsonage was purchased at 301 East Seventh Street. When the United Brethren and the Evangelical Church merged in November of 1946, they became known as the Evangelical United Brethren Church.

Because of the lack of Sunday School space in 1950, an educational unit was built and dedicated. Then in April of 1968, the merger of the Methodist and United Brethren churches took place. This formed the United Methodist Church.

With two other United Methodist churches in Cheyenne, the name Faith United Methodist Church was chosen. The parsonage was sold in 1981.

The first person to preach in the original church was the Reverend O. E. McCracken. The present pastor is Reverend Gary Goettel.

Although the affiliations of the church have undergone several changes, the congregation remains very much a neighborhood church serving a third generation.

ZION CONGREGATIONAL CHURCH

The Zion Congregational Church observed its fiftieth anniversary during the weekend of October 20th, 1973. The church organized October 15, 1923 under the name "Die Kongregational Zions Gemeinde zu Cheyenne, Wyoming." Through donations of charter members, friends of the church and businessmen, Jake Reiter, acting for the church, purchased property from A. D. Kelly on October 20, 1923 for $675.00.

The Congregation was incorporated on January 29, 1924 with a Board of Directors made up of Jake Reiter, John Hardung, C. M. Greenwald, John Reiter and Peter Stang. Other charter members included David Tempel, H. Walker, John Gettman, J. Burchmann, Fred Lebsack, Sr., Conrad Reiter, Fred Reiter, Henry Schnell, Henry A. Siefried, Henry Wambolt, W. H. Kleinke, John Fletcher and George C. Fleer.

The charter members were all of German ancestry. Many had come to the United States from Russia and had originally settled in Colorado and Nebraska as farmers. However, in 1922 the Union Pacific was hiring workers, and seeking a better life for their families, they moved to Cheyenne.

Prior to the Church's construction, members held services in a building which was located on the two-hundred block of East Twelfth Street. The services were held whenever Conference Minister, Reverend Helzer of Denver was in Cheyenne. Sunday School and Prayer Meetings were held every Sunday in the home of Mr. and Mrs. Peter Stang. The first Sunday School Christmas Program was also held in the Stang home. Services were conducted in German for many years.

Some years later when the directors had obtained enough money to start the building of the first church, someone was hired to dig a basement at 711 Maxwell Avenue. The remainder of the church was built by the members, working each night and all day Saturdays until it was completed.

Nine ministers served the church from its inception until 1950. Reverend William Strauch served the church from 1950 until 1958. During this period the membership growth enabled the congregation to build a new church edifice in 1953, at 600 East Seventh Street, which adjoins the original property, according to historian Edvina Weiderspahn.

The original building was then converted into a parsonage; again, all the work was done by the members. In December of 1967, a new parsonage was purchased at 716 Shoshoni Street. The original building now serves as the Sunday School Annex.

The wives of three of the incorporating members are living and active in the church. They are Mrs. John Hardung, Mrs. Peter Stang and Mrs. David Temple. They were honored at the Confirmation Reunion Banquet during the fiftieth anniversary celebration.

SAINT JOSEPH'S CATHOLIC CHURCH

We are privileged to have this excerpt from a "History of the Diocese of Cheyenne," written by Bishop P. A. McGovern in 1941.

"Cheyenne had shown a steady growth through the years, and the congregation attending the cathedral had increased *pari passu*, until the people could no longer be accommodated with three Masses. The isolation of the south side, due to the railroad tracks, suggested the advisability of a church for that section of the city. Two lots, therefore, were purchased at Sixth and House Avenue, and two more donated by Mrs. Mary Schmidt. St. Joseph's Church, an attractive brick building in Spanish Mission style, with a capacity of 300, was erected at a cost of $30,000.00.

It was solemnly blessed and set aside for divine worship January 28, 1929. Solemn high Mass was celebrated by Reverend James A. Hartman, assisted by Reverend John Henry as deacon, and Reverend Leo Morgan as subdeacon. Bishop McGovern preached the sermon, and had as his chaplains Right Reverend James W. Stenson, V.G., of Omaha, and V. Reverend John T. Nicholson, V.G., of Laramie. Thereafter Mass was said in the new church every Sunday at nine o'clock. However, in the course of a few years, it was found that four Masses were not sufficient to provide for the ever growing flock, and on November 29, 1938, the bishop created St. Joseph's — separate parish with Reverend Jerome Denk as pastor. From that date four Masses were celebrated every Sunday in the cathedral, and two in St. Joseph's Church. Before leaving this subject, we may remark that the new parish began its autonomous existence free from debt; but the erection of a parochial residence created an obligation of $3,500.00."

Since that time a Parish Hall and a Catechetical Center have been built.

OTHER SOUTH SIDE CHURCHES

Today there are eleven other churches in the city and county south of the Union Pacific Railroad tracks. They are: United Pentecostal Church, 1712 Park Avenue, Orchard Valley; Spanish Assembly of God, Fourth and Van Lennen; Harvest Time Tabernacle, 708 East Prosser Road; Fellowship Baptist Church, 1317 Avenue 6; Blessed Sacrament Catholic, 19 South House Avenue; Open Bible Center, West Leisher and Cribbon Avenue; Holy Temple Church of God in Christ, 567 East Fifth Street; and Church of God in Prophecy, 421 East Eighth Street.

NOSTALGIA TIME

As we reminisced with our friends and gathered these stories, almost forgotten scenes, people, customs and events came to mind. It was nostalgia time, our youth revisited.

We recalled how our lives were regulated by the great steam whistle on the Union Pacific Steam Plant beside the viaduct. The plant supplied heat for the shops. The whistle was hand operated and accurate to the split second. It could be heard all over town but especially on the South Side. It invaded our homes, got us out of bed and off to school or work. If it happened to blow when we were passing close by, momentary deafness resulted.

Depending on the weather and the wind direction, the cloud of steam from the plant was a gauntlet we had to run to keep from getting too many visible specks on ourselves. It was the same with trainsmoke crossing the viaduct. We thought that an underpass was an idea whose time had come.

Most of the people interviewed for this book had some anecdote involving the whistle. One woman recalled how, when the noon whistle blew, Mama would put the food on the table. The kids raced home from school trying to beat Pop. Pop came in the back door, shucked off his greasy outside overalls, kicked off his shoes, washed, and won most of the time.

A typical meal would be potatoes and gravy, homemade bread, beans and greens, home-canned tomatoes and pie, always pie. In hard times and in families whose main meal was in the evening, lunch was usually a big bowl of hearty soup and crusty homemade bread.

Most shop craft people carried lunch buckets. One man walked from West Twenty-Ninth Street and carried the same lunch bucket for over thirty years. Another carried his grandfather's three level miner's bucket. There was a "beanery" in the yards patronized mainly by single men and trainmen.

Everyone walked to school or work, even if there was a family car. We remember the parade of men on the viaduct, going to and from work, north and south. In the confines of the pedestrian walk it was like a marching army at shift-changing time. Busses began to run in 1924 but shop people usually walked.

Remember how we watched for the mail man driving his old grey horse hitched to a two-wheeled cart? And the rag man with his spring wagon came to the neighborhood every few weeks calling, "Raaks, old iahn, bottles, raaks, iahn." We took the leaky teakettle to him. Mama gave up plans to make a rug from a sackfull of wool rags and he bought them. Anything no longer useable might bring a few cents from the rag man. It gave us a righteous feeling, not wasting something of value. Five cents bought a kid a movie ticket.

Farmers brought produce to town in horse-drawn wagons; live poultry, fruit, vegetables and potatoes in hundred-pound sacks. Local merchants put a stop to that.

How the kids would come running when the Crystal Ice wagon came down the street. The driver would give them chips of ice. Boys would hitch a ride on the back of the wagon and brag how cool they were. And do you remember having to empty the ice water pan without spilling? Then you are over fifty years old.

And remember when everyone burned coal in the kitchen range and the heater, or stoked the furnace by hand? There were ashes to be taken out

Frontier Days Special, July 24, 1931, at Cheyenne, Wyoming.

PHOTOS COURTESY OF JAMES L. EHERNBERGER

1937 — Looking from viaduct in a northeasterly direction, showing Union Pacific yards at Cheyenne.

to the ash pits. Sometimes the trash on the garbage collector's wagon would catch fire from the hot ashes. Even the horses seemed to be in a hurry then.

The horse and buggy days were drawing to a close.

On windy nights the dump hill would have a ruddy glow and sometimes break into flames. The kids said, "That is what hell looks like." That was followed by an argument about heaven and hell. The KKK burned a cross up there!

There was once a deep gully on that hill. Old timers remembered that in winter they could slide down one side on their sleds and half way up the other. Gradually it, too, was filled with the refuse of Cheyenne. The antique bottle collectors have found bottles dated circa the 1870s, however, they could have been old before being deposited there.

Women learned not to hang wet laundry out in winter unless there was a good west wind to keep the soot spots off the white sheets. Over a period of time the fall of cinders built up on the lawns to several inches above the sidewalks. The passing of the steam trains was not too often mourned by housewives. How we envied the railroaders with their passes; we all missed train travel and the luxury of the dining car.

For the most part, families were large and the pay was low. It took more people working to sustain a family. Before World War I more tasks were done by hand. Gradually automation came to the shop crafts and finally labor-saving appliances came into the home.

Extended families with grandparents and grown married children sharing the same roof were not uncommon in the twenties. When older children went to work, they usually paid for their board and room at home, until they established their own homes. Sometimes, too, there was a little nest egg Mama had saved to help them get started. An extra room was rented, bath shared — no problem.

Often neighborhood boys grew up and married neighborhood girls as did these well known pairs: Anna Jessen who married Glen Hendershot and her sister, Edna, who married Orville Hendershot. Three of the four Fahrenbruch girls who lived at 208 West Eighth Street also married neighbor boys. Lydia married Howard E. Drake, Edvina married J. Arling Weiderspahn and Irene married Robert Weiderspahn. Rosie married a service man, Fred H. Freeman.

Most of the Italians, Greeks and Slavic people moved away from the South Side after the 1923 demolition. The only minorities we knew were those of numbers, rather than political power. Blacks were a minority because there were only six of them. Henry and Mary Asberry lived in the square two-story house at 922 Capitol Avenue. They had a little girl named Lily. Charles and Lillian Horn, 614 West Tenth Street were divorced. Lillian moved away. And then there was Mary Burk and her husband, George (Kid Fox) Burk.

Henry Asberry, listed as "driver" in the Directory, hauled sand and gravel, and dug basements. His beautiful, well-groomed mules and his hard work won the respect of everyone. (In 1931, he bid on the garbage hauling contract and lost to Art Trout.) Charles Horn was a cook at the Union Pacific.

The "demolition" and the advent of the chain stores in the early thirties eliminated most of the little neighborhood grocery stores in every section of Cheyenne. Finally, the family bakeries disappeared. We missed the Tagliavore's Bake Shop and the Purity Bakery on Central Avenue.

The newspapers cartooned about the HCL, High Cost of Living, and the inflation. Meanwhile, we had learned to cope. We knew the "Art of Making Do." Thrift was a habit; making over clothes, letting down hems, turning the faded coat wrong side out, then handing it down to a younger child. It helped us to keep our pride. "Use it up, wear it out or do without," was our motto through the years. We saved for a rainy day, made the house payments and helped those less fortunate. We managed our own affairs. Dogs and cats ate table scraps.

Eventually the small efficient, warm houses were mortgage free, and in the 1980s the cars again fit inside the 1920 garages.

ALICE MARVEN HEBARD

A Speech by Lavinia A. Cole

(Presented at Johnson Elementary School)

— year unknown —

Alice Marven Hebard was the first primary teacher at Johnson School. She did not teach in this building but over in old Johnson School which was torn down in 1923, before any of you children were born. The old school was located between Eleventh and Twelfth and House and Evans Streets. It was bought by the Union Pacific Railway Company in 1922 when they extended their railroad yards. The block on which old Johnson School stood is now part of the Union Pacific Railroad yards.

It was in this old school that Miss Hebard taught many of your grandfathers, grandmothers, fathers and mothers how to read, sing and do their number work. The red school house soon became so crowded with children that the school board bought an old depot, moved it on the north corner of the playground and converted it into a school house. Here Miss Hebard taught some of your fathers and mothers. She had many pupils in her room, often sixty to seventy, but she taught them the best she could and seldom complained.

Miss Hebard was one of the first teachers in the old Johnson School when it opened in the spring of 1884. She had taught my three older brothers and when I was a little girl, five years old I was sent to school so Miss Hebard was my first grade teacher. My class was so crowded that I could attend school only one half day, so one half of the children went in the morning and the other half attended in the afternoon. Miss Hebard never grumbled about these large classes because at that time it had not become the fashion to have thirty-five or forty pupils in one room. She took all who came and patiently worked harder with her large classes so they could be passed to second grade the next year. We had very little individual instruction, so some of the boys and girls who were slow about learning stayed in the first grade two or three years. Miss Hebard's older boys used to carry large coal scuttles to her room for the old heating stove. By the time these larger children stopped two or three years in each grade they were great trouble makers and very mischievous by the time they reached the fourth grade.

We did not have the great number of books that you children are privileged to read.

We bought all of our books from Mr. Logan's newsstand and bought only one reader for first grade. In the upper grades children had to buy a reader, an arithmetic, a language book, a geography and a history. These were all the books we had for the year. You children are very lucky indeed to have so many lovely books furnished free. In our first grades today the children have thirty-one readers, thirty in the second, twenty-eight in the third, twenty-six in the fourth, twenty-three in the fifth and seventeen in the sixth grade.

Children who had only one reader had to study it and then when the class time came to recite, every child read some part of the same story, so by the time thirty-eight or more children had read the same lesson, many of us knew it by heart. We could have only one lesson a day because the one book had to be stretched over the whole year. When we finished it we began at the first and read it over again, sometimes three or four times. I can still remember whole stories that I learned in the first few grades. Would you like to have me tell you one just as it was written in my old Barne's *Second Reader*?

"His Cure for Idleness —"

"When I was a boy in school," said an old man, "I was often very idle, even while at my lessons I used to play with other boys as idle as myself. Of course we used to try to hide this from the teacher, but one day I was fairly caught. 'Boys,' said he, 'you must not be idle. You must keep your eyes and minds on your lessons. You do not know what you lose by being idle and now when you are young is the time to learn. Let any one of you who sees another boy look off his lesson, come up and tell me.' Well, said I, to myself, there's Fred Smith, I don't like him. If I see him look off his book, I'll go up and tell the teacher.

Not long after I saw Fred look off his book so up I went and told the teacher that I saw Fred look off his book.

'Oh! you did, did you,' said the teacher, 'and where were your eyes when you saw him. Were they on your book?'

I heard the other boys laugh and I hung my head while the teacher smiled. It was a good lesson for me. I did not look for idle boys again."

The teachers and pupils were surely pleased when the school board furnished a set of sight readers. They were books without even one picture but they gave us new stories and that made us very happy.

Some of the children who bought their books had to be very careful with them, as most families saved the books for the younger brothers and sisters. Some with no little brothers and sisters had to sell them back to Mr. Logan at the end of the year to help pay for next year's books.

Many of these pupils were not really as careful with these books as you are with yours. If you soil, tear or get ink on a book you have to pay a fine; your parents and grandparents did strange things to their books and wrote many foolish rhymes in them. Of course, they thought they were doing something fine. When the girls got new books most of them would write such rhymes as these on the inside covers in their very best penmanship: "Don't steal this book for fear of shame for in it is its owner's name"; — Peggy Ward. Or "Do not steal this book away for if you do God will say, 'Where is that book you stole from Eileen Milward?' And when you say, 'I do not know.' Then God will say, 'Go down below.' "

The boys would write in big bold writing — "If my book should start to roam, — give it a kick and send it home," Robert Slames. Or "Don't steal this book for fear of your life, for the owner carries a big jack-knife," — Dale Collins.

Of course Miss Hebard's children didn't mark their books like this, because they hadn't learned how yet. Her little first graders sat at double seats and she kept them busy making their letters and copying from the board. They could copy anything and did it very nicely too. They did not have to be punished much but sometimes the girls whispered or erased something from another's slate for meanness, or a boy pulled a girl's hair, they punched or kicked each other when she wasn't looking, those naughty children were in disgrace and had to sit behind the stove in the wood box, or stand in the corner, or sit under the teacher's desk. Sometimes the naughty girl had to sit with a boy, or they couldn't help Miss Hebard by passing the water pail so that the boys and girls could wet their sponges and rags to wash off their slates. They tied their sponges and rags on strings to the sides of their desks, or poked them through the holes on the sides of their desks to keep them from getting lost. Children didn't have any free paper furnished until they were old enough to take examinations. They had no drawing paper. They did all of their writing and drawing on their slates, then washed them off after the teacher looked at them, to have clean slates for the next lesson.

Miss Hebard loved to see children happy. She would play with them at noon and recess such games as "Drop the Handkerchief," "Here Comes a Blue Bird Through the Window, Hey Diddle De Day, Day, Day," "Farmer in the Dell," "Here I come," and many, many fine games.

PHOTO FROM THE COLLECTION OF CASSIE COLE

Left to Right, standing: Lavinia A. Cole, principal, Alice Marven Hebard, 1915. Lower right, Miriam Kelliher — later Mrs. Frank Crowley.

Friday was the time for her dance and how much fun the children would have at that. Each boy would choose a girl for his partner, they would take hold of hands and slide sideways across the floor while the band of children clapped and sang. We had no piano, radio or victrolas in those days, so the children sang "Yankee Doodle" when they danced fast, and "Go Tell Aunt Rhodie That Her Old Grey Goose is Dead," when they had to go slower. Sometimes the children just flew across the floor and would get all tangled up and tumble around, then they had to dance to "Go Tell Aunt Rhodie." We had just as much or more fun than you have in your nice little folk dances with the piano or victrola.

We had no steady music teachers and no pitch pipes, but Miss Hebard had an old tuning fork. She struck it against the desk and it hummed. Then we all sang do, me, sol, and started to sing. I never did understand how we got in the right key but I guess we did.

Miss Hebard always said that the first party she ever had in school was my party when I was five years old. My mother wanted to give me a party and I wanted to invite all the children in my class, but the house was too small to hold them all so she went to school and asked Miss Hebard if she could make a cupcake and furnish an apple and some animal crackers for each of the children in the room as a surprise for my birthday. Miss Hebard had to ask the superintendent who gave his permission but said that he thought it was a very strange request for any mother to make. After this party, Miss Hebard's boys and girls had many parties and always had a joyous time. Sometimes when there were very poor little children in her room, she would take them, on their birthdays, to her home for dinner and she would write their names on the blackboard and draw a colored ball, doll or bugle after the name to please them.

At Halloween we ducked in a big wash tub for apples. If we weren't lucky in catching an apple with our mouths, we got an apple just for trying.

Perhaps the happiest time of all the year was Christmastime. Miss Hebard planned for this for a month in advance. Sometimes Old Santa Claus himself arrived with bells and a great deal of noise and delivered a big bag of candy and nuts and a little doll for the girls and a jumping jack or monkey for the boys. Those who had younger brothers and sisters brought them to school and each of them had a treat. Miss Hebard knew every child in every family she taught. Sometimes when old Santa was delayed at the North Pole, or was too busy way off west, he would come at night and hide his fine treats under the benches along the walls where the children would find them at a given signal. Miss Hebard always seemed very much surprised to find out that he had been there and left all those lovely things.

Miss Hebard's birthday was February 21. On one birthday the Parent Teachers' Association surprised Miss Hebard and gave her a large bell to hang up in the tower of the school house. Before that time she called all the pupils with this hand bell. She rang it ten times and all the youngsters had to run fast and be in line before the tenth tap. When Miss Hebard received the big bell she was so happy she couldn't speak one word. She just cried to think that the South Side mothers loved her enough to spend so much on a bell. That bell hangs in the Community Church today, and you hear it all over the South Side every Sunday.

I told you Miss Hebard's birthday was February 21, just the day before Washington's. As we always had a holiday on Washington's birthday, she always had a party on her birthday to celebrate both occasions. She would make hats for the children out of newspapers and would pin some red, white and blue paper on the very tip top. She wore a paper hat also. Then with each child and the teacher carrying a flag, they would march around the South Side and sing as they passed the pupil's house. This delighted the parents and the little folks at home as well as the pupils. When they returned to school some treat was already on the desks, some ginger snaps and jelly beans usually. How these ever got on the desks Miss Hebard never knew unless some good brownie fixed it while they were gone.

In the evening the teachers of the building were invited to Miss Hebard's birthday party at her home. Every birthday Miss Hebard was just six years old when the children asked her how old she was.

Miss Hebard taught the children of the South Side for thirty-three years. She could have moved over town to teach many times, but would never go because she loved the children over here and their parents. She made many home calls when the children were ill and left many glasses of jelly, a few oranges and apples or a few fresh eggs. She visited every new baby brother and sister that came to live at her pupils' homes to see if she would let them keep it. The mothers told her their troubles and asked her advice about many things.

She not only helped the boys and girls and their parents but she counseled and gave valuable assistance to the young teachers in the school building. Her room was always the meeting place for all the teachers before they started their work for the day. They went there because she was a cheerful friend to those younger than she, and always knew some good story, or joke, or interesting news.

Miss Alice Marven Hebard was my first teacher. Later we taught side by side for thirteen years, for her last three years in Johnson School, I was her principal.

She was always a cheerful, faithful, loving friend and I am glad to honor her here today.

Miss Hebard's sister Dr. Grace Raymond Hebard has kindly given to Johnson School a memorial tablet in honor of her dear sister, Alice, our beloved, pioneer primary teacher.

I hope every child will read this plaque — you know where it is, on the north wall at the central entrance.* Now you will understand why these words are written on the tablet.

* (The Hebard tablet was moved to Hebard school in 1948.)

THE PLAQUE AT HEBARD ELEMENTARY SCHOOL

ALICE M. HEBARD

SERVED

The Johnson School of Cheyenne

1884-1917

Alice M. Hebard will long be remembered
as one of the most beloved
pioneer primary teachers in Wyoming.
She was a lover of
little children and a sincere
friend and confidant of their parents.
A kindly advisor to her fellow teachers,
A benefactor to those in need,
A sympathetic cheerful companion whose gracious humor
and cheerful spirit made her welcome in any group.
She was loved by all who were privileged to be her friend.

THE ALICE MARVEN HEBARD SCHOLARSHIP

Alice Marven Hebard was the second child of George Deah Alonzo Hebard and Margaret Elizabeth Dominick Marven Hebard, born in Clinton, Iowa, on February 21, 1859. George D. A. Hebard was a Congregational minister.

The family moved to Iowa City, Iowa, where Alice studied at McClain's Academy and Iowa State University. After that she studied for one year at Des Moines, in the field of primary education.

In 1882, she came to Wyoming with her family, consisting of her widowed mother, her brothers, Fred and Lockwood and her sister Grace. Grace became the well-known engineer, lawyer, historian, professor of political economics at the University of Wyoming and exponent of Woman Suffrage. The Hebard's Cheyenne home still stands at 508 East Seventeenth Street.

On arrival in Cheyenne, Alice immediately set up Cheyenne's first private kindergarten. She began teaching at Johnson Elementary School in 1884, and until retirement in 1918, taught beginners there. She was as revered by the community as by her pupils. She became involved to the extent of helping people to buy their homes on the South Side. Her name can be seen on the mortgage records.

Upon retirement, she went to live with her sister Dr. Grace Raymond Hebard and Dr. Agnes Wergeland at their Laramie home, "The Doctor's Inn."

After Alice's death, October 1, 1928, Grace set up a scholarship trust fund at the Stockgrower's National Bank of Cheyenne, (now known as the First National Bank and Trust). The original amount was five thousand dollars.

After Dr. Hebard died, October 13, 1936, according to an editorial in the *Wyoming State Tribune*, she had, "only recently, when she realized that she would not much longer have need of her material resources, Dr. Hebard increased this endowment."

The Memorial Book published by the Faculty of the University of Wyoming, June 1937, stated that the Alice Marven Hebard Scholarship Fund then stood at $11,000.00.

"The purpose of the scholarship is to award scholarships to freshmen or sophomores in the University of Wyoming. The recipients of the grants must be graduates of Johnson School (now Junior High) and of the Cheyenne Senior High School. They must qualify mentally, morally and physically in order to receive the honored recognition. All things being equal, the scholarships should go to those least able to pay for their own education." (From a statement by the First National Bank.)

The Scholarship Committee currently consists of the principal of Johnson Junior High School, the principal of Cheyenne High School, presently East and Central branches, and the Superintendent of School District Number One, Laramie County, with a bank trustee as an ex-officio member.

The first scholarship was given in May 1930, amounting to $100, each semester. In later years, according to the bank, "the fund has increased, due to interest rates and wise investments by the bank, two scholarships have been granted yearly."

In 1956-57 there were two scholarships of $200 each; 1957-58 there was one at $300; 1958-59 there were two at $200 each; 1959-60 there were two at $200 each. In 1960-61 two scholarships of $250 each went to Lorene Bowles and Donna Ehlers. As of May 1960 the Hebard Scholarship Fund stood at "more than $10,000."

NEW JOHNSON SCHOOL, CIRCA 1923

When the news of the mass demolition for the new Union Pacific terminal broke in the *Wyoming State Tribune*, there was consternation in many a South Side home. There had been a large number of new homes built since World War I, old and new would have to be moved or torn down. The most universal concern was for old Johnson School.

PHOTO COURTESY OF CHEYENNE NEWSPAPERS, INC.

SCHOOL IN TRANSITION — The 1923 Johnson Elementary School became Johnson Junior High School. The transition to a junior high school began in 1947 with the opening of Orchard Valley - Rossman Elementary School, when a seventh grade was added. An eighth grade was added in 1948 and a ninth grade in 1949 as the Alice Marven Hebard and Lavinia A. Cole schools made space available. Additions in 1953 and 1959 failed to accommodate the growing enrollment of nearly 700.

South Siders were generally skeptical about any of the beneficial results of the expansion, highly praised in the article, trickling down to the residents of the South Side.

This change in the geography implied greater social change. A mass meeting was held at the J. T. Clark Fire House. Delegates from the Parent-Teachers' Association and the South Side Improvement Association were chosen to take these concerns to the School Board.

In varying accounts of this meeting with the board, the delegates were, at first, locked out. Finally a smaller delegation was allowed in. Assurances were given that land would be traded with the Union Pacific for a new school.

It was later announced that the site for the new school would be all of block 596, bounded by Warren and House Avenues between Seventh and Eighth Streets. According to county records, this block had been owned by the school district since 1890!

South Side people waited and watched in anticipation as the new school materialized. Many local building trades people were employed. It was a busy time. Homes were being moved to new locations on both sides of the tracks over the Russell Avenue crossing. Many residents left the South Side. In 1923 there were no houses south of Sixth Street and few east of Central below Seventh. The southeast blocks began to fill with houses.

Finally the seventeen room building was open for classes. The whole community rejoiced. There was room enough, teachers enough, at last. There was a gymnasium with a stage at one end which would be well used. More than ever Johnson became a community center although the firehouse was spared for some years.

When the new school was opened the block east of it was littered with construction waste. It was the site of a "hoped for" city park. A flagpole had been dedicated about 1914 at the corner of Eighth Street and Evans Avenue, according to best recollections. Julia Huffer recalls that her friend, pretty little Minna Lafferty had raised the flag that day.

The block had once been a small hill, until someone used the earth to grade the streets, leaving a depression. After cleanup by the South Side Improvement Association, a sunken garden seemed a good idea. Ed McKay, whose barbershop stood at the foot of the old viaduct, deeded the block to the city for a park in 1921.

The impetus of the new school renewed the effort to complete the park. The Parent-Teachers' Association decided to let the children contribute something. A "Penny March" was set for Fridays at school to help to buy trees for the park.

One day sister Ethel announced that she would not go to school. "It's Penny March Day and we haven't any pennies! I looked in the sugar bowl on the top of the ice box and there are none in the dresser drawer," she wailed.

J. T. Clark Volunteer Hose Company
Memorial in Lincoln Park.

Little brother Joe ran his chubby hand under the piano to try to reach the one that rolled under there. Papa laughed and gave each a dime. "Stop at the grocery store and get it changed into pennies, if you must. But hurry, you'll be late for school."

There were benefit dances at the fire house and numerous bake sales by the Parent-Teachers' Association. The Bolleana poplars were ordered for spring planting. The Parent-Teachers' Association took a justifiable pride in being the first organization of its kind in the State of Wyoming, and for its support of the best in education. The Johnson School kindergarten was the first in Wyoming.

The park dedication was set for a cold windy day on the east front of the building. The flagpole, given by the D. J. O'Connell family, was erected by Charlie Wallace. A patriotic program with a salute to the flag and lusty singing of the "Star Spangled Banner" and "America the Beautiful," ended with the announcement of the name chosen by the children.

They named it for the man on the penny, amid cheers and tears. Lincoln Park was a symbol of their children's heritage to the generations of blue-collar people represented at the gathering. They knew the meaning of America.

During the fifties, a patchwork of ten classrooms, a new auditorium, a cafeteria and gymnasium had been added; further stressing the inadequate plumbing and heating capacity; against the advice of experienced building technicians.

A pool had been installed in Lincoln Park, in front of the school, during that period. In the summer of the Bicentennial Year, 1976, culture shock swept over the residents of the neighborhood to see a mural painting of Che Quevera, the exponent of Communism in Latin America, emblazoned on the pool house. Trash cans were painted red, white and green — the colors of the Mexican flag. There were racial incidents. Mayor Bill Nation ordered a "cooling off" period. The militant expression did not represent a majority of the Hispanic people who had grown to one-third of the total South Side population since 1950. The sense of outrage and the ensuing uproar seemed to convince the officials that their ghettoization policies had gone too far.

Johnson School, Circa 1923, stands empty after sixty years of service.

OLD TERRITORIAL JOHNSON SCHOOL, 1883

In the fall of 1981, rumors began to fly about changing the name of Johnson Junior High School. At the City-County Planning Office, the new school site was labeled "Cornerstone!" A new subdivision had sprung up at the long forgotten southwest corner of the original city of Cheyenne. A large substitute cornerstone had been placed there, in 1890. In recent years the stone had been fenced and a plaque placed on it by the Arp family.

No one could remember for whom the school had been named. It had always been Johnson. A school official said that it didn't matter anyway. "The name is going to be changed."

"Over my dead body." I blurted it out. "For what earthly reason?"

"It would improve the image of the school."

I told him that this historic neighborhood had centered around Johnson School for almost a hundred years.

It wasn't fair to the generations of children who had grown up in the neighborhood. Many are prominent in business, government and education. Buildings may change, or be torn down, but a "school is the children." Sociological changes are being forced upon the South Side by the cynical planners and the "Johnny-come-latelies," who envision revenues and profits in its destruction.

I resolved to learn more about the person who was honored by having a school named for him.

PHOTO FROM COLLECTION OF JULIA GREGORY HUFFER

EDWARD PAYSON JOHNSON ELEMENTARY SCHOOL, 1883 — with 1911 addition. From torn 1915 postcard.

JOHNSON JR HIGH SCHOOL

ARCHITECT'S RENDERING COURTESY OF SCHOOL DISTRICT NO. 1.

JOHNSON JUNIOR HIGH SCHOOL 1983 — Relocated near the southwest corner of the original city of Cheyenne, with large campus, playing fields and educational advantages unheard of when Cheyenne was young in 1883. Edward Payson Johnson Elementary School near the railroad yards was comprised of four rooms.

On file at the Wyoming State Archives, Museums and Historical Department was a record of the achievements of Edward Payson Johnson, the man for whom the school and the county had been named. His photograph had been made by D. D. Dare, before Dare had become the enterprising financier. Later, the museum staff discovered an oil portrait of Johnson in its collections.

I prepared an article for the *Tribune-Eagle* Sunday issue of November 1, 1981. It appeared in the sport section, page 27, headlined: "Edward Johnson Is Pioneer Cheyenne Should Remember." (It had been given a new lead.)

> After so many years it's sometimes easy to forget the men who helped to build Cheyenne. The namesake of Johnson School and Johnson County, however, certainly deserve to be remembered.
>
> Edward Payson Johnson came to Cheyenne in the summer of 1867. He had settled in Denver but was persuaded that Cheyenne was the place to be.
>
> During a short brilliant career he was elected county attorney at a time when it required "not only ability but great courage to enforce the law." In 1868 he was deputy district attorney for the Second Judicial District of Dakota Territory, an area covering the eastern half of present-day Wyoming.
>
> At that time he was listed in the city directory as "E. P. Johnson, Attorney at Law, City Hall." His advertisement in the directory read: "E. P. Johnson, General Conveyancer, 1608 Eddy (Pioneer)."
>
> In 1869 Johnson returned to Ohio to marry Miss Susan Riner. He built a house at 2201 Ferguson (Carey Avenue) when they returned. Cheyenne attorney, William A. Riner is a member of that family.
>
> President U. S. Grant appointed Johnson Attorney General for the new Wyoming Territory in 1871. This was considered, in itself, to be a great compliment, since government officials were seldom selected from the citizens of the Territory.
>
> As Attorney General, Johnson was instrumental in organizing the educational system, its funding and administration. In addition, he was the Territorial Librarian, whose ex-officio assignment was Superintendent of Public Instruction. He was an advocate of free education.
>
> Johnson is credited with the formation of the school board and Central School, which some criticized as being "too far out of town." (Twentieth and Central.) This school was considered to be the "finest in the Territory." He was also one of the organizers of the Congregational Church, Sabbath School and the literary society.
>
> In 1879, shortly before he died, at age thirty-seven, he was chosen to serve in the Upper House of the Legislative Assembly. The pioneers keenly felt his loss and honored him in the naming of Johnson Elementary School, when the four-room building was erected in 1883. The Legislative Assembly had renamed Pease County for him at the time of his death.
>
> Another four rooms were added to old Johnson School in 1911. It was the center of the South Side of Cheyenne until 1923. The forty-year old building was demolished with 300 homes and businesses in the Union Pacific expansion of the yards. A new Johnson School was built the same year.

> Three former teachers at Johnson School were similarly honored by having schools named for them. They were Alice Marven Hebard School, located at 413 Seymour Avenue, the Lavinia A. Cole School, 820 O'Neil Avenue on the South Side, and the Lulu Lebhart School, 807 Coolidge Avenue, in Sun Valley.
>
> Truly the name Johnson is synonymous with education, and the story of Johnson School is better told in the lives of the people who were influenced by the outstanding educators, who taught within its walls.

Shortly after the article came out, we heard that the students had voted to keep the name Johnson, however, the school officials were still "stonewalling it."

Although we tried to explain to the school officials that a name change for Johnson would not be in the best interests of the school and local tradition, we were repulsed. Finally, May 7, 1982, we held a coffee for former students of Johnson. Three generations of alumnae attended. No one wanted to see the name changed.

We worded the following petition to the Board of School District Number One, Laramie County, Wyoming:

> We, the undersigned, former students of Johnson School, friends and families, wish to state our support for the retention of the name Johnson, for the name of the new junior high school. The name has great historical and sentimental value, having been used since 1883, when the territorial school was named for Edward P. Johnson, an early settler. It has remained Johnson, as a grade school and as a junior high school.

The petition was delivered to the next school board meeting. The board voted to retain the name of Johnson Junior High School!

At last, the new building was ready for occupancy and the students made it a "school" on January 3, 1983, one hundred years after the original Johnson Elementary School was ready for children.

Dedication for the newest Johnson Junior High School building was set for February 27, 1983, 1236 West Allison Road.

It was a Sunday afternoon, under a clear blue sky in the courtyard of the impressive new school. The Stars and Stripes and the Wyoming State flags snapped, cracked and tugged at the rigging of the shiny new pole. The band played. There were prayers and speeches and the crowd moved inside to see this spacious new building. We entered the carpeted halls, saw two gymnasiums, two shops, music and art rooms, light spacious classrooms and a large well lighted cafeteria where we had refreshments before we realized that there was no auditorium!

AMERICANIZATION OF THE NEW PEOPLE

"This is America, the language of the Americans is English. Our Constitution, our laws, and our money is expressed in this tongue, and the man or woman who deserves to partake of the hospitality, freedom, civil rights and prosperity that represents the outstanding features of our Country, should as quickly as possible learn the language of this, their adopted country."

That statement was given to an interviewer in a 1977 study of ethnic groups in Wyoming, in answer to the question: "Why is the Union Pacific Employees' Magazine not bi-lingual?" The study, "Peopling the High Plains," was published by the Wyoming State Archives, Museums and Historical Department, Gordon O. Hendricksen, Editor. The statement reflects the attitude that generations of immigrants also held. They hastened to learn as much English as possible and as fast as they could. They were anxious for their children to get a good education and to be good Americans.

The European and Asiatic immigrants often suffered incredible hardships coming to America. In the early days they were sometimes transported to the area where their labor was needed in freight cars having a barrel of water at one end of the car and a barrel of bread at the other, according to stories handed down to their children. They tended to congregate in neighborhoods for mutual assistance, for learning the language and coping with the new environment. America did not have ghettoes where foreigners were forced to live. The newcomers were welcome to progress at their own pace and to the limit of their abilities.

No government assistance, welfare or bi-lingual programs were available for the newcomers. All they asked was an opportunity. The majority became American citizens and took pride in their accomplishment.

THE CROW CREEK DAIRIES

In Cheyenne before 1900, anyone who could, owned a cow or bought milk from a neighbor who did. There were a few dairies, however, all who sold milk were registered with the State of Wyoming at that time. It was not until 1924 that the Federal Pasteurized Bottling Standard, making it illegal to sell raw milk, was adopted by the State.

Large families found it prudent to keep a cow for their own milk supply. A summer chore for the young Berkley children was herding the family cow. Mrs. August Johnson also kept a cow, staked with a long rope, grazing the lush grass of Crow Creek meadows, below Sixth and Evans.

Registered dairies were: 1905 to 1907, Sloan and Bell, 112 West Twelfth Street; 1905-1915, Anthony Robitaille, home, 916 O'Neil; John Hughes, Jr., 602-620 West Tenth Street, (moved to 522 West Tenth Street in 1909 and operated there until 1915, when he sold the dairy to Harry C. Taylor, his son-in-law, and moved to Oregon. Taylor operated it less than one year, and he, too, moved to Oregon).

Other Crow Creek dairies registered for short terms were: 1909-1910, Con Hodges, 816 O'Neil, (Clear Creek); G. H. Haskell, 810 West Fifth Street; 1913-1914, J. A. Reichart, 1109 Dillon; 1910-1911, Nels H. Jensen, home,

103 West Sixth Street; 1909-1911, J. B. Blamey Dairy, 908 O'Neil; 1916-1927, William Ferguson, Snyder between Eleventh and Twelfth.

The southwest dairies pastured the hills and Clear Creek drainage.

The price of bottled milk in 1922 was ten cents per quart.

O'CONNELL'S

As next week will be a busy week for all of us, a few suggestions by us now can help immensely. With our own battery of trucks we can deliver your order any time you wish; that is, barring another blizzard, but at that we can get along very well even in the worst blizzard.

Competent clerks ALWAYS at your command which, coupled up with our line of groceries and meats and "let live" prices, WE GUARANTEE TO SATISFY—those contemplating opening an account with us, or if you are one of our many patrons you already know of our service. We solicit new accounts always, both over here and on the north side, also Fort Russell.

Our Christmas trees have arrived and are surely pretty, nice and bushy, at 65c to $1.25.

A complete line of decorations. Sweetwood wreaths, 35c; holly wreaths, 35c; evergreen wreaths, 30c.

Let us lay away a tree for you and we'll bet old Santa Claus will surely agree with our judgment.

We have everything in fancy and staple groceries, both package and bulk.

We have a ton of the finest quality of Christmas Candy, 25c and 30c per pound. Fancy Box Candy, 1-lb. boxes 75c; 2-lb. boxes $1.40; 3-lb. boxes fancy Chocolates $2.00.

Best quality of Mixed Nuts, pound 30c

English and Black Walnuts, Pecans, Almonds, Filberts, Brazil, Peanuts and Chestnuts. A complete line of new packed Shelled Nuts.

All the ingredients for mince meat and fruit cake can be found here.

Fancy Jonathan Apples, box $1.90

Extra fancy Jonathan Apples, box $2.25

Fancy Delicious Apples, per box $2.25

Extra fancy Delicious Apples, box $2.60

We also have a dandy Cooking Apple at, per bushel $1.50. This is really a good buy.

Best Navel Oranges, from, dozen 30c to 80c

Indian River Grape Fruit, each 10c, 15c and 20c

How about a pair of the original Daniel Green "Comfys" and slippers for Christmas. We have them—the original Daniel Green Juliets for ladies $1.60

Men's Leather Slippers, per pair $3.10

The Hamilton Brown Shoes cannot be beat in either price or quality. Our expert fitters can fit each one in the family and guarantee both price and quality to be just what you want.

Overshoes and Rubbers, too.
Underhill Overalls.

Great Western Dress and Work Gloves—per pair .... $1.50 to $2.75

Silk and Lisle Hose, from, per pair ... 25c to $1.40

Silk and Wool Hose, per pair $2.50

All Hosiery Guaranteed.

MEAT DEPARTMENT

A REAL TREAT FOR ANY TIME

Ralph's Pure Pork Sausage—both link and bulk

Pure Beef Hamburger

Prime Rib Roast—rolled or standing

Beef Rump Roasts Beef Shoulder Roasts

Milk Fed Veal Genuine Spring Lamb

Corn Fed Pork Pork Loin Roast

Pork Shoulder Roast Spare Ribs

Side Pork Fr. Hams

Pig Tails Pig Liver

Lunch Meat Hams

Bacon Picnic Hams

Empire Brisket Bacon Swift's Premium Bacon

Morris Supreme Bacon

Weiners Frankfurters

Liver Sausage Bologna

Minced Ham Baked Loaf Boiled Ham

We have now, as always, the best supply of both Dressed and Live Poultry in the city. Leave your order now for a Live Turkey or any kind of Fowl.

Fresh Fish Oysters

Let Ralph and his assistants take care of you poultry for Xmas and you'll be satisfied

Hay, Grain and Feed in Any and All Quantities

O'CONNELL'S

120-22 East 11th Street **Phones 273 and 274**

WYOMING STATE ARCHIVES, MUSEUMS AND HISTORICAL DEPARTMENT

Advertisement appearing in the *Wyoming State Tribune and Cheyenne State Leader,* 1922.

SOUTH SIDE CHEYENNE RESIDENTS, 1922

EXCERPTED FROM R. L. POLK DIRECTORY

R. L. POLK & CO. Publishers
Casper, Cheyenne, Laramie and Sheridan Directories
COPIES ON SALE AT 615 DOOLY BLDG., SALT LAKE CITY

USED WITH PERMISSION OF R. L. POLK & CO.

Adams, Charles F. (Kath.), 618 W. 9th
" Fanny, (Mrs.), 618 W. 9th
" Floyd P., Mach, UP 618 W. 9th
" James H., teamstr 618 W. 9th
" Margaret, student 618 W. 9th
Adolph, Geo. (Kate), hlpr UP 407 E. 9th
Aginaga, Nicanor, trucker UP 111 E. 12th
Agridis, Thos. rpr UP
Akitoma, Suchi, lab UP
Akerson, Minnis, waitress UP cafe 710 E. 10th
Allen, Frank M., d 8.8.21 expresmn 316 E. 10th (Ida)
" Morton, farmer 316 E. 10th
" Ray, d.10.2.20 age 25 316 E. 10th
" Rufus, d.9.7.20 age 73 316 E. 10th
" Wm. L., Expresmn 316 E. 10th
Allison, Harry L. (Ethel), whsmn McCord Brady 205 E. 9th
Amschel, Emil (Temperance), brkmn 501 E. 7th
Amty, Geo., hlpr UP 116 E. 11th
Anderson, Thos., Driver, South Side MKT 119 W. 10th
Arnold, Cleland, appr UP 101 Warren
" Cath., student
" Clinton B., lineman Postal Tel Cable 1001 Warren
Arp. Henry A., rms. 216 E. 11th
Arroyo, Delfino, trucker UP
Asberry, Henry, driver (Mary) 922 Capitol
Ashburn, Hilda, clk Roedels 7 Eddy Apts
Ashizawa, Henry, lab UP 113 W. 12th
" Shinji, lab UP 113 W. 12th
Ashley, Jos. (Matilda), 715 W. 9th
Ault, Clarence C. (Mary), hlpr H. S. O'Brien
" Ray, H. S. O'Brien
Baker, Benj. F. (Myrtle), hlpr 818 W. 9th
" Mrs. Bessie, Albany maid 818 W. 9th
" Chas., carp 119 W. 7th
" Edward, 818 W. 9th
" Geo. I. (Ella), 107 W. 9th
Bare, Walter (Anna), rpr UP 301 E. 10th
Barling, Swan, stower UP
Barjar, Howard S. (Blanche), Grds 818 E. 10th
Barros, Manuel (Marie), trucker UP 421 W. 12th
Bassett, Geo., carp 112 W. 10th
" Jos., lab 112 W. 10th
" Leroy (Erna), clk South Side MKT 112 W. 10th
Bates, Wm. (Ella), mach UP 106 E. 10
Bauer, Henry (Kate), mach UP 516 E. 9th
Beckler, Phoebe, (wid. John) 1010 Central
Bellaires, Keith M. (Gertrude), formn UP 1000 House
Benson, Albert (Myrtle), 400 E. 8th UP
" Frank W. (Naomi), 121 W. 8th
" Jas. W. (Carrie), blksmth UP 301 E. 9th
" John W. (Ada), 411 E. 9th
" Mary Ann, 610 W. 10th
Bentson, John A. (Evelyn), appr UP 220 W. 10th
Beranek, Jos. J. (Dorothy), blmkr 610 E. 11th
Berkley, Adeline, steno State Game and Fish 121 W. 8th
" Benj, mach UP 121 W. 8th
" Frank (Minnie), mach UP 121 W. 8th
" Granville, appr UP 121 W. 8th
" Madeline, steno 121 W. 8th
" Roland (Estella), mech UP 423 E. 9th
Bezene, Jos. (Emily), mach UP 114 E. 9th
Birt, Henry C. (Anna), 601 Capitol
Bittner, Darwin A., mach UP 909 Seymour
" Myrtle (wid Wm.), 909 Seymour
Bleecher, Louise, 508 E. 10th
Blehm, David (Kate), lab UP 621 E. 11th
Bolden, Earnest F., foremn UP 108 E. 11th
Bonham, Clinton, rpr UP 221 E. 9th
" Helen, clk 221 E. 9th
" Thomas (Emma), 221 E. 9th
Bonner, Ode, appr UP 821 Seymour
Bonser, Cecil E. (Leah), opr UP 113 W. 9th
" Wm. A. (Sarah), real estate 1009 Warren
Bowman, Frank C., cond. UP 100 E. 10th
Bowyer, Bert (May), trucker UP 118 E. 11th
Boyd, Saml., Antler Cafe 715 Bent
Boyle, Edwd. (Florence), 910 Central
Brandon, Floyd B. (Mary), clk UP 206 E. 8th
" John H. (Lizzie), tmstr 700 E. 10th
Bryant, Harry, mach UP 221 E. 9th
Buckley, Isabella, student 109 E. 9th
" James (Ida), Editor WYOMING LABOR JOURNAL 109 E. 9th
" Marv. (Laind), 109 E. 9th
Bullara, Peter (Mary), barber 120 W. 11th
Bundy, Frank A. (Mollie), contr 922 O'Neil
Burk, Geo. (Mary), lab rear 1010 O'Neil
Burns, Horace C., lab 301 E. 9th
" Jennie (wid Fred), clk Cheyenne Creamery 301 E. 9th
Caiones, Thiro H., hlpr UP 300 E. 10th
Calabrase, Jos. (Josephine), lab 209 W. 12th
Callahan, John W., 805 E. 12th
" Patk. (Cath.), lab Ft. D. A. Russell 805 E. 12th
Callas, Geo. (Louise), inrnwkr UP rms 805 E. 12th
Candler, Florence D., rms 1000 House
Carlan, Louis (Thelma), eng UP 904 E. 11th

Chamberlain, Edw. H. (Mary), Brkmn UP 311 E. 10th
Chambers, Jennie (wid Frank), 503 E. 9th
" Manley E. (Ina), insp UP 501 E. 9th
" Jesse M., rpr UP 501 E. 9th
" Marshall M., d. age 78
" Merle F., insp UP 501 E. 9th
Chocas, Geo. (Helen), rpr UP 901 Central
Christensen, Chris L. (Annie), jan UP 111 E. 11th
" Dewey, lab UP
" Earl V. (Mildred), hlpr UP 215 W. 9th
Christoff, Wm., rpr UP
Chiupec, Stephen L., Carrier P. O. 110 E. 7th
Clancy, Ella, laundrs Ft DAR 814 Capitol
" Gus (Mabel), Supt County Infirmery 814 Capitol
" James, 814 Capitol
Clements, Louis H. (Lillian), Mach UP 8 Lillian Terrace, Central
Clevenger, May, clk Ft. DAR rms 1014 Evans
Clifford, Frank W. (Maude), Cond UP 710 Seymour
Clyma, Fred W. (May), welder UP 423 E. 9th
Coffman, Jacob S. (Mary E.), 821 E. 12th
Colba, Minnie K. (wid Jacob), 213 E. 12th
Cole, Jessie M., (teacher Converse) 320 E. 9th
" Charles C. W., Blksmth UP 320 E. 9th
" Emmett J. (Irene A.), mach UP 212 E. 9th
" Geo. H., farmer 320 E.9th
" Gladys E., Dep. Co. Supt Schools, 301 E. 9th
" Harry M., oiler UP 301 E. 9th
" James T., eng Hammond Pkg plant 320 E. 9th
" Jane (wid Harry), 301 E. 9th
" Lavinia A., Prin, Johnson School 320 E. 9th
" Olive M., cashr Chey. Creamery 301 E. 9th
" Wm. (Kate), 320 E. 9th
" Wm. D., farmer 320 E. 9th
Collenburg, Chas. K. (Johanna H.), painter 306 E. 9th
" Lloyd, apptr UP
" Pattee L. W., electrn 306 E. 9th
Collins, Robt. S. (Dena), carp 1013 Warren Av
Cooper, Arleigh J. (V. Inet), rancher 908 E. 11th
Cowles, Benedict E., pipeftr 412 E. 11th
" Clara (wid Cyrus L.), 412 E. 11th
Cronin, Jas. J. (Theresa E.), swtchmn 602 E. 10th
Crum, Dermot D. (Nora M.), mach UP 911 House
Curtis, Jas. W. (May), hlpr UP rms 404 E. 11th
Daniels, W. Henry (Alta), pipftr 900 E. 8th
Darden, Ray, (Eliz.), foremn freight dept UP 512 E. 9th
" Homer F. (Lillian), mach UP 1000 House
Dasanes, Gust., hlpr UP rms 108 E. 11th
Dauterman, Jesse G. (Anna S.), timekpr UP 912 House
Delgado, Artmo, lab rms 117 W. 11th
Diaz, Pedro (Mary), lab 112 W. 11th
Dietz, Chas A. (Lillie), Blksmth 811 Central
Demoff, Peter, prp UP 710 Warren
Doak, David (Mary A.), rpr UP 208 E. 9th
Doody, Chas. E., firmn C & S 216 W. 11th
" John J., student 216 W. 11th
" Kath M., 216 W. 11th
Doody, Patk F., lab UP 216 W. 11th
" Wm. J., firmn C & S 216 W. 11th
Dorman, Benj., lab UP 320 W. 11th
Drube, Earnest, rpr UP 900 Thomes
" Margt., 900 Thomes
" Otto H., 900 Thomes
" Wm. A. (Fredricka), 900 Thomes
Du Boyace, Jennie (wid Amos), 508 E. 10th
" John L., (American flag, sig: in military service)
Dunphy, Edw., blmkr UP 203 W. 7th
" Edw. A., expresmn UP 203 W. 7th
" John J., mach UP 203 W. 7th
" Michl., appr UP 203 W. 7th
" Richd., clerk UP 203 W. 7th
Durante, Alex (Maggie), cook 1101 Snyder
" Domingo, lab 209 E. 12th
" Louis (Mary), hlpr UP 209 E. 12th
Dyer, Mrs. Ina, clk Ingersolls Store 904 E. 11th
" Walter (Ina)
Echoa, Conception, rms 115 E. 12th
Eckhardt, John, d. 518 E. 9th
" John J. (Kate), carp 518 E. 9th
Eckstrom, Carl, rpr UP
Edgar, Charlotte, (wid Andrew M.), 208 W. 12th
Ekstrom, Carl G. (Louise), 815 E. 10th
Elix, Jas. E. (Ethel E.), Blmkr UP 421 E. 11th
Elkar, Nels, Fire Dept rms 421 E. 11th
Elliott, Nona, waiter UP Cafe 608 E. 5th
Emerson, Wm. (Josie), mach UP 308 E. 8th
Escobedo, Cruz, trucker UP
Evis, Kate (wid Chas.), 216 E. 11th
" Wilhelmina, student 216 E. 11th
Ewing, Art (Elva), farmer 122 E. 9th
Faber, Bertha A., steno Int. Harv, rms 105 E. 10th
Fahrenbrook, Alex (Kath.), hlpr UP 519 E. 11th
" Fred, mach UP 307 E. 11th
" John (Kate), rpr UP 307 E. 11th
Farris, Floyd B. (Mary), driver UP 501 E. 8th
Feiber, Geo., ranchnd Hammond Pkg Co.
" Harry (Etta), ranch mgr. Hammond Pkg Co. (East of city)
" Roy, ranchnd Hammond Pkg Co. (East of city)
Ferguson, William (Maude), Dairy, Snyder between 11th and 12th
Ferry, Van A. (Herma), clk UP 317 E. 10th
Finder, Wm. O. (Minnie J.), blmkr 122½ E. 11th
Fischer, Eliz., 112 E. 10th
" Lena (wid Henry), 112 E. 10th
Fitzgerald, Mrs. Lottie A., clk UP rms 412 E. 11th
Foellmer, Jos. A. (Anna), formn C.R. Inman Constr. 508 W. 9th
Forcum, John S. (Ella M.), carp UP 500 E. 8th
" Lloyd O., appr UP 500 E. 8th
" Vivian B., 500 E. 8th
Fox, Roy (Hazel), mach UP 7 Lillian Terr.
Fraley, Everett (Ida), blmkr 504 E. 11th
Frazier, James (Eliz.), insp. UP 116 W. 8th
" Geo., rpr UP 116 W. 8th
" Jas. E., lab UP 116 W. 8th
" Roy, Blmkr UP 116 W. 8th
" Thos., lab UP 116 W. 8th
" Wm. M., rpr UP 116 W. 8th
Freeborn, Edna, student 414 E. 9th
" Wm. D. (Eliz.), hlpr UP 414 E. 9th

Freeman, Thos. (Anna M.), carp r. 310 E. 9th
" Thos. A., hlpr US Air Mail Serv. 310 E. 9th
" Wm. H., 310 E. 9th
Fuller, Wayne H., lab UP 310 W. 11th
" Wm. B. (Iola M.), hlpr Chey. Creamery 310 W. 11th
Futa, Masaka, mach. UP 121 W. 12th
Gage, Chas L. (Letitia), eng UP 207 E. 9th
" Fred D. (Helen M.), clk, O'Connells MKT 810 House
" Edna L., steno UP 207 E. 9th
" Francis E., clk, O'Connell's MKT 207 E. 9th
" Harry, rpr UP
" Mrs. Helen, clk, O'Connell's MKT 810 House
" Herbert, clk O'Connell's MKT 207 E. 9th
Gale, John B. (Odetta), lab 817 W. 9th
" Kath. B. (wid Rudolph), 817 W. 9th
Galloway, Hazel, clk b. 105 E. 6th
" Jas. W., lab b. 105 E. 6th
" Thos. F. (Maude M.), whsmn Devine Grain 105 E. 6th
Garcia, Alphonse (Perfetitia), hlpr r. 601 E. 12th
" Pablo (Concepcion), lab UP 409 W. 12th
" Mrs. Rosa, rms 209 E. 12th
Garvin, Ross (Eva), painter 415 E. 10th
Gothman, Aug. H. (Anna), eng CLFP Pub Sev 406 W. 5th
Gavin, Mary (wid John), 419 E. 9th
Geary, Michl., 220 W. 7th
Geiger, Walter W. (Erma), clk UP 508 E. 11th
Geist, Jacob (Mary), South Central MKT 210 W. 11th
" John (Kate), 1010 O'Neil
Gelardi, Carmelo (Minnie), hlpr 118 E. 11th
" Carmelo, appr UP 118 E. 11th
Genera, Eliceo (Marie F.), lab UP r. 115 E. 12th
" Marcos, lab 115 E. 12th
Goodwin, Claude E. (Evelyn), firmn UP 618 Warren
Graham, Edw. H. (Emma), lab UP rear 202 W. 8th
Grant, Leroy N. (Anna B.), exprsmn 623 W. 10th
Gregory, Albt. W., lab UP 508 E. 9th
" Alex, lab UP rms 219 W. 11th
" Charleton L. (Laura G.), brkmn 115 E. 9th
" Francis W. (Leona), brkmn 508 E. 9th
" Walter L., b. 508 E. 9th
Hackthorn, Jas. B. (Flora), rms 415 E. 10th
" Jess W., farmer 415 E. 10th
Hahn, Albert J. (Laura), South Side MKT 1014 Central
" Mrs. Laura, clk South Side MKT 1014 Central
Hall, Jas. (Harriet), formn UP 420 E. 11th
Hallett, Warren J. (May), carp 4 Lillian Terr.
Hamada, Harry (Jennie), lab UP 500 E. 7th
Hamblin, John H., Shoemakr 922 E. 8th
Hamilton, Wayne, lab C R. Inman 219 W. 11th
Hannigan, Jas. B. (Effie), swchmn 614 E. 11th
Hardesty, Jet (Capitola), tmstr 814 Capitol Av
Hardwick, Geo. J. (Emma), firmn Chey LF&P 502 Snyder
Harper, Odell E. (Emma), condr. 611 E. 10th
Harris, Elmer. J. (Etta), rpr UP 417 W. 12th
Harvey, Edw., hlpr rms 718 E. 11th
Harvey, Lorene, 411 E. 11th
" Mrs. Maggie, 411 E. 11th
Hastings, Oliver H. (Margt. M.), Brkmn 220 E. 11th
Hatcher, Bernard F. (Nora), eng 1011 E. 11th
" Bernard M., lab 1011 E. 11th
" Martha J., b. 1011 E. 11th
Hathaway, Delbert (Sophie), rpr UP 10 Eddy Apts.
Hayes, Mrs. Maggie M., 417 E. 12th
" Walter, appr UP 417 E. 12th
Heicher, Donald M. (Mrs. Edna), clk 505 E. 12th
" Mrs. Edna, cshr. Atlas Theater 505 E. 12th
Hein, Wm. N. (Bertie), formn UP 108 E. 11th
Hendricks, Roscoe L. (Ada), driver 415 E. 9th
Hermansen, John A., tine UPP 123 E. 8th
Hermetet, Chas M., Soldier Ft. DAR 913 E. 11th
" Mrs. Effie L., amp Fed Bldg 911 E. 11th
" Ira E., driver UP 911 E. 11th
Hernandez, Francisco, trucker UP rms 115 E. 12th
" Ignacio, lab UP 111 E. 12th
Hess, Mack (Lucy E.), mach UP 1010 Central
Hill, Clem (Jessie), tmstr 223 W. 7th
" Warren (Katie), firmn Chey LF&P 810 Central
Hilsco T. (Yem), hlpr 215 W. 12th
Hodge, Floyd L. (Anna), rpr UP 600 E. 9th
Hofferber, Geo. (Maggie), repr UP 621 E. 10th
Hoffhine, Frank E. (Minnie), formn 922 E. 11th
" Robt J., student 922 E. 11th
Hoke, Conrad (Mollie), repr UP 900 E. 11th
Homan, Earl, 822 Capitol Av
" Jas. W. (Rose), painter 822 Capitol Av
" Ray, appr painter 822 Capitol Av
" Wm., driver O'Connell's
Honda, Jas., firmn 313 E. 10th
Hoof, Gustave P. (Estella), mach 522 W. 10th
Horikawa, Geo. (Turu), lab 219 W. 12th
Horn, Chas., cook UP cafe 620 W. 10th
Howarter, Jas. V. (Alice), driver Chey Transfer 622 E. 11th
Hubbard, Benj. (Sarah), carp UP 503 E. 10th
" Carl F. (Mabel), clk PO
" Mrs. Mabel, steno UP
Huffer, Simon J. (Julia), mach UP 810 E. 9th
Huggins, Lula (wid Wm.), 107 E. 11th
Hughes, John, 610 W. 10th
" Thos. H., pipftr UP 610 W. 10th
Hunter, John W. (Pearl), 122 W. 8th
Inglesche, Erasmo, hlpr r. 201 E. 12th
" Jos., hlpr b. 201 E. 12th
" Moreno, hlpr 201 E. 12th
" Rose, hlpr b. 201 E. 12th
Ishmeal, Benj. F., lab C.R. Inman Contr.
Iwaoka, Makhiko (Shiziano), lab UP 123 W. 12th
Jam, Victor, painter 700 W. 10th
James, Geo. (Mollie), lab 719 Bent
" Jacob W. (Marjorie), lab. r. 219 W. 7th
" Verne, lab r. 219 W. 7th
Jankovsky, Albrt. (Mary), painter UP 112 W. 7th
" Carl (Elsie B.), pipftr 512 E. 9th
Jemerson, repr UP rms 921 E. 9th
Jennaway, Geo. A. (Sadie), hlpr UP 207 E. 11th

Jensen, Iver C. (Viola E.), driver Chey Poultry House 620 E. 9th
" Jens E. (Marie), repr UP 909 Evans
" May H., emp Cheyenne Steam laun 103 W. 6th
" Nels H. (Helen), chkr UP 103 W. 6th
" Roy L., mach UP 103 W. 6th
Jessen, John P. (Winifred), Cond UP rms 301 E. 9th
" Lawrence R. (Christine), mach UP 902 Van Lennen
" Marie D. (wid Peter), 401 E. 10th
Jewell, Earnest E., repr 111 E. 8th
Johnson, Albert H., tailor S&K Clothes Store 403 E. 7th
" Aug. (Mary), carp 703 E. 10th
" Aug. (Anna), eng. 920 House
" Chas. A. (Christina), mach 901 E. 11th
" Edna, student 920 House
" Edwd., student 920 House
" Carl A., lab UP 920 House
" Elmer, mech Plains Auto Co. 703 E. 10th
" Elmer, student 920 House
" Helen M., clk UP 703 E. 10th
" Henry J., clk M.A. Disbrow Co 703 E. 10th
" Oscar S. (Martina), mach UP 702 E. 10th
" Vendla, clk b. 702 E. 10th
" William, b. 403 E. 7th
" Art C., clk b. 603 E. 10th
" Delmar A. (Ada), swchmn UP 603 E. 10th
" Edwd. C. (Rose), pipeftr 705 E. 9th
" Howard C. (Dorothy), mach UP 823 E. 11th
Juarez, Felix, trucker UP 1114 Central
Kake, Shawicki, r. 117 W. 12th
Kalber, Henry (Christine M.), eng UP 315 E. 9th
" John (Edith), clk O'Connell's 210 E. 10th
" Minnie (wid Jacob), 213 E. 12th
" Wm., eng UP 213 E. 12th
Kammerer, Chas. C., lieut, Fire Dept 517 E. 6th
Karos, Henry, warehsmn 1100 Pioneer Av
" John, hlpr 1100 Pioneer Av
Katsube, Henry, asst baker UP Cafe 107 E. 12th
Kaysbier, Fred (Lillie), formn UP 401 E. 11th
" Fred Jr., hlpr UP 401 E. 11th
Keelan, Mary (wid James), rear 809 Central
Keeley, Wm. (Mary), repr 419 W. 12th
Kelley, Earl, messgr Chey messgr serv 720 W. 9th
" John E. (Bessie), Kelly & Kelly 802 E. 11th
Kenchi, Ketoria I., lab UP
Kerr, Chas. F. (Sarah), eng C.R. Inman Contr. 705 Russell
Ketchios, Geo., lab UP
" John, lab UP
Kidcos, John, lab rms 211 E. 11th
" Thos., lab UP 211 E. 11th
Killebrew, Geo., hlpr UP rms 905 E. 9th
Kirchner, Louise, starcher San Home Laun 400 E. 9th
Kitchas, Nicholas, shiner Chey Shoe parlor 211 E. 11th
" Thos., shiner Chey Shoe parlor 211 E. 11th
Kitson, Geo., lab 119 E. 12th
Kitsos, Louis, blksmth UP
Kosbau, Otto, appr UP 723 E. 9th
Koster, Robt., lab UP rms 805 E 12th
Krager, Emerson J. (Jennie), hlpr UP 720 E. 9th
Kubeta, Katia, lab UP
Kurupus, Gust, hlpr UP
Kusuyana, J., hlpr 115 W. 12th
Lacatio, Wm., trucker UP rms 205 E. 12th
Laferty, Harry G. (Georgia), welder 822 Warren
Lafkas, Agiro, b 211 E. 11th
" John, lab UP
" Thos., hlpr UP 211 E. 11th
Lahr, Caroline, jan 513 E. 11th
" John (Myrtle), repr UP 513 E. 11th
Larr, Willis H. mech Dildines 208 E. 8th
" Mrs. Nora 208 E. 8th
Larson, Thos. O. (Bertha), firmn UP 416 E. 11th
Lee, Chas. W. (Florence), rms rear 505 E. 12th
" Chester, lab UP
" Rosabelle, rms 900 E. 8th
" Wm. M. (Essie), 207 E. 11th
Leeder, Chas. (Mary), 722 E. 9th
Leslie, Walter A. (Katea), clk Chey. Poultry 715 E. 9th
Lewis, John (Roberta), 219 W. 10th
Lillian Terrace, The, 813 Central Ave.
Link, Chris (Kate), So Central MKT 210 W. 11th
" Jacob (Eliz.), hlpr 614 W. 10th (Licata)
Liota, Thaznor, hpr 614 W. 10th
Lona, Elenterio (Frances), pipeftr UP 320 W. 11th
Lopez, Anastacia (Petra), lab UP 311 W. 12th
Luck, Fred W. (Pearl A.), brkmn 215 E. 11th
Lyon, Harry B., mach UP 215 E. 11th
" Henry E. (Mary), carp UP 215 E. 11th
McCauliffe, Mrs. Frances, rear 119 E. 11th
McCloud, Boyd, clk 515 E. 7th
" Geo. E., hlpr UP 515 E. 7th
" Harry L. (Bessie), welder 515 E. 7th
" Laura W., steno Chey Fruit Co 515 E. 7th
McCord, Bessie M., starcher Geyser Laun
" Jos. E. (Cora), ftr UP Lillian Terr
" Walter F. (Lorna), wringer Geyser Laun 219 W. 8th
" Wm. H., lab 220 W. 9th
McCullough, John F. (Amanda), hlpr UP 210 W. 10th
McDonald, Jas. J., 719½ Bent
McFarland, Gladys B., elev pilot 1st Natl Bank (16th and Capitol)
" John A. (Lucille), blmkr UP 1114 House
McGough, Geo. E., appr b. 400 E. 11th
" Geo. E. (Loretta E.), blmkr 1114 House
" Mrs. Lena, maid Plains 400 E. 11th
" Philip H. (Lena), driver O'Connell's
McGuirk, Clarence M. (Flora), asst chg clk UP 602 E. 10th
" Frank, hlpr UP 602 E. 10th
McHugh, John D., rancher 316 E. 8th
" Martin, (Nora), Chey LF&P formn 316 E. 8th
" Sarah, clk Athens Candy Co. 316 E. 8th
McIver, Wm. R. (Minnie), mach UP 201 E. 10th
McKay, Art E. (Jessie), carp 215 E. 10th
" Chas., carp 815 E. 12th
McLaren, Hugh J., sawyer UP
" Hugh S., hlpr UP
" Lloyd, welder UP
McLaughlin, Jos. (Sophia), lab 820 W. 9th
" Thos. J. (Annie), mach UP 604 E. 11th

McLees, Jos. (Ellen), mach UP 814 Central
McNair, Edw. (Alice), tmstr Hammond Packing Co 818 W. 9th
McSweeney, Dan'l., lab 202 W. 11th
" John, UP 202 W. 11th
" Mortimer, (Mary), formn 202 W. 11th
McVeigh, Peter, mach UP
McWain, Fred, lab UP
MacKay, Edwin (Marie), barber 1022 Central, r. 409 E. 10th
Magnussen, Einar, student Chey. Bus. College 702 E. 10th
Mahoney, Abner J. (Lydia), lab UP 212 E. 10th
" Jas. E. (Olive), clk 1013 Warren
Malone, Thos. F. (Fanny), blmkr UP 800 Thomes
Maltby, Otto, brkmn UP
Manarolla, John, oiler UP
Manos, Geo., blrwshr UP
Marino, Tony, lab UP
Mario, Natzo, lab UP
Martin, Earl, brkmn UP 509 E. 10th
" Eldorado, asst mgr. Woolworth's 814 Capitol Av
" Lewis (Hattie), lab UP 814 Capitol Av
" Roscoe A. (Orilla), brkmn 509 E. 10th
Martinec, Thos., 713 Central
Martinez, John B., lab UP
" Juan, mach UP
" Manuel, hlpr 411 E. 12th
Matinsen, Adolph C. (Mattie), repr UP 500 E. 10th
" Karl A., mach UP 500 E. 10th
Mason, Alice (wid Adam), 821 E. 9th
" Martin, 821 E. 9th
Matheson, Saml. (Ele), insp UP 911 Evans
" Wm., d. May 8 20 age 51
Matson, Sarah, 219 W. 11th
Matuska, Frank J., hlpr UP 113 E. 10th
" Jas. C., tinr UP 113 E. 10th
" Jas. (Adeline), 920 Warren
Maynard, Hezekiah (Myrtle), eng UP 103 E. 10th
" Lucille, student 103 E. 10th
Means, Garfield A. (Maggiea), 114 E. 7th
Meek, Emma (wid Clinton), 401 E. 7th
" Irving (Alice), btchr Hammond Pkg Co 401 E. 7th
" John, clnr UP 401 E. 7th
" Merrill, meat cutter Hammond Pkg Co 401 E. 7th
Melgoza, Salvador, 715 E. 12th
Mendenhall, Milton, brkmn 708 E. 11th
Mendoza, Ompara, lab 109 E. 12th
" Raphael (Marie), 109 E. 12th
" Rosanna, 109 E. 12th
Menelis, Gust, rms 106 E. 11th
Merna, David, d. age 75 May 30
" Jas., trucker UP 521 W. 10th
" John H. (Cecilia M.), welder UP 521 W. 10th
Mike, Saml. (Irene), blmkr UP 200 E. 11th
Miller, Frank J. (Anna), hlpr 410 E. 8th
" Fred A., 410 E. 9th
" Fred L. (Mary), 410 E. 9th
" Marguerite G., student 410 E. 9th
Mills, Gilbert, farmer 618 E. 11th
Mills, Harry E. (Gertrude), repr UP 618 E. 11th
" Paul, repr UP
Miover, Bell, waiter UP Cafe 608 E. 5th
Mohrlang, Alex, appr UP 201 W. 11th
" Chris N. (Kath.), hlpr UP 201 W. 11th
Montgomery, Robt C. (Edith), blmkr UP 515 E. 9th
" Wm. D., appr UP 515 E. 9th
Moore, Geo. A., lab UP
" John F., storekpr UP 815 E. 11th
" Mabel, drsmkr 118 W. 7th
Morford, Jas. A. (Vida), lab UP 906 E. 8th
" John W. (Nellie), he ter UP 707 Russell
" Melinda (wid Abner), 707 Russell
" Wm. N. (Ella), jan UP 900 E. 8th
Mortellari, Jos., lab UP 309 W. 11th
Mumm, Hans (Anna), carp UP 315 E. 9th
Murphy, John D., clk Schwartz Bros. 1115 Carey
" Julia, 1115 Carey
" Mary, clk So. Side MKT 1115 Carey
Nakano, Mormo, clnr UP
Neece, Emmett (Edda), lab UP 611 Capitol Av
Nelecoff, Daisy, Geyser laun 822 Central (Niddlecoff)
" Saml. (Eva), lab UP 822 Central
Nelson, Anna (wid Nels), 510 E. 10th
" Benj. S. (Mary), insp UP 911 E. 11th
" Edith, rms 1106 Pioneer
" Nels T. (Olga), carp 907 E. 11th
" Robt., hlpr UP 907 E. 11th
Neuman, Chas., welder 808 E. 11th
Nichols, Claude C. (Ethel), swchmn UP 320 E. 10th
" Leroy (Tillie), rancher 822 Morrie
Nielson, Elmer (Mary), hlpr UP 215 E. 9th
Notsell, Ford R., eng UP
Nunota, M., 121 W. 12th
Oakley, Julia T. (wid Wm.), 212 E. 9th
" T. Wm., mach UP 212 E. 9th
O'Brien, Bert E. (May), 3 Lillian Terrace
" Wesley, tmstr 3 Lillian Terrace
Ohlund, Isaac O. (Mary), rdmstr UP 900 E. 10th
" Roy F. (Augusta), 900 E. 10th
Oshel, Boyd (Gwen), repr UP 300 E. 10th
Oslund, Emil (Bertha), insp UP 910 Van Lennen
Packard, Chester, driver rms 401 E. 7th
Page, H. Roy (Anna), mgr Wyoming Filling Station 419 E. 9th
Painter, Jas. S., repr UP
Palmer, Roy, appr UP
Pappas, Strat. (Helen), lab 5 Lillian Terrace
Parker, Chas. C. (Anna), lab UP 411 E. 12th
" Everett M. (Carrie), clk Schwartz Bros. 1014 Evans
" Marshall A. (Minnie), clk PO 507 E. 10th
Patton, Ora (Leola), firmn C R Inman Contr 1114 Pebrican
Paulos, Geo., mach UP rms 119 E. 12th
Paulsen, Wm. (Irma), mach UP 311 E. 11th
Peacock, Wm. F., mach UP
Pearce, John (Emma), jan Carnegie 120 W. 10th
" Wm., appr UP
Perkins, Lewis A. (Stella), mach UP 314 E. 10th
Perry, Jas. H. (Myrtle), insp UP 910 E. 11th

Peterson, Gus (Ellen), 511 E. 12th
Petty, Grover C. (Edna), oiler UP 1118 House
Pfalzgraf, Edwd. (Leona), mach W. H. Heinkl 200 W. 11th
Phelps, Vernon C. (Mary E.), electrn UP 809 Central
Pollos, Steve, 116 W. 11th
Polzin, John M. (Anna), hlpr UP 219 W. 11th
Porter, Glen E. (Iola K.), tmstr 203 W. 7th
" Henry, repr UP
" Jas. B., brkmn UP
Potts, John A. (Carrie A.), cond UP 900 O'Neil
Poulson, Bernice, steno 604 E. 9th
" Mrs. Kate E., 604 E. 9th
" Leo C., electrn 604 E. 9th
Powelson, Chas. H. (Nora), 522 W. 10th
Preston, Mrs. Susan N., maid Plains Hotel 114 E. 9th
Pritchard, Chas. R. (Mattie T.), cond UP 814 Evans
Puppello, Jos., appr UP 118 E. 11th
Purdy, Geo., mach UP
" Jos. J., hlpr UP
Radowsky, Paul, hlpr UP 604 E. 11th
Ramirez, Edugegas, trucker UP
" Guadalupe, student 400 E. 9th
" Ignacio, trucker UP
" Jos. M. (Mattie), physician Bresnahan Blk., 400 E. 9th
Redmon, Chas. V. (Clara), herder 615 E. 10th
Reich, Carl, lab C R Inman
Reichen, Otto (Frances), blmkr 520 W. 5th
Resser, Geo. (Lillian), tmstr 618 W. 9th
Ressler, Harry, lab UP
Rice, Pete (Eliz.), jan Johnson Sch 922 Central
Richer, Alfred H. (Agnes), chf dep US Int Rev 416 E. 7th
Ridderstedt, Arnold, student 202 E. 8th
" Emma, student 202 E. 8th
Ridenhour, Clarence E., hlpr UP 112 E. 10th
Rider, Jacob (Elsie), lab 913 Evans
Rizzuto, Jos., lab UP
Robert, Mark E. (Alma), rpr UP 718 E. 9th
" Mary E. (wid Oliver), 1004
" William, appr UP b 718 E. 9th B
Robinson, Russell, lab UP
" Thos. V., Insp UP
Robitaille, Anthony (Stephanie), 916 O'Neil
" Emma, clk 916 O'Neil
" Laura, 916 O'Neil
Rodgers, Embry M. (Mary), r 812 E. 11th
Rodriguez, Salvadore (Marie), hlpr UP 111 E. 12th
Roe, Thos A., hlpr UP
" Thos. D., lab UP
" Wm. R., trucker UP
Rogers, Geo. F., watrtnde UP
Rollman, Frank (Ida), rancher 116 W. 7th
Root, Thos. J. (Rosa), trucker 419 E. 12th
Rosebloom, Jesse (Florence), Cond UP 213 W. 10th
"Leone, steno Int Harv. 213 W. 10th
Roshek, Jos. J. (Nancy), 805 E. 10th
Rowe, Roy J., emp Maneway Cafe 505 E. 12th
Rowland, Guy, trucker UP
Ruch, Gertrude, student 518 E. 11th
Ruchen, Walter J., mach UP
Saito, M., lab rms 111 W. 12th
" Taino, hlpr 1122 Carey Av.
Sakaguchi, R. M., lab 109 W. 12th
Sakais, John, lab UP
Samuelson, Seamon S. (Susie), 406 E. 8th
Sandberg, Anna C. (wid Chas), 208 E. 10th
" Elmer, lab 208 E. 10th
Sanfield, Corean, bkpr 307 E. 9th
" Fred (Esthina), firmn 307 E. 9th
Sara, Michl., lab UP
Saul, Wm., firmn UP
Scheidmiller, Peter (Marie), rpr UP 611 E. 11th
Scherf, Mabel, smstrs 116 W. 7th
Scheuerman, Geo., hlpr UP
" Gottlieb, hlpr UP
Schilling, Henry A. (Alice), washer Geyser laun 116 W. 9th
Schimpf, Jas. J. (Laura), lab rms 905 E. 12th
Schmutz, Harriet (wid Chas), 805 E. 12th
Schriner, Henry P. (Pearl), lab 201 W. 7th
Schroeder, Louis J. (Emma) rpr 1118 House
Schwerdt, Annie, 112 E. 10th
" Esther, student 112 E. 10th
" Lawrence (Minnie), rpr UP
Scott, J. Lawrence (Nellie), rpr UP 905 E. 9th
" Melvin B., hlpr 720 E. 9th
Sellin, Jacob F. (Millie E.), welder 1006 Capitol Av
Sempeck, Adam A., brkmn UP
Sennicksen, Carl F., brkmn UP
Setzer, Wm. (Beulah), hlpr UP 1013 Evans
Shea, Harry, appr UP
" Margt., messr US Weather Bureau 413 E. 10th
Shenefelt, Harold F. (Jessie), formn 205 E. 9th
Sherman, Geo. (Eliz.), hlpr 205 E. 10th
Shuipek, Stephen S. (Mae), clk 110 E. 7th
Shellenberger, Earnest, appr UP 921 E. 9th
" John F. (Minnie), rpr UP 921 E. 9th
Shultz, Glenn E. (Lena), 315 E. 10th
Shutts, David J. (Frances), 109 W. 8th
Simon, Saml. (Misma), mach UP 104 E. 11th
Simpson, Margt. E. (wid Geo. W.), 914 E. 8th
Sinon, Frank H. (Mabel), tmstr 907 E. 12th
Slagle, Chas. W. (Flora L.), pipftr 115 E. 8th
" Wiley A. (Ruth M.), 209 E. 12th
Sloan, Alfrd., hlpr H. S. O'Brien 1122 Seymour
" Harry J. (Katie C.), ftr UP 1122 Seymour
Smith, Earl F., foremn C R Inman
" Harry, welder UP 820 E. 9th
" Mrs. Mercedes, prsr San Home Laun 822 E. 9th
Sorenson, Jorgen E. (Ella), blksmth UP 302 E. 9th
Sorrentino, Michl., opr UP 209 W. 12th
So. Central MKT, (Jacob & John Geist & Kris Link) 1020 Central Av
So. Side MKT, (Theo. Anderson & A. J. Hahn, Geo. Thiel) 101 East 11th
So. Cheyenne Improvement Assn, 1021 Warren Av (J. T. Clark Volunteer Hose Co.)
So. Side Fire Station, 1020 Warren Av
Spadt, Alinda, hlpr Shadowette Tea Rm 214 E. 11th

Spadt, Alex (Mary), 214 E. 11th
Spires, Albt. R., appr UP 500 E. 9th
" Myrtle G., 500 E. 9th
Stadler, Paul, 801 E. 11th
Stainbrook, Henry (May), mach 604 E. 10th
Stanfield, Corean, bkpr Singer Sew Mach 307 E. 9th
" Oscar C. (Anna W.), Chey Stamp and Novelty Wks 400 W. 6th
Staples, Elwood (Tillie), 723 E. 9th
Tagliavore, Gaspare (Angelina), hlpr UP 210 E. 11th
" Louis, hlpr 210 E. 11th
" Gaspar (Frances), 118 E. 11th
" Vincent, b. 118 E. 11th
Taylor, Frank H., hlpr 811 E. 11th
" Lewis E., b 811 E. 11th
" Myrtle M. (wid Jas. H.), 811 E. 11th
" Mrs. Susie, 1010 Evans
Terry, Alby., lab rms 219 W. 7th
Teschmacher, Wm., emp Hammond Packing Co.
Thier, Frank (Bessie), ironwkr UP 712 Central
" Jos. (Blanche), tinr 424 W. 17th/712 Central
Tipton, Russell (Gladys), firmn UP 821 Seymour
Torrey, Mrs. Myrtle, r 504 E. 11th
Tottenhoff, Theo., foremn UP
Traxler, Findley A. (Theresa), formn 918 E. 11th
Tuarez, Felix, lab 1110 Central
Tuner, Robt., hlpr 112 E. 10th
Ulrich, Anna C. (wid Henry), 801 House
Underwood, Clark C. (Belinda), hlpr 701 E. 10th
Union Pacific System, A. W. Woodruff, Gen Supt.
" J. W. Highlyman, Master Mech
" O. B. Stapleton, Ticket Agent
" C. B. Irwin, Gen Agt. Frt Dept.
Unsell, Geo. (Mary), swchmn UP 413 E. 10th
Urich, Geo. (Mary), lab UP 721 E. 10th
Valdurama, Anastasia (Antonia), lab 108 W. 11th
" Asuncion (Theresa), lab 108 W. 11th
" Dario (Lonor), 108 W. 12th
" Lermina, 112 W. 11th
Vallas, Gust (Vancula), mach 416 E. 10th
Van Allyne, Walter (Charlotte), brkmn 919 E. 12th
Van Auker, Jessie, rms 918 E. 11th
Van Buskirk, Jesse, hlpr UP 301 W. 10th
Vanek, Frank J. (Mary), tinr 112 W. 8th
" John (Martha), blrmkr UP 107 E. 8th
Van Zandt, Byron D. (Minnie), driver 404 E. 11th
" Verna G., clk 404 E. 11th
Varnum, Don S., 501 E. 12th
" Harry F., carp b. 501 E. 12th
" Harry L., lab 501 E. 12th
" Mrs. May C., 501 E. 12th
Vergas, Wm., hlpr UP
Vieit, Wm., trucker UP rms 512 E. 11th
Vigis, Wm. (Mary), hlpr 117 W. 11th
Wade, John A., hlpr UP
" John F. (Carrie), firemn Fire Dept. 222 E. 9th
" Luella, clk F. W. Woolworths 408 E. 9th
Wagner, Wm. C. (Leola), formn UP 1005 E. 11th
Walker, Reed (Dona), rpr UP 908 O'Neil
Wallace, U. Grant, formn rms 112 E. 10th
Ware, Ralph M. (Maude), carp 220 E. 11th
Warner, Fred, brkmn UP 507 E. 9th
" Geo. E. (Gwendolyn), hlpr UP Lillian Terrace
Watts, Chas., tmstr C. R. Inman
Weaver, Albt. J., lab Hammond Packing Co.
" Frank A., wchmn 523 E. 9th
Wedge, Alfhild, student Chey. Business College 208 E. 10th
Wedgey, Anna M., maid Plains Hotel 112 E. 9th
Welch, Mrs. Eva, rms 200 E. 11th
Wellnitz, Edw. H. (Matilda), electrn rms 111 E. 11th
" Mrs. Matilda, Chief Operator UP 111 E. 11th
Wesche, Earnest (Edith), painter 1014 Warren
Wilcok, Thos. (Ellen), blmkr 202 E. 11th
" Thos. L., appr b
Wilder, Albert A. (Carrie), brkmn 814 Warren
Williams, Albert A. (Bertha), mech Walton Motor Co 1009 E. 11th
" Clarence A. (Ivera), carp 815 E. 12th
" Geo. W., 207 E. 11th
Wilson, Sam T., firmn UP 615 E. 9th
Woods, Chas. W., firmn UP 615 E. 9th
" Glenn S., carp 615 E. 9th
" Jas. O. (Merl), 615 E. 9th
" Rebecca (wid Wilson), 615 E. 9th
" Saml. (Bertha E.), wchmn 615 E. 9th
Woolf, Effie M., steno Tel Co 1002 Central
Wright, Earl J. (Carrie), rpr UP 900 Thomes
" Howard (Anna), rpr UP
" Robt. L. (Nellie), brkmn 919 E. 12th
Yagi, Imago, lab UP
Yama, Geo., jan UP
Yamanka E., rms 115 W. 12th
Yamashita G., 207 W. 12th
Yonkoff, Kolin (Mary), rpr UP 111 W. 11th
" Venke, rpr UP 111 W. 11th
Yoshi, E. N., firmn UP 111 W. 12th
" Gensis, lab UP 221 W. 12th
" Keno, 221 W. 10th
Young, Clarence, hlpr Brien's Quality Bakery 218 W. 9th
" Clarence (Elsie), firmn UP 903 E. 9th
" Claude, hlpr Brien's Quality Bakery, 218 W. 9th
" Fredk, asst eng UP
" Jas. S. (Jennis), lab 218 W. 9th
Ziegler, Mary, Mangler, San. Home Laundry 223 W. 8th
Zimmerman, Henry (Mollie), mach UP 1012 House
Zoggas, Gust, rpr UP 600 E. 8th

(Errors in the original 1922 R. L. POLK AND CO., DIRECTORY OF CHEYENNE, *where possible have been corrected. Names left out have been added.)*

STREET ADDRESS DIRECTORY

BENT STREET

715 Saml. Boyd
719 Geo. James
719½ Jas. McDonald
901 T. A. Adams

CAPITOL AVENUE

611 Emmett Neece
814 Lewis Martin
822 J. W. Homan
922 Henry Asberry
1006 J. F. Sellin

CAREY AVENUE

404 G. L. Wales Jr.
1022 J. K. Keefe
1115 Cornelius Murphy
1116 Nematella Rouhana
1120 Jos. Barrajos
1122 Taino Saito

CENTRAL AVENUE

712 Frank Thier
713 Thos. Martinez
809 V. C. Phelps
rear Mary Keelan
810 Warren Hill
811 C. A. Dietz
813 Lillian Terrace
1 Joe McCard
2 J. G. Ennis
3 P. O. O'Brien
4 W. J. Hallett
5 Strat. Pappas
6 G. E. Warner
7 Roy Fox
8 L. H. Clements
814 Jos. McLees
822 Saml. Nelecoff
901 J. H. Cole
903 Geo. Chocas
910 Edwd. Boyle
911 H. J. Johnson
914 Frank Check
922 Peter Rice
1002 O. C. Gilliam
1010 Mack Hess
1016 J. A. Garcia
1020 So. Side MKT.
1022 Edw. MacKay
1110 Felix Rodriguez
1114 Jose Martinez

EIGHTH STREET, WEST

109 D. J. Shutts
112 F. J. Vanek
116 Jas. Frazier
121 Frank Berkley
122 J. W. Hunter
219 W. F. McCord
223 Mrs. Mary McCord

EIGHTH STREET, EAST

107 John Vanek
111 Earnest E. Jewell
115 Chas. W. Slagle
123 John A. Hermansen
202 Arnold Ridderstadt
Emma Ridderstadt
206 Floyd B. Brandon
208 Willis H. Larr
308 William Emerson
316 John D. McHugh
Martin McHugh
Sarah McHugh
406 Seamon Samuelson
410 Frank J. Miller
500 John S. Forcum
501 Floyd B. Farris
600 Gust Zoggas
900 Wm. N. Moroford
Henry W. Daniels
Rosabelle Lee
906 Jas. A. Moroford
914 Margt. E. Simpson
922 John H. Hamblin

ELEVENTH STREET, EAST

100 Jacob Link
101 South Side MKT.
104 Saml. Sinon
107 Mrs. Lulu Higgins
108 Wm. Hein
111 C. L. Christensen
118 Carmelo Gelardi
119 Mrs. Frances McAuliffe
120 D. J. O'Connell's MKT.
112½ W. O. Finder
200 Saml. Mike
202 Thos. Wilcock
207 W. M. Lee
210 Gaspare Tagliavore
211 Thos. Lafkas
214 Alex Spadt
215 H. E. Lyon
216 Mrs. Kate Evis
220 R. M. Ware
307 John Fahrenbruch
311 Wm. Paulsen
400 P. H. McGough
401 F. H. Kaysbier
404 R. D. Van Zandt
410 E. J. Wright
411 Mrs. Maggie Hardy
412 Wm. C. E. Cowles
416 T. O. Larsen
420 Jas. Hall
421 J. E. Elix
504 Mrs. Myrtle Torrey
508 W. W. Geiger
513 L. M. Lahr
515 L. J. Schroeder
518 A. J. Wykoff
519 Alex Fahrenbruch
604 T. J. McLaughlin
610 Jos. Berenek

611 Peter Schneidmiller
614 J. B. Hannigan
618 H. E. Mills
621 David Blehm
622 J. V. Howarter
708 M. A. Mendenhall
804 M. M. Douglas
808 Chas. Neuman
810 Paul Stadler
811 Mrs. M. M. Taylor
812 E. M. Rodgers
819 G. W. Hosking
823 H. C. Jones
900 Conrad Hoke
901 C. A. Johnson
904 Walter Dyer
907 N. T. Nelson
908 R. W. Collins
910 J. H. Perry
911 B. S. Nelson
913 Mrs. E. L. Hermatet
918 F. A. Traxler
922 F. J. Hoffhine
923 L. A. Corlin
1001 K. W. Kelly
1005 W. C. Wagner
1009 A. A. Williams
1011 B. F. Hatcher

ELEVENTH STREET, WEST

108 Anastasia Valderrama
111 Kolin Yonkoff
112 Lermina Valderrama
116 Geo. Amty
117 Wm. Vigio
118 Gaspare Tagliavore
120 Peter Bulara
200 Edwd. Pfalzgraf
201 C. N. Mohrlang
202 Mortimer McSweeney
210 Chris Link
216 C. E. Doody
219 J. M. Polzin
220 O. H. Hastings
309 Jos. Mortellaro
310 W. B. Fuller
320 Elenterio Lona

EVANS STREET

814 C. R. Pritchard
819 C. M. Stone
909 J. E. Jensen
911 Saml. Matheson
913 Jacob Rider
914 E. H. Faulk
1010 Gordon Cramer
1013 Wm. Setzer
1014 C. F. Packer
1022 Stanley O'Brien
1123 Henry Weber

FIFTH STREET, EAST

600 Robt. Sheahan

FIFTH STREET, WEST

406 A. H. Gathmann
520 John Reichen

HOUSE STREET

801 Mrs. A. C. Ulrich
805 T. P. Brown
810 D. E. Gage
911 D. D. Crum
914 J. G. Dauterman
920 Aug. Johnson
1000 A. M. Bellairs
1004 Fred Bastron
1008 F. J. Kehl
1012 Henry Zimmerman
1020 O. B. Simmons
1021 W. L. Bonnell
1024 Albt. Martinez
1114 G. E. McGough
1114 W. E. Bain
1118 G. C. Petty

MORRIE STREET

822 Leroy Nichols

NINTH STREET, EAST

112 Anna Wedgey
114 Jas. Beztne
115 C. L. Gregory
122 Art Ewing
205 H. L. Allison
207 C. L. Gage
208 D. A. Doak
212 Mrs. J. J. Oakley
215 Elmer Nielson
221 T. J. Bonham
222 J. F. Wade
301 J. W. Benson
302 J. E. Sorenson
306 C. K. Collenburg
307 Fred Sanford
310 Thos. Freeman
315 Henry Kalber
320 Wm. Cole
400 J. M. Ramirez
407 Geo. Adolp
408 Mrs. Louella Wade
410 F. L. Miller
411 J. W. Benson
414 W. D. Freeborn
415 R. L. Hendricks
423 F. W. Clyma
500 Otto Reichen
503 Mrs. Jennie Chambers
507 Fred Warner
508 F. W. Gregory
512 Carl Jankovsky
515 R. C. Montgomery
516 Henry Bauer
518 J. J. Eckhardt
523 F. A. Weaver
600 F. L. Hodges
601 J. O. Woods
604 Mrs. K. E. Poulson

615 C. F. Griffen
620 I. C. Jensen
705 E. C. Jones
715 W. A. Leslie
717 B. H. Chamberlain
718 Mark Roberts
720 E. J. Krager
722 Chas. Leeder
723 E. L. Staples
810 S. J. Huffer
821 Mrs. Alice Mason
903 C. O. Young
905 J. L. Scott
921 J. F. Schullenberger

NINTH STREET, WEST
107 G. L. Baker
113 C. E. Bonser
116 H. A. Schilling
209 F. N. Studler
215 E. V. Christensen
218 J. S. Young
220 W. H. McCord
508 J. W. Foellmer
618 Mrs. Fanny Adams
715 Jos. Ashley
817 Mrs. K. B. Gale
818 B. F. Baker
820 Jos. McLaughlin

O'NEIL STREET
900 J. A. Potts
908 Reed Walker
916 Anthony Robitaille
922 F. A. Bundy
1010 John Gust
1010 r. Geo. Burk

PEBRICAN STREET
1110 McDouglass
1112 J. J. Goins
1114 Ora Patton

PIONEER STREET
1020 Saml. Mitoma
1021 Mrs. A. B. Moffatt
1022 F. W. Chapel
1100 Thos. Poulos
1106 Anton Rosenthyne
1109 Adrian Barajas
1110 Mrs. Mary Gomez
1114 Arch Davis

RUSSELL STREET
705 C. F. Kerr
707 Melinda Morford
1115 Elmer Kolous

SEVENTH STREET, EAST
108 H. M. Ashford
110 S. S. Shinpek
401 Irving Meek
403 A. J. Johnson
500 Emil Amschel
515 H. E. McCloud

SEVENTH STREET, WEST
112 Albt. Jankovsky
114 G. A. Means
116 Frank Rollman
118 Mrs. Mabel Moore
119 Cahs Baker
201 H. P. Schriner
203 G. E. Parker
205 Mrs. Anna Dunphy
219 J. W. James
220 Michl. Geary
223 Clem Hull

SEYMOUR STREET
816 Chester Robinson
821 Russell Tipton
909 D. A. Bittner
1122 H. J. Sloan

SIXTH STREET, EAST
105 T. F. Galloway

SIXTH STREET, WEST
103 N. H. Jensen
420 O. C. Stanfield

SNYDER STREET
1101 A. O. Clayton

TWELFTH STREET, EAST
101 John Condos
Henry Katsuba
109 Rafael Mendoza
111 Ignacio Herrera
115 Elicei Genera
119 Geo. Kitson
201 Erasmo Inglesche
205 Tony Lecato
209 W. A. Slagle
213 Mrs. Minnie Kalber
411 Gus Peterson
417 Mrs. Maggie Hayes
419 T. J. Root
501 Mrs. C. Varnum
505 J. W. Carlisle
505 r. J. A. Curtis
601 Alfonso Garcia
P. A. Garcia
605 J. A. McFarland
715 Salvadore Melgoza
805 Mrs. Harriet Schmutz
815 C. A. Williams
821 J. S. Coffman
905 J. I. Engstrom
907 F. H. Sinon
919 R. L. Wright

TWELFTH STREET, WEST
100 R. W. Sakoguchi
111 E. N. Yoshi
113 Henry Ashizawa
115 K. Kusuyoma
117 Shamiki Kake
121 M. Nunota
Masaka Futa

123 Matchiko Iwaoke
207 Mrs. Charlotte Edgar
207 G. Yamashita
209 Michl. Sorrcutino
215 T. Hilsco
219 Geo. Horikawa
221 Gensia Yoshi
309 J. M. Diaz
311 Anastacia Lopez
315 Frank Doninquez
409 Pablo Garcia
415 C. C. Ault
417 E. J. Harris
419 Mrs. Mary Gavin
421 Manuel Barros

TENTH STREET, EAST

100 G. W. Bowman
103 Hezekiah Maynard
106 W. H. Bates
109 Jas. Buckley
112 Mrs. Lena Fischer
113 J. C. Matuska
122 Schwert Lorence
201 W. R. McIver
205 Geo. Sherman
208 Mrs. A. C. Sandberg
212 A. J. Mahoney
213 Jesse Roseboom
215 A. E. McKay
300 Boyd Oshel
301 Walter Bare
311 B. D. Carey
306 S. T. Wilson
314 L. A. Perkins
315 G. E. Schutz
316 F. M. Allen
317 V. A. Ferry
320 C. C. Nichols
400 S. T. Wilson
404 John Swanson
409 Edwin MacKay
413 W. R. Unsell
415 Ross Garvin
416 Gust Valoskas
421 T. L. Bretton
422 R. J. Crews
500 A. C. Martinsen
503 B. F. Hubbard
506 H. F. Darden
507 M. A. Parker
508 J. L. Du Boyace
509 R. A. Martin
510 C. R. Nelson
600 G. J. Klein
603 D. A. Jones
604 Henry Stainbrook
608 F. W. Lucks
611 O. E. Harper
615 C. V. Redmon
621 Geo. Hoffeberg
700 J. H. Brandon
701 C. C. Underwood
702 O. S. Johnson
717 C. R. Steiber
711 Geo. Urich
805 J. T. Roshek
808 Mrs. Maude Coates
815 C. G. Ekstrom
818 H. S. Bargar
900 Ike Ohlund

TENTH STREET, WEST

120 John Pearce
122 LeRoy Bassett
210 J. F. McCullough
220 John Bentsen
301 Jesse Van Buskirk
521 J. H. Merna
522 G. P. Hoof
602 V. T. Cleland
610 John Hughes
614 T. M. Licatta
620 Chas. Horn
623 L. N. Grant
700 Victor Jam

THOMES AVENUE

1114 Mrs. Mary Jordan

THE ECONOMY, 1919-1945

THE NEW WYOMING HOLIDAY

After the troubles of the "teen" years, Wyoming was still suffering from wide divisions between Capital and Labor. Governor Robert D. Carey issued a proclamation noting that by Act of Congress of June 1894, Labor Day was designated to be observed on the first Monday in September.

September 7, 1920 was scheduled to be Wyoming's first official Labor Day celebration in City Park, near the Capitol Building. Labor Day arrived with a deluge which swamped Cheyenne's storm sewers and invaded cellars. The downpour prevented the celebration. Water swept down Capitol Avenue and surged into the Union Pacific depot. A hasty dam was erected in front of the depot to prevent further damage.

The headline of September 4, 1921, seemed oblivious to the economy of the day, "NO STRIKES, NO FOREST FIRES, NO INSURRECTION — NOT ANYTHING BUT HAPPINESS AND CONTENTMENT IN WYOMING."

The next day, September 5, (Overline Head) "CHEYENNE'S UNION LABOR MEN DEMONSTRATED ONCE MORE MONDAY THAT THEY ARE AMONG THE LIVE WIRES OF THE WEST," and framed, across the bottom of the page, as an overture to Labor, the *Tribune-Leader*, through the Newspaper Enterprise Association had requested President Harding to send the people of Wyoming a Labor Day message. The President complied with the following message:

PRESIDENT HARDING'S LABOR GREETING

"The White House, Washington, D.C. September 5. It makes no undue demand upon optimism to extend a cheerful and confident greeting to the American People on Labor Day of this year. Conditions are improving and there is every indication that they will continue to do so. For this the largest measure of credit is due to the American people themselves. They have recognized that they must get back to work and useful production and with their unwonted good sense have accepted the situation. The administration has undertaken to give every encouragement and assistance and will continue, without wearying, to seek out and apply the measures calculated to help people so generously willing to help themselves."

signed by Warren G. Harding

CHART OF STOCK MARKET AND OTHER FLUCTUATIONS

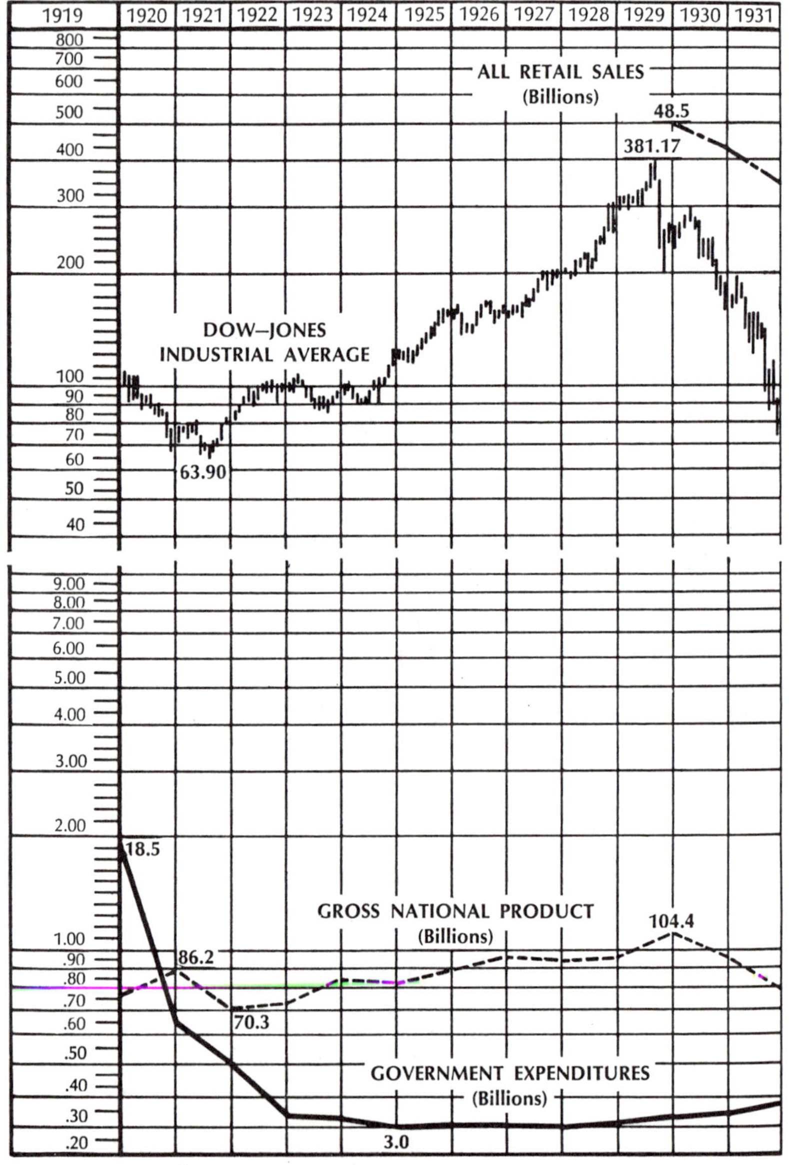

Excerpted from *The Oxford History of The American People* by Samuel Eliot Morison

1920 - 1945

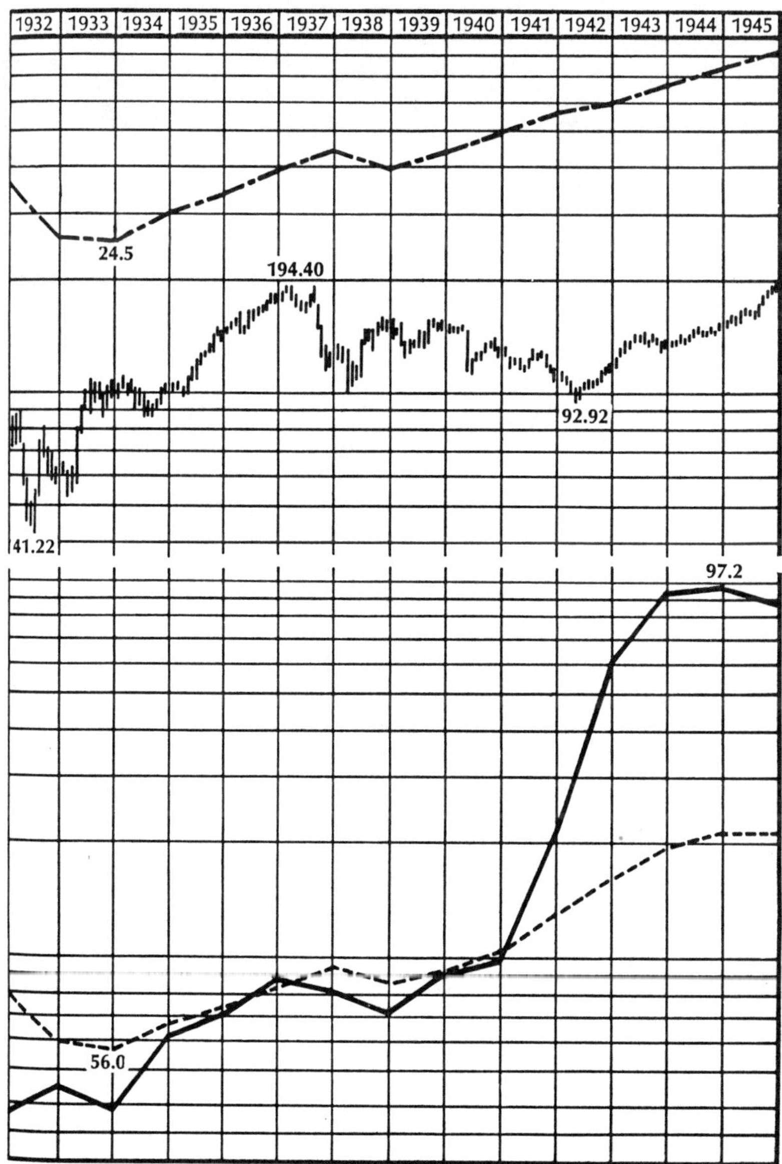

courtesy Forbes Inc., New York.

These resounding platitudes on the front page of the *Tribune* seemed to be intended as something of an olive branch to the blue-collar world out there.

After many years of vituperation against all forms of blue-collar working people, siding with Capital against Labor, regardless of the unsafe conditions in the mines and the work place, or the low pay, the editorial policy of the *Wyoming State Tribune - Cheyenne State Leader* was beginning to soften.

O'CONNELL TELLS KIWANIS ABOUT CHEYENNE

Wyoming State Tribune

On St. Patrick's Day, 1922, D. J. O'Connell addressed the Kiwanis Club on his favorite subject, the South Side. He advocated the "building of a tunnel on Warren Avenue, which had been approved by W. M. Jeffers, general manager of the Union Pacific Railroad, under the Union Pacific shops and yards, doing away with the present viaduct. O'Connell stated that estimates had been secured on the building of a tunnel and that engineers all agreed that the cost would be approximately $250,000, while the cost to replace the present viaduct would be approximately the same amount. The advantages of a tunnel, he said, would be that the upkeep would be far lower than on a viaduct.

As a bit of history, he pointed out that the original viaduct cost Cheyenne $65,000 and the city had paid, up to the present time, about $91,000 in interest and upkeep, and that the original bonds were still in force, never a cent having been paid on the principal.

Improvements which are taking place on the South Side include the new sewage system, which will deposit the city drainage below the old Hammond Packing Plant and thus remove the sewage from the residential section of South Cheyenne.

O'Connell recommended that the city dumps (which had occupied the Denver Hill site north of present I-80 for forty years) be moved farther away, so that the higher section to the south side could be used for residences. (Interior Heights.) "As it is now," he said, "the smoke and filth of the present dumping grounds are very close to the most convenient part of Cheyenne.

He pointed out that South Cheyenne lacked the proper police protection. While he accepted it as a compliment, crimes are committed that could be avoided if the section had police protection.

He stated that the new cutoff routes were surveyed and laid out across the tracks at both east and west ends, which would be a big saving of time to people who wanted to cross the tracks.

He further called attention of the club to the fact that the South Side is increasing in population rapidly and that a new school in this section is needed at once. "The school board owns one block of property in this section which should be used for a site," he said. (End of quote.)

As a matter of record: the city did not keep its promise to empty the sewer east of the packing plant. Instead, the new outfall was placed on Evans Avenue. There were also outfalls between Fifteenth and Sixteenth at Ames Avenue and above Nineteenth at Cribbon. These were not diverted to the line but continued to empty into the creek. Fort D. A. Russell diverted its contribution of sewage into the Cheyenne system.

Mr. Oscar Stanfield, Mr. Herman Kinstrom and my father went before the City Council to ask that the sewage from the western part of the city be diverted into the new line, and empty east of the packing house. In those days little thought was given to the treatment of sewage before emptying into a convenient stream.

Mayor Ed Taylor said, "If you don't like it, move away from there."

The two others did move. Eventually, in 1927, we too left the neighborhood. Sewage continued to flow throughout the entire length of the creek through the city until the Crow Creek Sewage Treatment Plant was built in 1951.

When the new 1929 Riner viaduct was built, a ramp on East Eleventh Street was built partially to accommodate access to O'Connell's store.

HARD TIMES, 1922

No economic group in Wyoming was immune to the problems of the twenties. The rancher, farmer, railroad worker, miner, merchant, banker, builder, all suffered. Like the Bedouin, "each thought his fleas were camels."

The prosperity of the "Roaring Twenties" of song and story did not describe Wyoming. Wyoming governors from Campbell to Carey had promoted its climate and productivity, the endless bounty of it all, luring investors, stockmen and homesteaders to plunge into the waves of boom and bust. The "Great Depression" started in Wyoming in the twenties.

Nature had created a semi-arid region of "short grass, no wood and little water" on the High Plains. Bill Nye, in 1885, had warned in the *Laramie Republican Boomerang*: "Don't founder the goose that lays the golden egg." Overgrazing, drouth and hard winters added up to financial ruin.

Since the terrible drouth of 1919, when one third of the state's cattle had to be shipped, either to market or to out-of-state pastures, the number of cattle had diminished in Laramie County from 47,971 to 39,055 in 1923. The number of antelope fell to 160. A moratorium on hunting them was in place until 1925.

With the passing of the open range, surviving dry farmers began to grow feed grains. Windmills pumped water from the largely untapped Ogalalla aquifer. Pine Bluffs farmers began to use gasoline powered pumps to irrigate crops.

After another cold, dry winter, March was by far the coldest month of 1922. Temperatures fell to fifteen degrees below zero on March 1 in Cheyenne. The cold wave extended to the Gulf of Mexico. Grass had a late start. Searing winds dried it in June, making 1922 another year of short grass and low prices.

One rancher recalled paying ninety dollars per head for cattle in the fall, wintering them on hay, for which he paid forty-five dollars and up, per ton, then selling them the next fall at forty-five dollars per head.

In the 1920 Census, urban population in Wyoming (towns of 2,500 or more), exceeded the rural population for the first time. Until 1910, rural population was double the urban population. Hard times on the farm and ranch sent many families to the towns to seek a livelihood in mine or railroad jobs. On account of the strikes, there were many opportunities.

There was much lingering bitterness amongst the workers stemming from the action of Governor Robert D. Carey in calling out the National Guard during the strike of 1919. The troops were trained at Fort D. A. Russell for "riot control."

The newspapers chronicled the nationwide strikes of the miners and railroad workers. In March, John L. Lewis said that he "did not ask the railway workers to strike in sympathy. His union desired only moral support."

Businessmen complained of freight rates. It cost sixty-eight cents per hundred pounds to ship gasoline to Sheridan, only fifty-eight cents to Minneapolis and nineteen cents to Omaha. Long hauls cost less than short hauls within the State.

The *Tribune* published lists of names gleaned in a "contest," to see who could name and give the addresses of the most people who had moved from the city. The prize-winner, Abraham Wellnitz, postman, submitted a list of several columns, which ran March 4th and 5th. Some people were said to have left "between two suns."

The Commercial Federation had organized in St. Louis in 1920 to fight organized labor. H. M. Haldeman, of Los Angeles, was elected permanent chairman. Federation spokesman, S. H. Halstead, charged that the "American Federation of Labor is the most dangerous force in American politics" and vowed to combat them taking over Congress.

In December of 1920, the Union Pacific Railroad laid off one-third of the work force. The Union Pacific continued to hire workers at a lower wage during 1921, however, although as the strike wore on they paid higher wages for experienced workers.

There were many refugees from the "Colorado Coal War" of the teens working in Cheyenne so there was much sympathy for the plight of the miners. The nation was shocked at the violence of the strike at Herrin, Illinois, when strike breakers were murdered. *The Wyoming Labor Journal*, however, pointed out that the "kept press" of Capital preferred to forget the "Ludlow, Colorado massacre."

Editor James Buckley kept workers aware of developments on the labor front, tried to keep up the courage of the strikers and to promote unity in the Wyoming Labor Movement through these trying times.

The *Tribune* headline of May 29, 1922 read: "Railway Employees Face Big Wage Reduction." Four hundred thousand Maintenance of Way men were affected by the latest order of the Railway Labor Board. Wages of these workers ranged from twenty-three cents to forty cents per hour, according to the report.

During World War I, the railroad workers had reorganized their unions and had gained shorter hours and better pay. With the return of management to the companies, these benefits were for the most part lost, according to a "History of the Labor Movement in Wyoming, 1870 to 1940," a Master's Thesis by Erma A. Fletcher. The eight-hour day and time and a half for overtime, Sundays and holidays were at stake.

Nationally, the mine operators refused to meet with the Union leaders. Of the 400,000 mine workers in America, 7,000 in Wyoming were involved in the strike which lasted for five months. The strike was peaceful in Wyoming and settled in five months with better working conditions and a return to the pay scale of 1920. In Cheyenne the shortage of coal was merely an inconvenience and did not disrupt industry as in some parts of the United States.

"Approximately fifteen hundred mechanics out in Cheyenne," according to the *Tribune* headline of July 1, 1922; the strike call had finally come. "There was virtually one hundred percent suspension in the railway shops. Five hundred machinists, boilermakers and mechanics, three hundred ninety-five car men, four hundred fifty-three helpers and laborers walked out." They were later joined by the stationary engineers and stationary firemen.

The strike was nation-wide. A White House spokesman said that, "the Labor Board is the government, when it speaks." President of the Union Pacific, William M. Jeffers said, "the strike is against the government."

On July 26, the *Tribune* said that a new rail strike threatened. Maintenance of Way Union President, S. F. Grable, denied the rumor, saying "negotiations are proceeding satisfactorily." The men later went back to work without the benefits sought. The Shop Crafts strike dragged on.

U.S. Attorney General Daugherty obtained an injunction against the unions, tying up their funds so benefits could not be paid. The pay cuts were but one grievance, the loss of the eight-hour day, time and a half for Sundays and holidays after twenty-five years was too much. Several railroads settled with their workers on a contract basis or set up the "Baltimore Plan" of Company Unions. Jeffers, however, refused to bargain with any organization.

He further ordered the loss of seniority for strikers and required new and returning workers to sign up with the company union.

President A. H. Smith of the New York Central Railroad said, "Ninety-five percent of this railroading is human. The other five percent is merely coal and steel, and it is not worth anything if you cannot get good men with it," Buckley reminded his *Labor Journal* readers. Further, the Supreme Court had ruled that, "No one owns the transportation industry. A large part of the physical properties are held in private ownership. But the ownership does not authorize the complete and unlimited "rights of property," because the service to which these properties are devoted is a public service and the right of any individual to control his property, when it is devoted to a public service is definitely limited by law."

At a Congressional hearing the Daugherty action was upheld.

In October 1923, the Union Pacific Railroad employees voted to go back to work. According to some old-timers, old animosities had played a part in the loss of the strike. The Shop Crafts had not supported the Brotherhood of Railway Trainmen in their strike of 1919 and the trainmen returned the favor. Some strikers simply went elsewhere on the line and went to work.

It would be decades before the workers again challenged the "feudal power" of the railroads.

CURRENT EVENTS, 1923

The *Tribune-Leader's* banner headline, January 22, 1923 read:

UNION PACIFIC TERMINAL BUYING SOUTH SIDE PROPERTY
TO SECURE ROOM FOR FREIGHT TRANSFER
ON EXTENDED SCALE

It was the story of the year and it changed the lives of many people as well as the history and geography of Cheyenne. "Two Tiers of Blocks Extending Full Length of Present Yards to be Added and New Viaduct Must Be Constructed." The story filled in the details.

> The establishment of a Union Pacific freight terminal at Cheyenne, the preliminaries of which are under way, means:
>
> Extension of the present yards from Twelfth Street to Tenth Street, from extreme east end of city to Crow Creek.
>
> Expenditure of $1,500,000 for freight terminal tracks and buildings.
>
> Construction of new steel and concrete viaduct.
>
> Closing of Russell Street crossing.
>
> Improved water system for city and Union Pacific railroad.
>
> Establishment of Cheyenne as a distributing point for Wyoming and adjoining sections of other states.
>
> Possible completion of Yoder-Cheyenne branch in very near future.

PHOTO COURTESY OF UNION PACIFIC SYSTEM

A Union Pacific #3588 Mallet Class 16611, 2-8-8-2 wheel arrangement, "MC" class designation. First of type built for freight service, shown in Cheyenne yards.

Probable change in handling of freight traffic from the south over the Borie cutoff, thereby minimizing the freight hauls over the mountain grades of Wyoming.

At least fifty new homes for the city, to house additional employees of railroad after completion of the terminal.

Construction of three hundred homes to take the place of those razed on the South Side by Union Pacific in improvements.

The making of a new and better South Cheyenne.

The Union Pacific Railroad Company is to extend its Cheyenne yards south from Twelfth Street to Tenth Street, and agents under the direction of J. A. Griffin, of the land department of the Company, are purchasing the necessary land on the South Side, extending from the Crow Creek valley on the west to the east end of the town site.

This expansion of the Union Pacific yards will be followed by the erection, at the cost of $1,500,000, of a large freight terminal plant. It is understood that the plans for this terminal call for 48 tracks and the erection of a freight terminal of brick and steel. Work will begin at once on the improvement and it is expected that it will be completed within a year.

Although no contract has been entered into between the city and the railroad company, it is known that the Union Pacific plans include the erection of a new steel and concrete viaduct by the railroad company, which will be maintained by the city after construction, the closing of Russell Street crossing over the Union Pacific tracks, and an enlargement of the city's water system to be partly paid for by the Union Pacific.

William Jeffers, general manager of the Union Pacific recently announced these tentative plans for Cheyenne improvements to a representative body of businessmen requesting the assurance of these men that the plans would be favorably accepted by the citizens of Cheyenne, before laying them before the Board of Directors of the Union Pacific.

Mr. Jeffers was assured that it was the opinion of the men to whom the proposal was made that the plan would be accepted, as announced by him, and that they would give their endorsement of the plans proposed.

It has been proposed that the viaduct be located one block east of the present bridge on Warren Avenue, and that it extend over the Colorado & Southern and Burlington tracks as well as those of the Union Pacific. Details such as this, however, remain to be worked out between the city and the railroad company.

Surveyors have made a preliminary survey of the available trackage space and the ground which will be occupied by the terminal. It is understood the plans are ready for work to start immediately.

With the widening and extension of the yards, the Union Pacific yards will be the largest on the entire system and will present an appearance similar to the large railroad terminals in Chicago and other large cities. The trackage will be laid as spurs leaving the main line in the extreme eastern portion of the city and connected with the west end of the main yards by trackage which will run south of the present coal chute and roundhouses.

The improvement will mean an expenditure in the city in the next two years or less of not less than $3,000,000 for improvements and buildings.

Mr. Jeffers stated recently that the railroad proposed to spend $1,500,000

> on the new freight terminal, $350,000 on the erection of the new viaduct and approximately $50,000 for either the enlargement of the present filter plant of the water system or the construction of a by-pass and pipeline for the settling of the water controversy which the city commissioners have had up with the railroad for some time.
>
> In addition to the improvements hereinbefore mentioned, it will be necessary to build new homes for at least 200 families already living here, due to the fact that they will be forced to give up their present homes on the South Side. It will also be necessary for homes to be built for the families of an additional number of men who will be employed in the freight terminal and on the necessary added freight crews.
>
> That General Manager Jeffers recognizes the strategic position of Cheyenne as a distributing point and a logical freight terminal is shown by his communication with the board of directors of the railroad that they anticipate the growth of this section now and establish this large freight handling terminal. Cheyenne is at the crossroads of north, south, east and west lines and it is hoped will soon be on a direct line with the North Platte valley, at Yoder, Wyoming.
>
> It is believed by many that this enlargement of the Cheyenne yards as a freight terminal means that ultimately the Union Pacific shops here will be much larger than at present, as the freight traffic to and from the city will all demand that more rolling stock is kept and repaired here.
>
> It is the general opinion that this announcement means more to Cheyenne's future than any other improvement since the locating of Cheyenne by the railroad engineers at the point "where the railroad crosses Crow Creek."

(Copy provided by Wyoming State Archives, Museums and Historical Department.)

THE DAY THE BANKS CLOSED

It was all over town Wednesday. Papa called from Grier's Lumberyard to say: "Don't let anyone go uptown. The First National Bank closed this morning. There is a big crowd. There might be a riot. Our bank (The American) is safe — for now." There was more when he came home for lunch.

Thursday's *Tribune*, July 10, 1924 had two stories about the closures on the front page. On the left, headlined: "TWO NATIONAL BANKS CLOSED IN CHEYENNE, First and Citizen's Suspend Payment Wednesday."

> The First National Bank of Cheyenne did not open its doors Wednesday morning. At 12:15 o'clock Wednesday afternoon the Citizen's National Bank closed its doors. A posted notice on the door of the First National stated that the bank was closed by order of the board of directors and was in the hands of the national bank examiner. The notice was signed

by J. F. Lorang, national bank examiner. No statement concerning the closing of the Citizen's National was issued, nor was any notice posted.

Officers of the Midwest Refining Company here Wednesday were arranging with other large depositors of the First National, it was stated, for reorganization of the bank.

According to the statements as of June 30th, the First National's assets and liabilities each were $6,986,209.14 and its deposits totaled approximately $4,750,000. The Citizen's National's assets and liabilities totaled each $2,285,656.65 and its deposits approximated $1,450,000. The First National is capitalized for $200,000 and the Citizen's National for $100,000.

George E. Abbott, president of the bank, when requested to give his opinion as to the causes necessitating the bank's closing, stated that he thought the three principal reasons were:

"First, extraordinary depreciation in values, more particularly cattle, agricultural products and lands.

"Second, excessive taxation.

"Third, the broad policy adopted by the bank, whereby, it undertook to render helpful assistance to smaller banks of the state in an effort to support the business interests of the state."

Mr. Abbott further stated that "the directors of the bank felt that the interests of the depositors would be best conserved by the closing at this time," and that he was "hopeful the final result would save the the depositors any excessive loss."

Officers of the bank in addition to Abbott are F. E. Warren, vice president; John A. Martin, vice president; A. D. Johnston, cashier; Daniel McUlvan, director.

Then in the middle of the page, right under the masthead, the latest story: "LOCAL BANKING SITUATION NOW NEARS NORMAL, Citizen's National is Taken Over by Examiner." (The *Tribune* was doing its part to calm the jitters.)

The banking situation in Cheyenne appeared Thursday afternoon to be rapidly returning to normality, following the disturbance of conditions resulting from the closing. The three other banks here — The Stockgrowers National, American National and Cheyenne State — Thursday were transacting an unusual volume of business, a large part of it represented by accounts that were being opened with these banks by new depositors. The receipt of deposits incidental to the opening of new accounts was steady throughout the day, this augmented by a virtually normal deposit business with old customers. Each of the three banks remained open Wednesday after the customary closing hour, 3 o'clock, in order that any customers desiring it may have service.

National Bank Examiner S. N. Sullenberger, who arrived Thursday morning from Casper, took charge of the Citizen's National. A posted notice on the banking house door stated that the bank had been closed by order of the board of directors and was in charge of the examiner.

"The public, or rather a few who lost their good judgement, temporarily, caused the Citizen's National bank to close its doors," declared the official statement from the bank, issued Wednesday night at 9 o'clock.

> "If the public had been orderly and content and not gotten excited, we would have been able to meet the few requests that were inevitable, due to the closing of the First National Bank of Cheyenne. Too, we did not know of the closing of the First National Bank until 3 o'clock Wednesday morning and that was too late for us to get any cash from our reserve members. Had we been able to call in any of our reserve cash, we could have handled the situation. Or, if we could have persuaded people to accept drafts, we would have been all right, but our cash on hand ran out and the bank examiner ordered us to close the doors.
>
> "In closing our doors, we did it more to protect our other depositors than anything else. There was not the feeling or thought of failure. Our course from now on depends on the national bank examiner."
>
> The State Bank Examiner's office here was notified of the failure of four small Wyoming banks to open for business Thursday morning. They are: Carpenter State Bank, resources about $65,000; Hillsdale State Bank, resources of about $65,000; and Bank of Upton, resources of about $100,000; Cowley State Bank, resources of about $50,000. All are State Banks. Carpenter and Hillsdale are small towns near Cheyenne, Cowley is in north-western Wyoming and Upton is in northern Wyoming.
>
> An unofficial report received at the examiner's office said that a bank in Grover, Colo., about 40 miles from Cheyenne, failed to open Thursday morning.

A short release from Denver confirmed the report.

The crowd in front of the First National Bank was reported to be large, pressing against the door and windows. A fat lady lay on the sidewalk, screaming and pulling her hair. Finally, she fainted and was carried away.

Chief of Police George H. Troastle drove up and shouted through a horn for the people to disperse. They paid no attention. He drove away and returned riding a horse borrowed from the Bon Ton Livery. This time he rode up on the sidewalk. The people moved back and gradually dispersed, according to observers.

Grandma Benson stopped by our house dressed for "going uptown on business." She said that she was going to draw out every penny and keep it in a coffee can. "I have little enough to keep me in my old age," she said.

On her way home she stopped in again. "It was crowded in the Stockgrowers," she said. "And there was Mr. Marble, walking around chatting with people, cool as you please!" She took out all her money, they didn't mind and there was plenty. "It was piled up on the counter, in plain sight." She had never seen so much money!

She headed for home, over the viaduct. Her handbag had a long handle, which she put over her shoulder, and clutched the bag to her bosom. About half-way over the bridge she decided that she had been foolish and took the money back to the bank.

The newspaper did not list the officers of the Citizen's National Bank. According to an advertisement in the 1924 edition of the R. L. Polk

Directory of Cheyenne, they were: C. W. Hirsig, President; J. L. Jordan, Chairman; G. E. Gilland, Vice President; Wesley I. Dumm, Cashier; J. C. Gans, Assistant Cashier; J. M. Garrett, Assistant Cashier; T. E. Rogers, Assistant Cashier.

The bank was located at the southwest corner of Eighteenth Street and Carey Avenue, in the Boyd Building. The First National Bank was located at the northeast corner of Sixteenth Street and Capitol Avenue.

Although an accounting was still being sought in court in February of 1926, for the First National Bank, the Office of Comptroller of the Currency gave the cause of the failure, in the cases of both banks as: "Local financial depression from unforeseen agricultural or industrial disaster."

Finally, December 10, 1924, the Cheyenne State Bank, 1610 Capitol Avenue closed. It had advertised in the R. L. Polk *Directory*: "State of Wyoming Supervison; Member, United States Federal Reserve System." Its officers were Harry S. Clark, Jr., President; John T. McDonald, Vice President; Tracy Newlin, Vice President; John A. Reed, Cashier; Edward A. Ryan, Assistant Cashier and Auditor; and Ewar W. Adolphson, Assistant Cashier. Thomas Hunter was the receiver.

Wyoming had been thoroughly shaken by the drouth, general depression, declining oil business and bank failures. Thirty-five of one hundred and twenty banks failed during this period. By 1930, only eighty-three remained, and by 1936, there were only thirty-two banks left in Wyoming.

William B. Ross, elected Governor in 1922, was the only Democrat among the top five state executives. He faced a Republican dominated legislature. In view of the depression of the twenties, Ross urged shifting some of the tax burden to the large property owners, a severance tax, improved child labor laws and a two cent per gallon tax on gasoline.

Ross was campaigning in Laramie for the severance tax when he was stricken with acute appendicitis, operated upon and died of complications following the operation, October 2, 1924.

Mrs. Nellie Tayloe Ross was nominated by the Democrats to fill the vacancy and won without campaigning. She followed the course outlined by her husband and remembering the ninety-nine who died in a mine disaster in Kemmerer, August 14, 1923, called for stiffer mine safety laws. She successfully urged ratification of the Federal Child Labor Amendment, and the restriction of work hours for women, giving some consolation to the cause of Labor. A one cent per gallon tax on gasoline was adopted by the Legislature.

Banking was not mentioned in the State Constitution, nor was there a banking code of laws at the time. Mrs. Ross called for and got a State Banking Code and an enlarged Farm Loan Fund as well as new mine safety legislation.

In spite of the bank failures of 1924, J. M. Snyder, State Treasurer, did not feel obligated to mention the economic disaster in his November, 1924

PHOTO COURTESY OF WYOMING STATE ARCHIVES, MUSEUMS AND HISTORICAL DEPARTMENT

Shop crafts men assemble to hear an evangelist during the depression.

report, although he accounted for $920.03 in checks returned from the defunct Citizen's National Bank.

While Mrs. Ross had the support of women in her election, she did not appoint women, except where they were already serving. The frustrated suffragists turned against her and helped to defeat her in 1926.

When I interviewed Mrs. Theresa Jenkins in 1923, she said that she was "disappointed because women were not taking advantage of their opportunities in the business world." Perhaps it was because they had not prepared themselves for executive positions in a "man's world," that they were not appointed.

Mrs. Ross developed her administrative abilities during the two years that she was Wyoming's first woman governor. She held the positions of Vice Chairman in Charge of Women's Activities in the National Democratic Party, and later served as Director of the United States Mint, under both political party administrations, lauded for being a capable administrator.

She was the first woman governor of any state and brought attention to Wyoming at a time when it was much needed.

THEN CAME THE DEPRESSION

The period of Cheyenne history between the election of Herbert Hoover in 1928 to World War II should be written about separately and in depth. The entire population was affected in some way in this High Plains city, although many would prefer to forget those times.

The unemployment, drouth, dust storms and poverty affected all sectors of the economy. The beginning of recovery through government intervention under Roosevelt meant public assistance to agriculture. There was a concerted effort to find new ways of learning to live with drouth through soil conservation methods. It revolutionized our agricultural economy.

There was a new philosophy of human service, public assistance to the needy. The notion that none should starve in a land of plenty gained recognition. No one is truly prosperous if anyone is hungry.

People who forget their history are doomed to repeat it.

THE NEW ERA, 1945

The reservoir of goodwill and the sense of neighborhood that had been recaptured on the South Side as a result of the people rallying around the city dump issue in 1944-45, brought about an unprecedented period of renaissance for the area. The issue had brought attention to environmental and social issues that affected the entire city. The South Side Community League was organized and continued to be a force in the community for fifteen years.

A full page subscription advertisement attracted the nucleus of membership. Prominent citizens gave their encouragement. An account of the first meeting appeared in the *Wyoming Eagle*, March 4, 1945, headlined: "South Side Recreational Requirements Emphasized."

> Gov. L. C. Hunt spoke Saturday night at Johnson School to a large group of Southsiders interested in community improvement.
>
> The governor emphasized the business and industrial future of Wyoming and Cheyenne's role in its development. He assured the cooperation of the state with the betterment of the individual community and advocated planning for the returning veteran.
>
> Mayor Bruce E. Jones commended the group on their "recognition of the needs of organized leadership." Referring to prospects for recreational requirements on the South Side, the mayor quoted figures from the city budget showing that some $6,000 is now set aside for playground supervision in the city plus $500 for Boy Scout work and $2,400 for band concerts.
>
> The mayor added that most of the money spent for playground supervision would be for wages and that "not much would be left for new equipment."
>
> He urged cooperation of all people in the city, stating that in that way only can the city "program."
>
> Esther Anderson, superintendent of public instruction, urged the group to work for the future citizens and to consult them in their plans.
>
> Jack Lowe, of the Frontier refinery, who is serving as publicity chairman announced that an election of officers will be held at a meeting Wednesday night in the music room of the Johnson School. At that time, Commissioner of Parks, George L. Kemp will address the group.
>
> Approximately 60 persons attended the meeting Saturday night and members made clear that the meetings are not only for southsiders within the city limits of Cheyenne, but said they "welcomed all persons in the southern part of the county as far as the state line."
>
> Other speakers included D. W. Caswell, Edward T. Lazear, John Goodman, Commissioner Gus Fleischli and James Greenwood. The meeting was presided over by Mrs. J. C. Willoughby.

SOUTH SIDE COMMUNITY LEAGUE

The South Side Community League organized March 7, 1945 and immediately set about forming committees on recreation, schools and scouting. Parks and library came later. Meetings were held at Johnson School.

When a committee met with the school board, it was well planned to give everyone a chance to make a point. Mr. J. A. Wilson, board president, complimented the group on its deportment. He recalled that once some South Side people threw bricks through the window.

We knew the story. One of the members said, "Why didn't you let them in so they wouldn't have to do that? All of your meetings should be open to the public."

The board recognized that these parents were informed and intelligent people and that they were going to have to address the problems. Again a board member voiced the Mayor's comment that "so little in taxes was paid by South Side residents." A South Side father of three children said, "We all pay taxes at the same rate." There was a moment when only the clock spoke.

Then a quiet voiced woman said, "The school district covers many square miles. Perhaps we may have to call a boundary commission and divide the district to get our fair share."

The board seemed to sense a new determination and promised to work on the problem and build another school, "if necessary, when the war emergency is over."

Friday evenings, once a month, were "Town Meetings." There would be a speaker, followed by discussion and sometimes action was taken.

Byron Hirst and the Junior Chamber of Commerce brought the idea of the city manager form of government to one of the early meetings of the group. In 1944, the Mayor Ira Hanna and Chief of Police Jesse Ekdall had been sent to prison for bribery to protect prostitution. Obviously, the three member commission form of government lacked safeguards. Decades of turmoil in local government lay ahead.

Everyone seemed to want to correct all of the ills of the community at one time. The condition of the streets, the viaduct, the sewage in the creek, the determination to have a good education for our children, more classrooms, a park west of Central Avenue and restoration of the library branch were among the urgent suggestions for cooperative effort.

A Boy Scout troup was soon organized. Girl Scouts had always been a project of the Parent-Teachers' Association. The school continued to be the meeting place until the radio building and headquarters of the State Highway Patrol on East Fifth Street near the refinery became available.

Although the Fox Farm Road Community people had succeeded in the legislative effort to force the City of Cheyenne to clean up its handling of solid waste, the matter still had to be taken to court. We had to keep the pressure on the city officials, while grinding a few axes on behalf of the South Side people and the quality of life in our community.

In 1947, the South Side Community League approached the officials of the new Blue Cross insurance plan to see if the League could serve as a test group to open the service to the public. It was a successful experiment and it increased the League's effectiveness and membership.

Among the League's major accomplishments were its efforts to publicize the educational needs of the South Side. Hebard School in 1946, Rossman School in 1947 and Cole School in 1950, as well as the transition of Johnson Elementary School into a junior high school were realized due to the constant pressure by the League.

At one point the League opposed the "package deal," whereby the South Side would get new classrooms only by supporting an additional $250,000 bond for Storey Gymnasium. Several years earlier the district had voted $300,000 for the gymnasium, however, school officials said, "You can't build much of a gym for $300,000, these days." The League wanted the ballot to be selective, enabling the voter to vote for or against the gymnasium, the classrooms or the shops, separately. While we lost the election, Cole School was built before the gymnasium was constructed. We considered it a victory for academic needs over sports.

Support of the Sewage Bonds in 1949 and the South Side Community Park, (now Optimist) in 1950 kept the League busy. The restoration of the south branch of the Laramie County Library in the new Ketchios Building at Eighth and Central was cause for celebration, September 17, 1953. We also taught the public to say "Laramie County Library," instead of "Carnegie" library, since it is a tax-supported county library. The Ketchios building became a casualty of the I-180 Highway Connector.

After World War II, the red-lining policies of the banking-real estate establishment caused the returning veterans to move away from the South Side, potential young leaders could not get loans to build on the South Side. The South Side Community League had always had an "open membership" policy, however, the "new people" moving into the neighborhood had little interest in democratic community organizations. The Boy Scouts had grown up and the old leaders were tired of the responsibility. In May, 1960, the South Side Community League relinquished its building and passed into history.

THE RAILWAY EMPLOYEES BUILDING AND LOAN ASSOCIATION

The Railway Employees Building and Loan Association was organized in 1901 by Joseph M. Carey, J. C. Costello, W. R. McKeen, Jr., John L. Murray, John Treacy, C. W. Riner and D. A. Jones to give its members an opportunity to acquire by monthly installments, capital for the building or the purchase of a house or the founding of a business, and to enable its members to invest their savings in a safe and profitable manner. (The name of the association did not imply eligibility to membership.)*

The stockholders met monthly in the district court room of the City and County Building and members would bid for the use of the money in a regular order of business called "Sale of money subject to loan."

The interest rates reflected the inflation of the period. Most of the blue-collar homes were financed in this manner until the mid-thirties when low interest government money fed the local loan market.

* (By-laws of the Railway Employees Building and Loan Association.)

INTERLUDE

THE REAL TRUE STORY OF LOST CAUSES ANONYMOUS

It was all because of a dear lady whom I shall call Bea. I had been given her name as a prospect for membership in an organization for good government, the League of Women Voters, of which I was the membership chairman.

"Good government, eh?" she asked with interested skepticism. "What do you know about libraries?" She had struck a nerve.

"What do I know about libraries?" I echoed. "In this town they are dying. We had a small branch library over here on the South Side. It was started by the Parent-Teachers' Association, a real, live branch of the public library, and the Library Board gave it to the school."

The branch library had been located in the basement of Johnson School. The population explosion following World War II had hit the Cheyenne Schools and they needed the room. The catalogue of adult books went into the Johnson Junior High School library, and the children's books went to Hebard School.

"Well," she huffed, pretending indignation, "I happen to be a member of the Library Board."

"Wonderful," I said. "You seem to be someone we can talk with. So far we haven't had much luck. However, I must not mix personal business with League business. We are in our first year of organization. As a prerequisite for national recognition, we must make a study of local government, then choose some phase for further study. Our town is ripe for some good, concentrated non-partisan attention."

After attending a membership coffee, Bea joined a discussion group, having satisfied herself that we were truly a non-partisan group.

The League had discovered a formula for encouraging the participation of citizens in government. It would take time to tell, but an organization with such a goal was worth exploring. The survey of local government included a brief summary of library services. The group chose to devote more study to jails and corrections.

Shortly after we had met at the membership coffee, Bea called to invite me to lunch and talk about libraries. I accepted, providing I could bring my friend, Doris, who had been the organizer of our branch library when she was president of the Johnson Elementary School Parent-Teachers' Association.

We arrived at one of Cheyenne's loveliest homes, with Doris determined not to be patronized or impressed. I was equally determined that Bea, innocent as a lamb, was not to be browbeaten by the old guard running the library.

Doris and I had been reminiscing about the building of the little South Side Community Park. Trees had been planted amidst publicity, and with lots of people helping, but the time came when the trees had to have hours and hours of watering. City park employees began to roll up the hose. We begged them to leave it so we could continue to soak the trees. They were skeptical; it was against the rules. I guess they thought we might steal the heavy, monstrous hose. Doris and I entered the dining room laughing.

As we took in the elegance of sterling and white napery, Bea explained that the lady who would be serving us ("So I won't have to be jumping up and down,") was a displaced person who did not speak much English.

At that point, a starched, white-aproned woman appeared with the first course. Bea pressed me to finish the story, and jokingly asked how I had managed to stay out of jail.

The displaced lady may not have spoken English, but she certainly understood it. She set my shrimp cocktail down with a sharp click, eyeing me with alarm.

"I do love hung-over shrimp," Doris said, clearing the air, daintily unhooking a fat shrimp for a dip in the pool of sauce.

"You are spoiling us, Bea," I said. "A sandwich in the kitchen would have been fine. But let's talk library, now that we are together. What have you done, so far?"

Her resumé was a brief, shrewd analysis of the problem, an acknowledgement of the entrenched establishment that controlled rather than governed our town. She was supposed to be part of it, but so far her individuality had not been completely subjugated.

When she finished, I could tell that Doris had decided to give her the benefit of the doubt. Doris gave a terse account of the short but useful life of the South Side Branch Library, accented by her eloquent hands. Parent-Teachers' Association members had taken training to act as substitutes for the librarian, who kept the branch open from three to five afternoons, and from seven to nine in the evenings, three days a week. No need for father to change from his work clothes to go to this library in the basement of the school, a room with an outside entrance.

Doris and I had been through many campaigns together. In the process of jarring a citizenry into action, we had learneed some people skills ourselves. True, we had begun to tire of the responsibility that falls to movers and shakers. While we had always acted with the utmost democracy, someone had to light the fire and fan the flame. Doris' forte was administration, and mine was publicity.

During the 1944-45 fight of the Fox Farm Road neighborhood against the city dump, we had managed to involve the entire community. The spirit we had nurtured must not be allowed to die. Together we had organized the South Side Community League, and we had discerned many needs. We had dreamed the improbable dream, and we had made some small gains.

In 1947, when Blue Cross was struggling to get started, they served only the Farm Bureau and a few businesses as group insurance providers. We went to the Blue Cross office in the old Colin Hunter residence on East Seventeenth Street to inquire about South Side Community League becoming an experimental group to open the benefits of a group health insurance plan "to the public." We could and they did. Doris served as the unpaid volunteer agent, working on a card table in the living room of her home. Our membership soared.

Community work is hard and takes stamina. I wanted to be free to pursue state and national issues, but I could feel myself slipping into another local project. I, who had promised Ray "no more campaigns."

Doris asked, "Bea, if we help you, will you help us get our branch library back?"

Doris could always deal. I knew I would help, whether or not Bea could help us. We began to plan. We needed a new location for the South Side library.

There was no real reason for these conditions. State statute allowed a one-mill levy, and Laramie County levied a mere .58 mill for the library system.

We thought the South Side Community League would work for the restoration of the branch library. Doris was serving as South Side Community League treasurer. Being in town only during school term, I preferred not to take an office. I like committee work better. That's where the action is, the brainstorming and the fun.

"Webster had a word for it," I told Doris on our way downtown. "Antidisestablishmentarianism: to be against depriving an entity, or one, of the status of being established, or to be against depriving (as a state church) of official connection with the government."

I had copied that definition in my book of quotations. Another quote appropriate to the moment was from *Time* magazine: "The ESTABLISHMENT is the cretatious equivalent of coral, animate life, clinging together for its own support until solidly cemented into a wall or reef — to challenge the Patrick Henrys of the world."

We found a county commissioner in his office and stated our case.

"The library is fine," he said. "The Board always returns a surplus to the general fund. It runs a very efficient operation. We haven't had any complaints until now."

"I guess you know what we're up against," I said to Doris on the way home.

Doris had been living in Panama when the library disappeared into the school. Returning to Cheyenne at the beginning of the war, she inquired why the teachers or the Parent-Teachers' Association didn't protest. "Or did they?" I asked.

"No guts." Doris wasted neither words nor sympathy.

Poor Bea! I was afraid she would bruise easily before being impaled upon the reef. I, who had promised Ray "no more projects," felt we had to give Bea support and backing.

It all comes back, like an old movie, with sound:

"I don't neglect my family, do I? I bake cookies, don't I? I sew our clothes and keep house, help the kids with their homework, don't I?" Ray had to admit that I did indeed.

"Bridge is boring. I like to do something that makes me think I am using my mind. Housework doesn't use up enough kilowatts."

Pat put in her oar: "You scheme and plot. I've heard you on the phone."

"Don't forget the dishpan," I answered. "Some of my best plots are hatched while I'm doing your chores."

And Lee complained, "Sometimes you don't listen when we talk."

"Ha! I can tell you everything you said about that carburetor. I am proud that you know so much about cars." (You, too, Brutus?)

"OK," I said, "campaign over; bills paid; money in the bank. No harm done. Just don't ask me to give up the LWV."

"Nobody is asking you to give up anything," Ray said. "We just don't want you to work so hard. Take some time for yourself. Go back to your painting."

A few days after our visit, the phone rang right after breakfast. It was Bea, crying. "I have resigned from the Library Board. I have just put my letter of resignation in the mailbox."

"Now, now, don't be hasty. Don't cry. Tell me what happened." The wind was howling and I could hardly hear her.

"Yesterday at the board meeting, I moved to raise the salaries of the librarians from $.70 to $1.00 per hour, effective immediately, using the reserve fund. They voted that down. (There were only three members on the board.) Then I moved to raise the salaries on the new budget. They voted that down. It's a lost cause."

"Hold everything, I think I have a germ of an idea. First get the letter out of the mailbox and put on the tea kettle. This could be an emergency operation. I'll be right over."

I called Doris and told her. "We have to get over there and do something."

"I can't. Johnny is home in bed with a bad cold and I don't feel so well myself. Tell me what happens."

Bea met me at the door, tall, ash-blonde, blue-eyed, model-thin, wearing an elegantly simple pink sweater and skirt, a red nose and puffy lids.

"I boiled water as you suggested. What do you say we make some tea with it?" She had a nice smile.

"Good. Doris couldn't come, she thinks she is getting the pip. Johnny is in bed with it."

Seated in the breakfast nook, I told her how the South Side Community League had appointed a libary committee. Guess who is chairman? During our refreshment break, we made a general plan, alert to county budget deadlines. A committee is scouting for a building to rent. We are to meet next Monday to plan for meetings with the Library Board and the county commissioners. A news release would report merely that a committee had been appointed, which could mean anything or nothing. "You know how committees are; other people's committees, that is." Discretion was vital.

"No one but Doris and I know of your interest. Now we must plan a diverting action, as the generals say."

Over tea, we read the "Library Letters" which had appeared in both daily papers. We had a modest pride in the first, but no clue as to the author of the second, which had a professional ring.

"Obviously, we have friends," I said. "We just don't know who they are. We had found this to be true when we started to get the tax off margarine, followed by the campaign for yellow margarine, and whatever else we undertook. You know the saying, 'God helps U.S. sailors, when their hearts are pure.' It works for us, too. Six thousand people signed our petition, 'WYOMING WANTS IT YELLOW, TOO.' People can't help unless they know about your project. Publicity is the answer."

"Oh, no! No publicity!" Her eyes suddenly welled with tears.

If I didn't have trouble enough, the one person who could help turns out to be a shrinking violet. "We will be discreet, don't worry," I said. "Then there was the Brimmer and Deming lost cause. You *had* to be there."

George Brimmer, a prominent attorney, had apparently been pleased with our efforts in support of a successful Sewage Disposal Plant bond referendum, which would aid in cleaning up Crow Creek, and our project creating a park bordering Crow Creek north of West Ninth Street.

The South Side Community League located a parcel of city owned land, the west half of block 530, bordering Crow Creek between West Ninth and West Tenth Streets, and petitioned City Council on Valentine's Day 1950 for permission to develop a park. The request was approved.

The Capitol Building Commission gave the city $500.00 to help defray the cost of moving the trees; seven buckeyes, five hackberrys and one pine.

Mr. Everett Copenhaver, Secretary of State, called Lillian to give her the news.

It was an impressive sight; fully grown specimen trees on flat bed trucks being moved from the city's oldest park to the city's newest park; a neighborhood bootstrap project.

Mr. Brimmer called a meeting in his office, inviting Dr. A. C. Hildreth, director of the High Plains Horticultural Station; Earl Hartchen, nurseryman; M. J. (Bud) Andrews, of the Izaak Walton League; Lewis Bates, editor of the *Wyoming State Tribune*; and anyone I wished to bring from the South Side Community League.

Bates couldn't make it, and asked for a report. (I gave him one.) W. I. Holmes, South Side Community League president, was a milk route driver and was unavailable for morning meetings. (It all seems like yesterday.) Doris Willoughby, South Side Community League treasurer; Lillian Hundley, South Side Community League secretary; and I, Gladys Jones, as park chairman, attended.

Brimmer spread out a large roll of plans on the conference table, which was covered with a buffalo robe. He explained that he and the late William C. Deming, former publisher of the *Tribune*, had commissioned S. R. DeBoer, noted designer of city parks, including the Denver Public Park System, to design plans for a scenic drive from the Ft. Warren gates to the Hereford Ranch, with little parks and flowering trees along the creek, through the west and south neighborhoods of the city.

Poor Lillian, the buffalo robe gave her the sneezes and she had to leave.

Mr. Deming, who died in 1949, in his will had bequeathed $10,000 to the city for the project. He had also, in 1930, deeded to the city for park purposes, all of Block 529, which is west across the creek and Deming Drive from the South Side Community League park, to initiate this "greenbelt" proposal.

Brimmer explained that three sets of park design plans had been prepared, one for Deming, one for himself, and one for the office of the City Engineer. "I guess you would call it a decent burial. The city put the money in the bank and forgot about the plans," he commented.

The outspoken Dr. Hildreth said, "What this city needs is a few large expensive funerals."

A Civic Works program, in cooperation with the Works Progress Administration project, had constructed a combination dike and roadway in the thirties, apparently spurred by the flood of 1929, channeling the Crow Creek floodplain into an unlovely ditch. The road was named Deming Drive.

"Unknown friends will help if they know what is needed. There are lots of lovely lost causes begging for someone to find them: a swimming pool, an auditorium, and the classic 'sidewalks around the cemetery.' "

"I've got it! How perfect! How about starting an elite new club and calling it 'Lost Causes Anonymous'?"

"You see, we could have crazy made-up names, like 'Tubby Pitied.' That's a man's name. What's a girl's name? We could be anonymous and still get publicity for our CAUSE!"

Bea caught on fast: "Hedda, for . . . had. Hedda Nuff!" She took over. "How about 'Pulda Boner'? 'Carrie Onner'?"

I called Doris as promised. She laughed so hard Johnny had to know what it was all about. Johnny had one: he says rumors at the Union Pacific shops come from "Gray P. Vine." Good work, now how are we going to use this idea and these names?

Bea on the extension phone: "We could have a party and dress up, wear masks, be anonymous and make heartrending pleas for our CAUSE."

"And charge admission," said Doris, always the treasurer.

"Yes," I said, "Or we could have an entry fee and a prize for the most worthy LOST CAUSE. The winner would get to promote his cause and we would all have to support it until it was accomplished." Doris had been relaying all of this to Johnny, everyone talking at once. Shared laughter had a way of relaxing tension. Our sense of relief bordered on the hysterical.

Bea asked, "who would decide and how?"

Johnny nominated a judge, "Hurd E. Nuff." "Hien Mitee," scoffed Doris. "I'm not going to tell Johnny anymore. It hurts him to laugh. I think he's got pleurisy."

"Hold it, hold it," I begged. "I'm trying to get this down."

The morning had gotten away. I was going to stop downtown at the *Tribune* to say goodbye to Lew Bates.

Lewis E. Bates, crusading editor of the *Wyoming State Tribune*, was taking a leave of absence to serve on the staff of Francis E. Barrett, newly elected Republican United States Senator from Wyoming. I wanted to wish him well, although I didn't approve of his mission. The Friend of the Little People would be missed. I decided to tell him about "LOST CAUSES ANONYMOUS."

"Sounds great," he said. "Wish I could be here to help. Take it up with Keith (Keith Osborn, his successor). I'm sure he'll help. If it comes off, I'll come back for the party."

We'll save a chair for Brother B,
Long he yearned to save a tree,
All he heard was chop, chop, chop,
Let the tears fall, drop by drop.

Lew's editorials had stirred the town to help us save the trees in the historic four block city park, laid out in the original city plat, when the park was ceded by the city to the State for the new Barrett Building. We had saved some specimen trees for the South Side Community Park. Whenever healthy trees fell in Cheyenne, there was public mourning in the *Tribune*.

I talked to Osborn. He went along with the idea of LOST CAUSES ANONYMOUS, and even wrote an editorial on the day my introductory letter came out on the front page (*Tribune*, March 15, 1953). This was followed midweek by two more anonymous letters.

I wrote the first. Many knew of my interest in playground supervision at the schools. I had been one of a group appearing before the Parent-Teachers' Association Council to get their support. Sometimes you have to stand up and be counted.

It was disappointing, but we had started a fad of sorts. Everyone was making up zany names and joining in unstuffing shirts. It was done at cocktail parties. Puns at the businessmen's lunches were rampant, they told me.

The next week two more letters came out. We hadn't planted them. I had phone calls: "You can't tell me that you're not at the bottom of this." "Who, me?" Some wanted in on the party but couldn't bring themselves to go public.

We went on planning for the party for April Fool's Night. The contestants would wear masks until after the winner was announced. The Master of Ceremonies, Worth E. Issue, would pass the crying towel to the first contestant, who would plead his cause, relate his sad story and in turn pass the towel to the next contestant. "Would a Crying Towel be unsanitary?" "No, it's OK, it's ceremonial only. You just hold it."

At one end of the judge's table, we would prop up a "straw man," a real "bucket head," topped off by a dunce cap, THE GRAND IMPOTENTATE, a stand-in for "so-and-so." That stiff expression was acquired from sitting too long on too many boards. (There ought to be a limit on terms of service.)

We would swear an oath "to abide by the decision of the judge/judges, to strive nobly, forsaking all other causes to right this 'miscarriage of justice,' 'progress,' and/or civic need of whatever category, until right once again triumphed!"

Besides the Master of Ceremonies, Worth E. Issue, judges nominated were "Overly Credulous," "Cleverly Odious," "Hurd E. Nuff," "Grave D. Meanor," and "Hien Mitee." No women's names were submitted for judges!

More names of men than of women were submitted as contestants, perhaps because fewer women were sufficiently liberated to make fools of themselves in 1953.

Women expected to attend were: Iva Haddit, Pulda Boner, Lasta Nalisis, Birdie Watcher, Ample Sample, Dema Gog and Peda Gog (sisters under the skin). Undoubtedly Sena Mall, Neva Makit, Hedda Nuff, Neva Moore, Carrie Onner, Civvy Theta, Sensy Umor, Parsie Monious, Keepsa Tryon, Fancie Frazer and Ima Sorhed could be counted on at the last minute.

Men nominated for membership were: Leadon McDuff, Spade A. Spade, Porbut Honest, Dyer Knead, Señor Pulno Ponches, Sano Moore, Ewar

Faded, Ron A. Rounds, Mel Arky, Gray P. Vine, Seam O'Line, Nuim Wen, Thizbe Trezon, Krine Inizbeer, Shorty Funz, Unby Knownst, Shudda Stadinbed, Puddup R. Shuddup, Junior Forster, Sean S. B. Levin, Dew U. Dert and Dowt R. Sanitee.

There could be a commercial angle. I could start my own public relations agency. The mad, mad month of March has caused the merchants to get mad at their buyers for loading up on such hare-brained merchandise. Their stores become a "Fool's Paradise", causing them to throw caution to the March wind and have a sale on All Fool's Day.

Clearer heads prevailed. The idea that someone could profit from such suffering was too repulsive. The winner would have to be content with our unswerving devotion to the CAUSE.

An unkind fate decided the issue. I pasted a few clippings onto black paper for my scrapbook. LOST CAUSES, ANONYMOUS, itself, was a lost cause!

Only these little pieces of paper keep falling out of my files: Doggerel was apparently off the leash. It was a time of giddy confidence, John Q. Public could fight City Hall, or the Powers That Be, and sometimes win.

Have a reservation for Ima Sorhed,
Long she sat upon a Board,
As she watched them count their hoard
Ne'er a cent could she divert
To her project. What a jerk!

Sound the knell for Civvy Theta,
She brought culture, tried the hard way,
Brought us shows right offa Broadway,
Four bells for Theta. Rise and greeta!

A low groan for Junior Forster,
Thought the world would be his orster
"Let the young'uns plant a tree
They'll grow to love and never harm it."
Alas, alak, and even darnit!
No cause could ever be more lorster.

Poor old Shudda had it bad,
Gave the Crusade all he had,
But, alas, t'was not enough
Poor old Shudda Stadinbed.

Why did we fail? Perhaps if the editor hadn't called us "do-gooders," when we know in our hearts that we are "good-doers." Whatever the reason, it was the most successful lost cause I ever had.

It may have helped. The new South Branch Library, in the Ketchios Building on East Eighth Street was dedicated September 18, 1953. At least it helped us to keep our sense of humor.

THE FOX FARM COMMUNITY FOLKS

It seems incredible, that pastoral scene, the "prairie organ," I had gazed upon that never-to-be-forgotten day in 1922, could have become a "blighted area" in fifty years, or ever. It happened. A visitor remarked that "it looks like the craters of the moon." Although it seems unlikely that it can be reclaimed, that is what the residents of the community are stubbornly determined to require. I feel an obligation to record the transition.

Crossing Crow Creek downstream of Morrie Avenue, the first road into the area made use of the abandoned roadbed and bridge of the Denver and Pacific Railroad. It crossed the Perry Organ-Hammond-Arp-Lummis meadow, coming out on the present Fox Farm Road at Avenue C 2, (also utilized as a pipeline right-of-way) thence, east to Archie Allison's Clearview Dairy at the end of the road.

Vera B. Persons, of Boulder, Colorado, platted a quarter section of land south of the meadow, lying north of the road. She divided it into thirty-two tracts and named it "Cheyenne Irrigated Gardens." From 1923 to 1936, some of the ground had irrigaton from Crow Creek. After that, irrigation was by well. Gordon and Persons Road were dedicated to the public use, "forever." Later a second plat of Irrigated Gardens was filed west of Charlie Turk's little farm, which joined the original on the west.

Turk built a beautiful "prairie style" house on the highest point, where he had a great flowing well. In 1946 he began to develop his farm into "Broadmoor Addition."

"Irrigated Gardens" was the little place in the country to many a blue-collar family. Most of the men had jobs in town. The garden tracts were a hedge against strikes and layoffs. Corn, potatoes and winter vegetables to supply the family table were the chief crops. Peas and beans were canned in quantities. Many had cows and chickens. In the late twenties there was also a goat dairy. Clarence Ekstrom raised rhubarb and aspargus for the local market.

In 1929, James Harper and Clarence Ekstrom established a fox farm on ten acres lying along the road to Clearview Dairy. The fox farm became a local attraction. They installed an observation deck.

After the Crow Creek flood of June 4, 1929, residents traveled west to the old "Denver Road" to get to town. The trail was improved and its name, Fox Farm Road, was to outlive its namesake. It was finally dedicated in 1966.

In spite of the depressed economy, the Fox Farm prospered. Movie stars and ladies of fashion draped themselves in silver fox stoles and capes. The best pelts came from Cheyenne where selective breeding and scientific handling increased the amount of silver hairs in a pelt, bringing premium prices. The more silver, the higher the price.

Earl Harper recalls that the tariff on furs was repealed in 1940. Silver fox coming from Canada and Norway cut the price to less than half. Mr. Ekstrom sold his interest to his partner. In 1947, the breeding stock was sold.

Archie Allison, mayor of Cheyenne from 1934 to 1940, also promoted "country gardens," with Allison and Clearview tracts. The cornfields of Clearview gave way to gravel pits. The gravel turned to gold. The Prossers platted a wedge of land bordered by the abandoned railroad. The Wilson brothers, Henry and Wayne, mined the Prosser placer.

This pit, when mined out, was leased for ten dollars to the City of Cheyenne for a garbage dump in 1944, bringing about the first confrontation of this rural neighborhood with the city, in court. Landmark legislation coming out of this issue provided considerable protection from attempted abuses until the "Enlightened Seventies."

A. C. (Cal) McClain and his wife Elsie, bought their little place in the country in 1931, in the second plat of Irrigated Gardens, west of Turk's on the road to the Fox Farm. Cal was a machinist for the Union Pacific. They operated a dairy from 1932 until 1940.

Elsie recalls the first time they went out to look at the place. They crossed Crow Creek after the flood, bravely driving over the bridge which was awash with sewage. The Hereford dam had held, enlarging the lake upstream to Evans Avenue, where boys launched a raft made of railroad ties.

In 1950, the McClains went out of the dairy business and developed the first trailer court east of the Greeley Highway and named it "Avalon." They had a fine well and planted many trees. The big playground next to the road was a popular place for ball games with all of the neighborhood kids.

Finally, the McClains retired. The new owner crowded six more mobile homes into the playground area.

The parents of Kenneth Fogg bought the Allison dairy in 1942. Kenneth grew up on the farm. Here, he and his wife, Norma Jean, raised four daughters. He says, that now, due to encroachment of the city and loss of pasture due to firecrackers, he may have to sell the farm.

Early mining of gravel by the Wilsons and Earl Vandehei began with horse power. Acceleration of the mining came with the increased demand after World War II. Although some tractors were in use during the thirties, the development of high-powered, specialized equipment speeded the creation of the pits, unhindered by permits of any kind, or any control.

Of the gravel miners, only the Wilsons were residents, until the McCard family entered the field, making small pits here and there in the neighborhood.

The Wilsons cleaned out several of the Clearview tracts. Some owners sold only the gravel, retaining the pits, and managed, for the most part, to keep dumping out. J. Gustafson planted golden willows around the pond of exposed water table in his pit, creating a sheltered swimming hole. He also pumped water from it to irrigate his garden.

The Wilsons moved down the road to mine out the west part of the old Fox Farm. McCann and Teton Construction mined the east part, while south of the road, the Reads were getting down to the water table. Friends would say, "If you are going east, be sure the road is still there."

The acreage of the pits increased rapidly. They were still clean, however. North of Fox Farm Road, behind the homes fronting the road and west of Turk Avenue, the City of Cheyenne had opened a new pit that eventually covered twelve acres.

When a June snowstorm broke down trees all over Cheyenne, the city engineer called on the neighbors to see if they would object to the tree limbs being deposited in that pit? The residents did not object. It was the humanitarian thing to do.

Another time it was bricks and dirt from a demolition. Then more and more, the assumption was that the residents did not care. However, when other refuse began to appear, the residents requested the State Health department to enforce the law. The law was very explicit. We were very vigilant. Later administrations were not as solicitous.

Gravel was running out and the big company controlled all of the available new gravel producing land. John Morandin and Son had several small pits, nearing depletion, in the neighborhood. When Harry Fitzmorris died, the Morandins acquired his small acreage between two residences. The operators took all of the gravel out, to the highway's right-of-way. Harry's pump, still attached to the rusty, exposed casing, bent at an odd angle, thirty feet above the bottom of the pit, a grotesque monument to the sick man who had tended geese and goats and tolerated curious children.

This pit, so convenient, alongside of the road, attracted the casual, passing dumper, as no other. Just dump and speed away! They came from all over. Sofas, stoves, dead televisions, trash and garbage spilled out onto the shoulder of the road. The county officials did not respond to our complaints. A dead antelope in August had to be covered by residents.

The road, which had been built up to accommodate the heavy gravel trucks and cement mixers, had been designated as State Secondary Highway number 221. The department send a bulldozer to push the trash further back, off the road. A barrier and a "NO DUMPING" sign failed to deter the determined dumper.

The pit continued to be a problem to the neighborhood until the Solid Waste Management Division of the Department of Environmental Quality had been created and was functioning.

Unregulated, illegal dumping of all this filth so close to residences was an atrocity against the people, the land and the underground waters. We can never forgive the indifference of the authorities, or the absentee owners.

The anatomy of the neighborhood was changing. Fox Farm Road was still the main artery, not yet connected to the "outer belt." Older friends were retiring, moving away. Kids were growing up, moving away. Younger families were moving in. The Air Force family next door went overseas. They left the house to be managed by a real estate firm, intending to return, some day.

The managers rented it to a "distressed" family. They arrived to find the water pipes ruptured. It was bitter cold and there was no coal for the furnace. The well-mannered children came over for water for several days.

The father had been a career Army man who had answered the call to preach the gospel. He drove a taxi and did some preaching here. Each member of the family played some musical instrument. In the spring he answered another call and the family was moving again.

The next tenants came from the opposite end of the social spectrum. A man and wife, supposedly a nurse, said that they were boarding several old men. It turned out to be an alcoholic household. Some of the neighbors suspected that the old men were mistreated. Then one day there was a flurry of sheriff's cars, an ambulance, and the house was empty again.

Ed Wederski and his wife, Josephine, bought the house, enlarged and renewed it beautifully. Their flower bordered lawn, fruit trees and bountiful garden became the envy of the neighborhood.

The Wilson Haul Road, an extension of South Morrie Avenue, (or Avenue C) had been carved through Denver Hill to shorten the gravel haul to town. The hill, itself, was eventually hauled away to build I-80, with an underpass for the road.

Trailer courts were filling up the little pastures and gardens, west, toward the Greeley Highway after the water and sewer district was formed. Few amenities, such as playgrounds and green space exist in the new courts. Open space for country quiet and serenity is disappearing. Absence of state regulation of the "manufactured housing" industry insures a high return for the new slum lords. Greeley Highway, US 85, has become a commercial strip.

A new school, Arp Elementary, named for the donor of the land, was located in Prosser Tracts, beside the long abandoned, historic railroad line, south of Fox Farm Road. Children would no longer have to be bussed to Rossman School in Orchard Valley. Students over a mile away were bussed until the recent "energy crisis." They take their chances with the increased traffic of Fox Farm Road, now a "feeder road" opening onto the College Drive "Outer Belt."

THE SOIL AND WATER REALITIES

By the early fifties, it was apparent that some of the wells in the area were polluted. A few were being chlorinated, using feeder pumps. Gasoline from buried tanks at a filling station on Denver Hill was said to be polluting nearby wells. Many were ill. A healthy baby died. Gerry Kirkbride's doctor said her problem was "just nerves." She suspected the water and took some over to the University of Wyoming laboratory. The biologist showed her how to take samples and gave her test kits for her neighbors.

The test results were alarming. Beside large amounts of nitrates, there was also typhoid germ present. Bottled water solved Mrs. Kirkbride's health problem.

She enlisted volunteers to help with the water sampling campaign. They met opposition from people who believed that their deep wells could not be contaminated. They also encountered apathy. Some just moved away. Public complacency had to be challenged.

A pile of detergent suds at the end of our garden hose had us buying Rock Crest water for cooking and drinking for eight years. The South Cheyenne Water and Sewer District was finally organized in 1960, having arranged to buy its water from the City of Cheyenne.

Wells in the area ranged from hand-dug shallow wells to two- and three-hundred-foot deep wells. Our well, drilled ninety feet deep, had water at twenty-five to thirty feet, depending on the fluctuating water table.

Laramie County soil is generally porous, sandy and gravelly. Poor septic system installation or aging equipment accounted for much of the pollution. Metal tanks are no longer allowed and percolation rates must be checked before new systems are installed. One may wonder how many rural Laramie County residents may be drinking their own sewage? Well water should be tested regularly. The safety of the new systems is questionable.

The suds disappeared from the garden hose as soon as the new sewer line was functioning. Although a few people resisted the necessity for water lines, all hooked onto the sewer lines.

We learned that no area is immune to environmental problems. Orchard Valley, a planned subdivision southwest of the city was developed by the P. J. Black Lumber Company in the late twenties. Their 500 foot deep well was thought to be an unending supply, however, two more wells have since been drilled.

Several artesian wells existed in earlier times. Cheyenne people used to drive out to the McGees during the drouth of the twenties to get the sweet unchlorinated artesian water, just west of Orchard Valley.

A flowing artesian well once supplied the Green Valley golf course east of Orchard Valley until new wells were drilled and it ceased to flow. In recent years, some residents have hooked up to the water lines of the district. However, the entire area is on the sewer line, made necessary by the type of soil and the failure of their sewer lagoon.

Much has been learned, at long last, about the ability of the soil to accept waste-water. The new study by the United States Soil Conservation Service will make it possible for governmental agencies to deal more intelligently with their development problems in the future. Soil conditions should be the primary environmental consideration.

Once the residents of the county, south of the city, had the water supply, they could afford the luxury of fire protection. The Laramie County Fire District Number One was organized in 1962. Until the eighties, these services made our taxes the highest in the county, currently 77.92 mills.

The people of Fox Farm Road Community took the initiative in bonding themselves to provide safe, clean water; others look to government grants.

The availability of water brought a proliferation of trailer courts. While it was argued that the density of population helped to keep our water bills down, few were convinced that the trade-off was worth it.

LARAMIE COUNTY COMMUNITY COLLEGE

After an abortive attempt to create a Community College in 1966, the voters approved the idea on May 21, 1968. Amid a storm of controversy, the site for the new school was selected to be on 140 acres south of the gravel pits, donated by the Arp and Hammond Hardware Company and Herbert Read, the mine owners.

The neighborhood generally favored the college and hoped for its good influence on the quality of life in the county. Unforgivable things had been said about the area with its illegal dumps and pitted landscape. On June 12, Governor Stan Hathaway turned the first "real shoveful" of earth with a backhoe and simultaneously, a suit was filed to stop construction of the college.

June 21, the neighborhood held a tea to start a "Well Wishers" fund for the college well. The drilling of the well and the pump were donated by the South Side Advanced Development Association. City-wide support was growing despite the Chamber of Commerce opposition to the site and yet another suit to block construction. This suit was dismissed.

Classes were held in various buildings in town until November of 1969, when the young college moved into the new buildings on the "cow pasture" campus undaunted by bad weather, strikes and lawsuits. Almost every family in the community has made some use of this truly "people's" college.

We looked forward to the "Enlightened Seventies" which began with the highline controversy. The new corridor for the Bureau of Reclamation power transmission lines would traverse the "very depressed" area of the gravel pits. Tall pine trees would have to come down. Not even our congressional delegates could help us. No building would be allowed in the corridor.

Occasionally, we talked about retiring from the strenuous business of soil conservation contracting. The Raymond R. Jones Company had developed water for ranching across southern Wyoming's mountains and plains. We had built roads in forests and deserts. After thirty-three years in the business, Ray retired.

Summers, the children and I had gone out on the job. After they were in college, I spent the entire season in the field, keeping house in a trailer, moving camp, studying and absorbing the clean, rugged environment, enjoying our ranch friends. We tended to lose touch with the neighborhood.

Wyoming's future growth requires sensitive planning. As an organizer and first state president of the League of Women Voters, I tried to keep informed on the League's study of "Land Use Planning." However, the local League's study seemed more real estate oriented, less people oriented; antiseptic and hypothetical. The individual citizen should observe, study and participate. "Know, care and act." I lobbied, as an individual, for strong state control in the handling of solid waste by local governments, a subject slighted by the study.

In the years after the children left home, I returned to my painting, and during the sixties, took up the study of mosaics. Although I had been an exhibiting artist in the thirties, I had to work hard to bring my work up to my expectations.

Having achieved some recognition for mosaics in regional exhibitions, I was asked to be the consultant-teacher on a five- by twenty-foot mural at Hobbs Elementary School in 1973-74. The project involved some 350 children and their teachers. The ceramic tile mural depicted "The Four Seasons at Hobbs." Permanent works of art for the schools had been a dream of retiring Art Coordinator Irene White. It was a privilege to help them achieve this goal.

It was easy to put "Solid Waste" in the back of my mind for long periods of time. The trouble was, it would not stay there. We are all a part of the problem. Someone had to say it!

SOUTH SIDE POPULATION

Cheyenne City Population

Year	Population
1870	1,450
1880	3,456
1890	11,690
1900	14,087
1910	11,120
1920	13,829
1930	17,361
1940	22,474
1950	31,935
1960	43,505
1970	40,914
1980	47,283

According to the Federal Records in the Wyoming State Library, unincorporated places listed separately from Cheyenne, included Orchard Valley and the Fox Farm Road Community in 1960 and 1970.

1960, Fox Farm Road	1,371
1970, Fox Farm Road	1,329
1960, Orchard Valley	1,449
1970, Orchard Valley	1,015

The 1980 Laramie County Census total was 68,649.

The 1980 demographic study of Cheyenne population by the United States Bureau of the Census seems to have been done the hard way, if not deliberately gerrymandered. The South Side area was divided into tracts, each were partly inside of the city and partly outside of the city. There were 7,243 people living south of the Union Pacific tracks inside of the city and 6,339 living outside of the city, a total of 13,582.

Tract 2, south of the Union Pacific Railroad, in the city	4,394
Tract 2, south of the Union Pacific Railroad, outside the city ...	94
Tract 3, south of the Union Pacific Railroad, in the city	2,795
Tract 3, south of the Union Pacific Railroad, outside the city ...	135
Tract 4, south of the Union Pacific Railroad, in the city	54
Tract 4, south of the Union Pacific Railroad, outside the city ...	6,110

The South Side Area Study, published by the City-County Planning Office December 28, 1981, addresses an expanded Fox Farm Road Community, south of I-80 and east of the Greeley Highway. The socio-economic data from the 1980 Census was available and provided useful information for future planning. The maps are more accurate than those used in the 1974 "Genesis Caper." The motive for the study came from the Tharpe family of Cheyenne Irrigated Gardens, who wished to subdivide their 4.5 acres into three lots for their own family.

The statement is made that the area (Fox Farm Road Community) is difficult to plan "*for*." Although the report seems intended primarily as a prospectus for the developer, it could be a valuable tool for future planning. Planning should be done *WITH the people* of the area, rather than for the exploitation of the real estate involved.

"The following individuals were consulted in preparation of this report: Shirley Francis, County Commissioner; Don Pack, Environmental Health; Don Heyne, Frontier Conservation Service; Mike Hackett, DEQ; Dennis Flynn, former County Sheriff; Red Jones, Fire District Number One; Floydine Gay, South Cheyenne Water and Sewer District; Neil Blair, President of the South Side Task Force and Donelle Fenwick, County Engineer's Office." Only Red Jones is a resident of the Fox Farm Road Community. The South Side Task Force is an organization of South Side business people created by the Cheyenne Chamber of Commerce.

Apparently no attempt was made to contact homeowners or to interview a cross-section of the people. However, residents of the area have been classified by the 1980 Census as to Age; Sex; Race; Marital Status; Year Round Housing Units; Dwelling Unit Status; Substandard/Overcrowded Units, having 1.01 persons per room; Median Housing Value; Household Type and Population Under 18 Years of Age.

Sixty-five percent of the population live in mobile home courts or "parks," numbers fluctuate, due to the economy and the condition of the construction business. Arp School has had as high as ninety percent turnover in some years, according to the Principal, Elmer Dykeman.

Enrollment in the South Cluster Schools	**1980**	**1981**	**1982**
Schools inside the city:			
Cole	296	302	316
Hebard	294	284	281
Goins	497	489	479
Schools outside the city:			
Arp	314	334	329
Rossman	278	282	279
Johnson Junior High School	583	748	738

The 1982 increase in enrollment at Johnson Junior High School was due to children being bussed from the Sun Valley area. The number of teachers and workers employed at these schools was not available.

Laramie County Community College has been steadily growing as indicated by the end of semester totals: Fall, 1980 — 5,181; Spring, 1981 — 5,797; Fall, 1981 — 5,652; Spring, 1982 — 6,065; Fall, 1982 — 6,465.

Racial Categories: 1980 Census, STFIA Tape Source, (compiled by South Side Area Study, Cheyenne-Laramie County Area Study).

(cy - 2)	**Total**	**White**	**Black**	**Indian**	**Asian**	**Other**
Cheyenne City	47,264	43,299	1,402/3%	246	380	1,937
South Side City	4,394	3,313	311/7%	47	43	680
Laramie County	21,385	19,828	565/2.6%	176	150	666
Fox Farm	2,850	2,643	41/1%	43	11	112

Number and Percentage of Spanish Origin

(cy - 3)	**Total**	**Percent**	
Cheyenne	5,382	11.39%	
South Side City	1,873	42.63%	
Laramie County	6,625	9.65%	(overall)*
Fox Farm	226	7.93%	

*Includes City of Cheyenne

POLITICAL SUB-DIVISIONS

Another population indicator is the South Cheyenne Water and Sewer Users Association. Floydine Gay, Secretary, says that there are 828 connections, as of November 1982, of which fifty are to mobile home parks. Of the 1,588 mobile home connections in the parks, 1,453 were in use. Each connection is taken to represent a single family occupancy.

The area served by the association includes Rossman and Arp Schools, the Laramie County Community College and Fire District Number One. It extends south to include the Race Car Tracks, businesses and homes along the South Greeley Highway and south of Fox Farm Road, as well as north of Fox Farm Road, east of House Avenue, also known as B3.

The South Cheyenne Water and Sewer District Number One and Fire District Number One are pioneer political subdivisions of Laramie County. The property owners of the area incorporated the districts, under State law, so that they could tax themselves to pay for these essential services. The Water and Sewer District was formed in 1960 and the Fire District in 1962.

The original bond for the sewer was paid off in 1981. In 1973, combined water and sewer bonds were refunded at a lower rate. The new bond will be paid off in March, 1991. Over fifty percent of the property owners and land area represented, according to State law, had to agree to annexation before the City of Cheyenne could sell water to the district.

Although the district buys its water from the City of Cheyenne, the people have no vote on water bonds, neither are there any representatives of the area serving on the Laramie County Regional Planning Commission. When asked why there were no representatives on the commission, an employee said that there was no one "qualified" out here.

At the present writing, the District's Waste-Water Treatment Plant is near capacity. The "201 Waste-Water Treatment Study" for the entire Cheyenne drainage area has recommended hooking the district lines into Cheyenne's Sewage Treatment System, which would be expanded under a Federal Environmental Protection grant through the Wyoming Department of Environmental Quality, to return safe, cleaned water to Crow Creek. It is expected that the plan will be implemented in the near future.

While the action has been made necessary through the extraordinary growth of the mobile home parks and Laramie County Community College, public acceptance of the responsibility for the environment, and the initiative to do something about it, is a matter of local pride.

Residents of the Fox Farm Road Community are not only "qualified" but entitled to representation in the decision-making process.

THE ENVIRONMENT

THE CITY DUMP SCANDAL

"Do no dishonor to the Earth,
Lest you Dishonor the Spirit of Man."

Henry Beston

Laura Kirk called early one crisp, blue October morning when the fences, roofs and trees sparkled with the season's first frost. Tumbleweeds piled in the fence-corner made a velvet throne for the "Frost King." A crystal-crusted newspaper hung limply over the three strands of barbed wire topping the six-foot wire fence enclosing the Burks and Company construction yard on Fox Farm Road. What a set for the "Nutcracker Ballet"!

Last night's roaring front was gone. The air was still. The steam at the refinery was going straight up. Laura's voice shook. Some frost fell from the telephone wires. (Did she do that?) We, too, were alarmed to learn that the City of Cheyenne had leased the mined-out gravel pit on Fox Farm Road across from her house and had begun to dump garbage into it!

"Isn't that against the law?" I asked. "They can't bring garbage and dump it right across the street, in front of a person's house, can they?"

"We are trying to find out," she said. "Can you come for coffee about two? We are getting the neighbors together. We will try to have some information and make plans. It is incredible that a city could be so ignorant and uncaring. Don't they know how dangerous it is to the health of the community? We will probably hire a lawyer."

Laura was a nurse. Her husband, Earl, worked for the telephone company. At last they had their little home in the country. They had worked and saved for it for so long. They had a cow, a nanny goat and some chickens. Laura made pets of them all. A road, now called Avenue C1, separated their place from the four acre pit.

It is almost forty years later. I will never forget the trauma of our first year back in my home town, Cheyenne. We had been happy when Ray's boss, G. W. Burks, an earth moving contractor, had bought the Blanchard Brothers construction yard on Fox Farm Road. There was an office, a big shop, six warehouses for equipment and supplies; and best of all, there was a house for the superintendent, Raymond R. Jones.

Except for the fact that the year was 1944 and World War II was going strong, on that rare breathless, iridescent morning, God was in his heaven and all was right in His world! The illusion melted like the frost.

I had grown up in Cheyenne. We were among friends. Patty was in the first grade at Johnson School. Although Cheyenne was swollen with wartime population, we were fortunate to have housing. There were "Wartime Housing Projects" and substandard trailer parks. Almost everyone had renters in their basements and attics.

When school started we realized that this was not going to be an ordinary year. There were over 1,000 children enrolled at Johnson, a school built for 350 children. The school board "solved" the problem by having eight shifts of first grade, four in the morning and four in the afternoon. Bus kids were on the morning shift. Patty was a bus kid.

I became a "battle-ax," going to Parent-Teachers' Association meetings, school board meetings, writing letters to newspapers, learning to organize meetings. There seemed to be an appalling lack of awareness, caring or planning, on the part of official Cheyenne, at the school board as well as at the municipal level.

"The war would soon be over," they said, "and all of these people will go away." Meanwhile, it was business as usual; and business was good.

We found that we could inspire people to action. We could turn out workers and make small gains. Children grow up. Wars come to an end. Problems are replaced with new ones.

Of all the ills a community is heir to, the problem that we were to face in 1944, would introduce us to the reality of the ever-growing monster "solid waste." We would develop, at first hand, an awareness of the danger to the environment, as perhaps few others have experienced it, in this great, wide, wonderful Wyoming.

My clipping books and the original carbons of all those letters to the papers and public officials, while incomplete, record the apathy and ignorance we faced. The state of the art had not developed much technology for handling the solid waste of a city, nor was there any willingness to bring Cheyenne into the twentieth century in this field.

Several neighbors had talked with city officials and the Wilsons who owned the pit, to no avail.

The *Tribune* carried the first of many newspaper stories of our historic battle, October 23, 1944, quote:

CITY FACING NEW THREAT

Location of Dump is Protested

City council members today faced threat of court action for the second time in one week.

Property owners on Campstool route east of Cheyenne, protested to city council members today in regard to the city dump adjacent to their property. Mrs. Earl Kirk, Box 48, represented the group. [Fox Farm Road had not been officially named at that time.]

In threatening court action, Mrs. Kirk asked Gus Fleischli, commissioner of streets and alleys, why the "city of Cheyenne started dumping into the pit before they had equipment ready to cover the refuse in order to avoid rats, odor and flies."

George L. Kemp, commissioner of finance, asked the property owners for "one week to get ourselves organized." Mrs. Kirk vehemently threatened court action after that time "if no clean-up was made."

Fleischli said that "eventually your property will be worth a great deal more, altho it may seem that the location of the dump is depreciating it now." The lots into which the refuse is being dumped by the city previously were "eye-sore" gravel pits, he said. Eventually, the pits will be filled and covered over, and the lots will be saleable, Fleischli noted. (end quote)

According to my clipping book, the neighbors had met several times with city officials, only to be discouraged by their stalling tactics. Patience was growing thin.

In reporting a fire on Lummis property north of the pit, due to wind-borne fiery debris at 3:20 on a Sunday morning, the *Tribune* stated that the site was one-fourth to one-half mile from the Fox Farm in Wilson's gravel pit.

The fire was one of many that filled our nights with horror.

The officials were "surprised" to learn that the people had finally filed suit asking that the council "be permanently enjoined from the dumping and disposing of garbage in the Wilson pit."

Wyoming Eagle, November 29, 1944:

CITY DUMP NEIGHBORS RAP ODORS

Nine persons took the witness stand in district court here yesterday to press their suit against the city council for an injunction to restrain the council from disposing of garbage in the Wilson gravel pit on the fox farm road.

First witnesses called by the group's attorney, J. A. Greenwood, were Mr. and Mrs. Earl Kirk, who testified they felt the value of their property had decreased materially due to odors emitted from the dump.

Raymond Jones, another resident of the area, told the court that since dumping of city garbage was begun at the gravel pit he and his family had noticed "very unpleasant odors" and many more flies in the area.

Asked during cross examination by City Attorney C. A. Lathrop if he knew whether the flies came from the dump, Jones replied, "I never followed any of them over."

"Did you ever notice a tractor down there?" asked Lathrop.

"Yes," answered Jones.

"Well, what was it doing?" asked the city attorney.

"Just generally stirring up the mess," Jones replied.

A. C. McClain testified residents of the area had met with the council on several occasions seeking removal of the dump and "the council kept promising in a day or two they would find another place, but never did." McClain said on a day when the wind blows hard "I can't recognize my place when I come home in the evening because of the papers and boxes that blow out of the pit and pile up against the fences and trees."

McClain told the court his renters had threatened to move if conditions were not improved. He testified he had examined the contents of the pit and found dead chickens, rotten vegetables and dead rabbits. Asked if the garbage was covered McClain said, "About half of it was covered and half of it was mixed with dirt."

Others testified they were constantly uneasy because of the fire hazard created at the dump and that they were embarrassed by the "sickening, stinking odor" which pervaded the air.

Greenwood rested his case late in the afternoon and the city called Commissioner of Streets and Alleys Gus Fleischli as its first witness.

Asked about the odor from the dump Fleischli said he had never "smelled anything, going by or coming around" the dump. He told the court the dump was infested with rats when the city leased it and that they had been eradicated through the use of lime and a tractor.

He testified that the fire hazard at the dump was to be eliminated through the use of an incinerator which would burn all boxes and papers.

Asked under cross examination by Greenwood "just how the tractor got rid of rats" Fleischli replied they were killed by the lime and then smashed into the dirt by the tractor.

"Oh, you kill them and then grind them up, is that it?" queried Greenwood.

"You testified that you found no odor at the dump, did you not?" asked Greenwood, "I did," Fleischli answered. "Have you ever been to the old dump on West 19th?" Fleischli replied that he had. "Did you notice an odor there?" was the next question. "Yes," replied Fleischli. "*Isn't that the same kind of garbage dumped in the present location as was dumped on West 19th?*" asked Greenwood. *Fleischli answered that it was but he had not noticed an odor at the new dump because the garbage there was being covered and he had not been there when it was not covered.*

"Then you don't know whether there is an odor emitting from the present dump or not, do you?" asked Greenwood. Fleischli replied that he didn't.

Asked if the dump wasn't "soft and spongy" Fleischli answered, "Not when that bulldozer goes over it. It gets pretty solid with 20 tons of weight on it."

"Yes, and when 20 tons more garbage is thrown in the odor gets pretty strong, doesn't it?" asked Greenwood.

The hearing adjourned about 6 p.m. until 9 this morning. Attorneys said they expected to conclude the hearing by noon.

November 30, 1944 *Tribune:*

The next day, City Attorney C. A. Lathrop called H. R. Wilson, who lives "on the bank of the pit," for the first witness. Wilson who owns the tract in which the pit is located, said that "the pit looks a great deal better now than before the city started dumping there."

Wilson said that there's more odor from Mrs. Bainbridge's hog farm than from the dump. Mrs. Mamie Bainbridge owns land directly south of the gravel pit. Wilson also stated that Mrs. Earl Kirk, who owns the residence to the west of the pit, came to him when she and her husband "bought their place and asked when the pit was going to be filled up."

Attorney James A. Greenwood representing residents protesting the use of the pit as a city dump, cross-examined Wilson with the question, "Do you mean that the garbage under your doorstep doesn't bother you at all?" Wilson's reply was "No."

Third witness called by the defense attorney was Willie Wilson, who lives at the H. R. Wilson residence, who stated that "before the city started dumping, the pit was a rat shooting gallery." He said he had not seen a rat since the first week in October when the "city took over."

Willie Wilson said that the grass, "as dry as it has been," enhances the fire hazard at the dump more than the paper brought to the pit by the collectors.

Walter Cotton, superintendent of streets and alleys, notified the court that prior to the time the city started dumping in the pit, the "sides were covered with dead animals — horses, chickens — all uncovered."

"INJUNCTION IS REFUSED IN DUMP ISSUE" *Wyoming State Tribune*, November 30, 1944:

An injunction to restrain the city of Cheyenne from dumping its garbage in the Wilson gravel pit on the Fox Farm Road was refused yesterday afternoon by District Judge Sam M. Thompson.

Attorney James A. Greenwood representing persons living in the vicinity of the pit and protesting the use of the pit for the depositing of garbage, declared today that "they were going on with the case."

Residents in the area met with their attorney last night and decided they would continue the fight against the council, "taking it to the state supreme court," if necessary.

Judge Thompson stated he was denying a temporary injunction, first, because the testimony showed that none of the residents lived close enough to the dump to be materially damaged by the odor.

Secondly, Thompson said, residents complained of the increase in flies in the area since dumping had begun there. He said he did not feel he could grant a restraining order on that ground due to the fact that this time of year flies either "die or hibernate" and thus would not constitute a nuisance this winter.

Regarding the plaintiff's contention that papers and trash blew off the garbage trucks and were scattered about the vicinity, Thompson said testimony showed that problem had been eradicated by the council through the use of screens on trucks hauling boxes and papers.

> "Neither have the plaintiffs offered any proof that decaying animal matter would drain into the resident's water supply," Thompson said.
>
> "The only nuisance shown therefore is odor," Thompson declared, "and the question is — *is the court justified in tying the hands of the city regarding the disposal of garbage because that nuisance exists?*"
>
> The removal of garbage in a city the size of Cheyenne is a necessary function, Thompson stated, and that while its disposal in a certain area may inconvenience some I am unable to find that it was a serious enough nuisance to authorize the granting of a temporary restraining order.

This statement by a man of some education illustrates the state of public understanding on the subject of "solid waste," a term that had not a yet come into general use, in November of 1944.

THE GARBAGE BALL

Wyoming Eagle, December 12, 1944 headline: "Group Reloads Guns for New Fight Against Dump."

> Fox Farm Road homeowners, who claim they got the "run around" in their battle to have the new city dump removed from the area, yesterday reopened their campaign with a surprise weapon — satire.
>
> In an advertisement telling the public to "laugh at trouble with us," the group will announce this week a "garbage ball" to be held Saturday night at Johnson School auditorium. A skit — a satire on life near the city dump — will be presented in pantomime during intermission at the dance, it was learned.
>
> Many attending the ball will wear aprons, overalls and other country costumes to carry out the country theme. Prizes will be awarded for the best costumes. Flower girls will offer corsages made up of vegetables. The dance will be advertised as a benefit affair.
>
> In a statement labeled, "The Facts," the Fox Farm Road residents declared yesterday that "the power of the press was demonstrated to the homeowners when city officials begged them to 'lay off the newspaper stuff.' " The group complied and got the "run around."
>
> Meanwhile, a spokesman revealed that the Laramie County Medical Society and the Cheyenne businessmen have been asked to consider the health and sanitation problems of the city dump in the midst of established homes.
>
> The neighbors assembled at the Jones' residence to write a skit to be presented during intermission at the "Garbage Ball." They made turnip orchids, carrot chrysanthemums and radish roses. They stuffed old socks to create rat puppets, which would be pulled across the stage set representing the city's dump.
>
> The J. C. Penney Store gave a "pair of shopworn corsets." Roedel's Drug Store gave a large window display sign for Chanel No. 5. The stage was set for a realistic "sanitized Dump," having a perfume of its own. Even the grapefruit rinds had been disinfected.
>
> Preceded by Ray Alcock, spraying perfume, Charlie Ahlbrandt, Earl Kirk and Cal McClain satirized the parts of the mayor and commissioners,

> visiting the City Dump and finding it altogether lovely. They shook hands and slapped backs, congratulating themselves. Little Jimmy McLees rode the freshly painted yellow tricycle with the attached bull-dozer, which was made by the mechanics in the Burks and Company shop. Jimmy went round and round the set, "grinding up the garbage with his 'twenty-ton dozer.' "

The "Garbage Ball" raised several hundred dollars for the legal battle, as well as an immeasurable amount of good public relations and neighborly cooperation.

There was a question as to whether the School Board would let us use the building for a dance. We convinced them that in Wyoming, schools are traditionally community centers, and we would continue to use them. They agreed that a dance would hurt the building no more than a meeting. Johnson School was our Community Center.

The ball helped to restore the community morale, as well.

Soon after the ball it was announced that Mayor Bruce S. Jones had called together a committee to discuss the advisability of acquiring land for garbage disposal. The committee consisted of Archie Allison, J. W. Walton, Cliff Bloomfield, Warren Richardson, J. A. Greenwood, Fred Warren, M. H. Chapman, R. J. Hoffman and Don Wageman.

After some discussion, it was proposed that the northeast quarter of Section 12, Township 13 North, Range 67 West, be investigated. A committee composed of Bloomfield, Allison, Wageman, Hoffman and members of the council visited the site.

The committee recommended that the city acquire the land with the least possible delay.

Our attorney, J. A. Greenwood, advised us to call off the publicity. He said, "The City wants to settle out of court. We must pursue a legislative solution."

Mrs. Maude Van Tassell protested that it was too close to her land on which was located the Van Tassell Terrace, a "wartime housing project."

The council was of the opinion that the only possible objection would be from the blowing of papers on a windy day. They proposed to erect a wire fence to "catch most of the papers."

At least, they were proposing to use "whole" land, so that there would be material for covering of the garbage. Civilization might yet bring a modicum of sanitation to solid waste disposal in Cheyenne.

The anger and frustration of the neighborhood was revealed in the many letters from residents. On January 2, 1945 Laura Kirk reviewed the situation to date in a letter to "VOICE OF THE PEOPLE," *Wyoming Eagle*: adding,

> Perhaps it is hard for you to visualize just what having a city dump in your midst would be like. Here are a few facts:

In July, 1944 a sample of water from the well on our property (E. R. Kirk) was examined by the state laboratory and found to be free from contamination. On October 30, 1944, (after the city had poured thousands of gallons of water daily for ten days into the pit, whose bottom is about the same depth as our well) another sample from this well was found to contain colon bacillus — the typhoid germ. It was found in amounts large enough to make the water unsatisfactory for domestic use, and our physician advised my husband and myself to take preventative shots for protection against this disease, which we did. A short time later a neighbor's well became contaminated with the same germ.

On December 26, 1944 a Walton Motor company service truck came past our place, dragging a dead horse, which they hauled over and deposited in the dump. Just as this was done, a city employee came over and made them remove it. Then he used my phone to call the foreman, Walter Cotton, who came out and instructed them where to dispose of it. Whereupon, they hauled it to another small pit in the vicinity, which, like the city pit is surrounded by houses, and dumped it there. A few shovels of gravel and frozen earth were its only cover. The next day, dogs had uncovered it.

Incidents of this type lead us to ask the following questions: See if you wouldn't like to know the answers too?

1. Where can dead animals be disposed of without trespassing on other people's rights?
2. What becomes of the money collected on parking meters? Is it available to the garbage fund?
3. Who was responsible for the accident to Wm. Ross, caretaker at the dump, and where was the foreman when it happened? (The man had been run over by a truck.)
4. Why is the city so insistent on maintaining their dump at this location over our protests, if $10 is the only sum they invested there?

The next day, George L. Kemp, City Commissioner of Finance, answered with a statement in the *Wyoming Eagle*, explaining that the parking meter money was not available to the garbage fund and that it was used to maintain the hard-surfaced streets. "All city accounts are published regularly, and the treasurer's office is audited by the state examiner's office yearly, and his report is published."

"Any information regarding any of the functions of this office are open to the citizens of Cheyenne at any time during office hours."

The *Wyoming Eagle*, Cheyenne, Wyoming, Friday, January 26, 1945, headlined: "LAY SIEGE TO BRESLAU." There, right in the middle of the war news was our news.

New Senate Bill Aimed at Garbage Disposal Problem.

Introduced in the Senate yesterday was a bill, which if it becomes law, will do what residents of the Fox Farm Road area have tried unsuccessfully to do for the past four months — halt the disposal of garbage in that vicinity immediately.

> The bill, S. F. 61, which was introduced by the senate committee on counties and municipalities, declares the disposal of offensive substances such as dead animals, refuse from butcher shops, spoiled fish, or any "putrid or decayed animal or vegetable matter, is a nuisance, and prohibits depositing of such matter by persons, cities or towns within a half-mile of any inhabited dwelling, public roadway or highway."
>
> Violators of the act would be guilty of a misdemeanor, and upon conviction would be subject to a fine of not less than $50 nor more than $200 and six months in the county jail.
>
> The Cheyenne city dump controversy dates back to Oct. 2, 1944, when the city council leased the abandoned Wilson gravel pit for use as a city dump.
>
> Since that time the residents of the area have been demanding its removal on the grounds that it was a menace to their health and safety.

Meanwhile, dumping continued. Our six-foot fence was so burdened by the debris, papers and cartons, rocking in the wind, that the steel posts, which had been set in cement, broke. Winds registered 105 miles per hour on several occasions. High winds were normal. We frequently woke to the sound of sirens in the night. We were about two blocks east of the pit.

We had found that there was nothing in the health and safety statutes to protect the people of Wyoming from having a dump move into a neighborhood of established homes.

We asked two Laramie County legislators to seek to amend the laws, so that no Wyoming citizens would ever again be subjected to such outrageous treatment.

State Senator W. A. (Pat) Norris, a Cheyenne machinery dealer, introduced an amendment, know as Senate File 61, in the Senate, where it passed. John Bell, a well-known Laramie County rancher, attended to its passage in the House. We were advised to ask for a committee hearing.

We are "working people." Husbands sent their wives. We "testified." Each of us, Laura Kirk, Grace Stallings, Elsie McClain, and I, Gladys Jones, made a statement, consisting of one point, briefly put. It was our first, ever, attempt at lobbying.

We backed this with letter writing to committee members, our own county delegation, state officials, the newspapers and five minute talks at club meetings. Almost everyone wanted a look at what kind of person would live out by the dump. *Were they unaware that the residents preceded the dump?*

Doctors K. L. McShane and Harry Newman came out and inspected the site. The Laramie County Medical Society sent a resolution to the legislature, as did the City Council of Parent-Teachers' Associations.

With a copy of S. F. 61 in hand, I would read, word for word, leaving out none of the fine detail as to the nature of the substances and objects which could not be deposited "within one-half mile of any inhabited dwelling, or within one-half mile of any public roadway and which shall be

S. F. No. 61 Introduced by Committee No. 7

A BILL

FOR

AN ACT relating to disposal of offensive substances, declaring such nuisances, prescribing penalties for violations and repealing Sections 32-709 and 32-710, Wyoming Revised Statutes, 1931.

Jan. 25, 1945. Introduced, Read first time, Referred to Committee No. 7, Delivered to Printing Committee.

Be It Enacted by the Legislature of the State of Wyoming:

Section 1. The depositing, placing, or causing to be placed or put, the carcass of any dead animal or the offal or refuse matter from any slaughter house, butcher shop, meat market, packing house, fish house, hog pen, stable, or any spoiled meats, spoiled fish, or any animal or vegetable matter in a putrid or decayed condition or which is liable to become putrid, decayed or offensive, or the contents of a privy vault, or any refuse or garbage or industrial waste, or any offensive matter or substance whatever upon or into any river, creek, bay, pond, canal, ditch, lake, stream, railroad right-of-way, public or private roadway, highway, street, alley lot, field, meadow, public place or public ground, or in any other and different locality, building, or establishment in this State so located that the said substances shall directly or indirectly cause or threaten to cause the pollution or impairment of the purity and usefulness of the waters of any spring, reservoir, stream, lake or water supply whether surface or subterranean, which are used wholly or partly as a source of public or domestic water supply, or where the same may become a source of annoyance to any person, or within one-half mile of any inhabited dwelling [amended: with exception of the dump caretaker], or within one-half mile of any public roadway, by any person or persons, association of persons, company or corporation, incorporated city, incorporated or unincorporated town in the State of Wyoming, or the knowingly permitting of such acts by the owner, tenant, or occupant of said places, upon, into, or on said places, or the permitting of said offensive substances or other offensive substances to remain thereon or therein, shall be unlawful and is hereby declared to constitute a nuisance detrimental to the public health and general welfare of the citizens of Wyoming.

Section 2. Any person violating the provisions of this Act shall be guilty of a misdemeanor and upon conviction thereof shall be punished by a fine of not less than fifty dollars nor more than two hundred dollars or shall be imprisoned in the county jail not to exceed six months, or shall be punishable by both such fine and imprisonment.

Section 3. Sections 32-709 and 32-710, Wyoming Revised Statutes, 1931, are hereby repealed.

Section 4. This Act shall be in force upon and after its passage and approval.

unlawful and hereby declared a nuisance detrimental to the public health and general welfare of the citizens of Wyoming."

Unfortunately, for enforcement, we found the penalties to be inadequate but always encouraged our listeners to write or call the following legislators: Robert J. Rymill, Ft. Laramie, Chairman, Senate Committee on Counties and Municipalities; A. H. Cordiner, Laramie; Roy Chamberlain, Lusk; E. Harold Josendahl, Casper; and W. A. (Pat) Norris, Cheyenne, sponsor of the bill.

Josendahl offered an amendment to delete "burning," since Casper, at that time had a burning dump. Another amendment was to "exempt the house of the dump caretaker" from the law.

A. H. Cordiner, Laramie, Chairman of the Senate Medical and Sanitation Committee was already getting letters from his constituents at the time of the hearing. John K. Phifer, Wheatland and Dr. J. A. Farlien of Worland, on that committee were sympathetic.

In the House of Representatives, John Bell of Iron Mountain, Laramie County, was a member of the Medical and Sanitation Committee.He participated in the joint committee hearing, making us feel at ease when we made our statements. Cecil Bon, Committee Chairman; Dr. C. H. Carpenter, both of Casper; Earl Chamberlain, Torrington; E. F. Shaw, Cody; Elmer D. Kinnamon, Rawlins; Orrin D. Jenkins, Afton; and Donald Hubbard of Laramie were attentive and encouraging. One of the legislators commented that they had never received so much mail in favor of a bill.

We had been told that the House Committee on County Affairs might be against the bill. Roscoe C. Austin, Newcastle, was Chairman. Clarence W. Brock, Casper; William Henry Harrison, later to be U.S. Congressman, Dayton; Glenn W. Hardy, and James Bentley of Sheridan; Louis Boschetto, Rock Springs and William E. Holland of Buffalo, made up the committee. We were worried.

At the hearing, I read from my hand-written notes: (They are still preserved in my scrapbook.)

"We think that S. F. 61 is constructive legislation. It will not only protect the rural community from abuses of this kind but it will encourage municipalities to keep their *outskirts safe for future growth.*

No matter how a city dump is cared for, it is a breeding place for flies. I live two blocks east of the dump and never saw flies around a stable worse than at my back door this last fall. I nearly went out of my mind fighting them with the baby going in and out. When I see a fly disturbing my sleeping child, or it comes to my table, I have very uneasy thoughts. I think of the seventeen disease germs which have been found on house-flies and wonder?

It will soon be spring and the thought of epidemics sweeping the schools is a very real possibility."

Speaking at a club meeting, I was asked, "How can you bear to talk about such things?" I answered, "I sincerely think that this legal language is purest poetry. In it, high ideals are expressed concerning the lowliest of situations, for the benefit of humanity and the environment."

On February 20, 1945, Governor Lester C. Hunt signed the bill, making it law, "to be in force upon and after passage and approval." Although the bill was regarded as landmark legislation, establishing the rights of citizens to be safe from abuses through the disposal of solid waste in a manner "detrimental to public health and the general welfare," the battle would have to be fought over and over again, as new barbarians came to power.

In spite of the success of the publicity and the passage of the new legislation, it was the following January before our new case could be brought to court. The neighbors said that the city was being more careful and it was *buying more dirt to cover the garbage.* A newspaper article pointed out the increased costs of garbage collection. An advertisement quoted the new rates to taxpayers.

When school was out, our family went out on a construction job in western Wyoming. We were spared the miserable summer with a garbage dump for a neighbor.

In a change of venue, Judge V. J. Tidball had been assigned to the case. On the evidence presented, the City of Cheyenne was enjoined from using the dump for garbage disposal after the first of May, 1946. "No dead animals of any kind were permitted to be deposited and all other garbage shall be covered with six inches of dirt, each day, and that the city should maintain enough equipment and manpower to see that this is done; The court further finds that on or before May 1, 1946, when dumping has ceased, the City of Cheyenne should be required to cover the area designated as said dump with 24 inches of dirt." (Copy of entire verdict follows:)

THE STATE OF WYOMING)
) ss.
COUNTY OF LARAMIE)

IN THE DISTRICT COURT
FIRST JUDICIAL DISTRICT

ARTHUR McCLAIN, et al.,)
Plaintiffs)
vs.)
THE CITY OF CHEYENNE,)
a Municipal Corporation, et al.,)
Defendants)

Doc. 29. No. 122

DECREE

The above entitled matter came on for trial on the merits on the 29th day of December, 1945, pursuant to assignment, before the Honorable V. J. Tidball, District Judge of the Second Judicial District, to whom the case had been assigned for trial, the plaintiffs being present in person and represented by their attorneys of record, A. Joseph Williams and James A. Greenwood of Cheyenne, Wyoming, and the defendant being represented by its officials and its attorney, Carleton A. Lathrop of Cheyenne. The parties having announced themselves as ready for trial, the court proceeded to hear the testimony offered in behalf of the parties; and having declared the testimony closed, argument was then heard by counsel representing said parties and the Court then took the matter under advisement. Being now sufficiently advised in the premises, the Court finds that the disposal of garbage under the disposal system established by the evidence, in and upon Prosser Tract No. 17, constitutes a nuisance to those plaintiffs living in the vicinity of said Prosser Tract No. 17 and referred to in the evidence as being the garbage dump; and that the City should be enjoined from using said dump for garbage disposal after the 1st of May, 1946.

The Court further finds that the City should be allowed to continue using said garbage dump from the date of the entry of this decree to the date of May 1, 1946, under the following conditions:

(1) That no dead animals of any kind will be deposited by the City or permitted to be deposited by others in the garbage dump;

(2) That all other garbage shall be covered each day by at least six (6) inches of dirt, and that the City shall maintain enough equipment and man-power there to see that this is done;

(3) That if any papers escape from the dump or the trucks hauling the garbage to the dump, the City shall immediately collect and bury such papers.

The Court further finds that on or before May 1, 1946, when dumping has ceased, the City should be required to cover the area designated as said dump ground with 24 inches of dirt.

NOW THEREFORE, IT IS HEREBY ORDERED AND DECREED that the City of Cheyenne be enjoined from using said dump located on Prosser Tract No. 17 for garbage disposal after the first day of May, 1946.

IT IS FURTHER ORDERED AND DECREED that between now and May 1, 1946, the City be permitted and allowed to continue using the said dump for garbage disposal under the following conditions:

(1) That no dead animals of any kind will be deposited by the City or permitted to be deposited by others in the garbage dump;

(2) That all other garbage shall be covered each day by at least six (6) inches of dirt, and that the City shall maintain enough equipment and man-power there to see that this is done;

(3) That the City shall immediately proceed to gather, collect, and bury papers which have spread upon the property of plaintiffs in the vicinity of said Prosser Tract No. 17, from said dump or from trucks hauling material to said dump in the past, and any papers which shall be similarly so spread or scattered, from the date hereof.

(4) That said City shall immediately on May 1, 1946, or any date prior thereto when it discontinues the dumping of garbage on said Prosser Tract, cover the entire garbage dump area with at least 24 inches of dirt.

To all of which findings, order and decree the parties hereto are each granted an exception to each and every provision thereof, and to the whole thereof.

Dated this 18th day of January, 1946.

/s/ V. J. TIDBALL, Judge.

Approved as to form:

/s/ John J. Miller
/s/ Carleton A. Lathrop
Attorneys for Defendants.

The new pit southwest of the city went into operation. A high chicken-wire fence was erected to catch the paper, there was daily covering, however, no scientific plan was followed for the operation of the dump (landfill).

A new subdivision sprang up between the dump and US 85, the "South Greeley Highway." Windblown debris was an acute problem for the residents. These people were not as patient as the Fox Farm Road group. One day, the mayor found garbage decorating his lawn.

We had always watched the legislature to guard against erosion of our protection against the dumping. In 1961 we missed some new legislation passed to allow cities and towns to fill in "low ground" or holes with refuse. (However, it required the permission of nearby residents.)

"The price of liberty is eternal vigilence."

In 1965, the city again started to dump refuse into an old city-owned pit, south of the original Wilson-City Dump pit of 1944, between Avenues C1 and C2. The neighbors retained Walter B. Phelan, former Laramie County Attorney and State Representative, to do their talking.

In a letter to Mayor Bill Nation, Commissioners Herbert Kingham and George Dubois, May 6, 1965, Phelan cited the 1961 law. They did not have the permission of the neighbors. Further, the pit was surrounded by residents, and it was in violation of the one-half mile limit of our hard-won protection.

The city immediately ceased operation.

The landmark legislation of 1945, having survived several recodifications, is now numbered 35-10-101 through 107. We consider this body of law to be an extension of the Constitution. We could get enforcement by the State Health Department.

All of the pits in the East Fox Farm Road area, have been and are, within one-half mile of one or more residences; making all of these dumps and so-called "reclamations," illegal.

The residents have the only "*grandfather right.*"

THE ENLIGHTENED SEVENTIES

A pink dollop of wild plum jelly missed the muffin and landed on the front page of the *Wyoming Eagle*, dateline, June 29, 1974. The headline read: "RELOCATING OF CITY DUMP UNDER STUDY." Trauma time, again!

Members of the "Project Genesis" committee were recommending that city and county officials move the Cheyenne landfill to the gravel pits on Fox Farm Road, according to Don Carlson, a member of the "planners."

I reread the article in disbelief! Incredible! Worse, I had to wait until Monday to call and try to reason with the "planner" quoted in the article. Don't they keep records? Haven't they learned anything from history or the laws?

The people of the Fox Farm Road Community had taken the problem to the legislature and the court and found justice. We would not tolerate this abuse again!

There was more:

"Before the relocation there would be an economic impact study, an engineering study and a sociological study done," said Carlson.

"If after the engineering and environmental studies have been completed," said Carlson, "the site is unsuitable for the deposit of refuse, it is still an excellent site for construction waste."

When I finally contacted him by phone, he told me that there would be no smell, no flies. They would use chemical deodorants! I tried to explain to him about the permeability of the gravel soil. The residents of the Fox Farm Road Community had been forced to bond themselves to create a Water and Sewer District due to the contamination of the wells caused mainly by the dumping in the gravel pits.

He agreed that there would be the inconvenience of papers blowing, temporarily.

I explained the law to him, quoting the more explicit language, language that had been on the books since early statehood days. In 1945 it had been amended to include a ban on dumping within one-half mile of established residences. Demolition waste, rubble, rock and dirt were not excluded.

"No problem, we will get the law changed," he said.

"Since you have not completed your study," I said, "be sure to take into account the cost of earth to cover your 'sanitary landfill,' there being none in the pits, plus the cost of litigation."

My next call was to Jack Mabee, then County Commissioner. He seemed surprised that I objected to the plan. The commissioners had been told that everyone out here wanted the pits to be filled. Again, I quoted the law. If anyone wanted a dump, it couldn't be a resident, except, perhaps, a gravel pit owner.

Since the "City Dump Scandal" of 1944 I had studied and participated in issues dealing with the environment, especially with regard to "solid waste." It seemed to be a subject that few people were willing to think about, much less act upon. Sensational headlines may fool some, but not the people of Fox Farm Road!

According to Webster, "Ecology, in sociology, is the relationship between human groups with reference to material resources, and the consequent social and cultural patterns." The saga of Fox Farm Road is a classic example of disregard for these relationships.

When the City and County Zoning ordinances appeared in 1971, I studied them carefully and wrote my recommendations to the Planning and Zoning Commission, pointing out that Solid Waste had not been properly addressed. Also better definitions of "Open Space" were needed. Regulations should be more specific, else, a "pandora's box" of problems would explode. I could not believe that the "planners" had so little scientific knowledge of the issues.

As for solutions, gravel pits could be reclaimed through sloping the sides, contouring or terracing, and seeding with grasses to make pastures or recreational areas. No new permits should be given without an agreement to reclaim the land through acceptable conservation methods. (I keep a copy of that letter on file.) Permits should not be given in residential areas.

December 2, 1965, the City of Cheyenne had acquired 1,042 acres of land, twelve miles west of the city "to be used as a Sanitary Landfill." It was whole land and there were no near neighbors to endanger, providing leachate water did not filter down into the underground water since the site lay in the city well field. At last, Cheyenne seemed ready to live at peace with the environment. It would be a long haul, however.

Solid waste is one of the greatest problems of civilization and we are all a part of the problem. All of us should accept some of the responsibility for it. After thirty years in the soil conservation business, we welcomed land use planning and the awakening to the necessity for protecting our own place in the environment.

The planning process had begun quietly in 1957 with enabling legislation. I had lobbied for it enthusiastically. The laws were compiled in 1965, after court challenge. We looked forward to the "ENLIGHTENED SEVENTIES."

Cheyenne was preoccupied with her new toys, Urban Renewal, Model Cities and "Revenue Sharing." New carpetbaggers were running around, making speeches, administering new programs, furnishing new offices. It seemed harmless. Officials were happy with it.

Our old Irish neighbor once observed that "Cheyenne is like the innkeeper's daughter, she takes up with every drummer who steps off the cars."

There were some new drummers in town.

A month before the "Genesis Project" was ready, Peter Inniss, the new program manager for the project, launched an intensive, all media, propaganda campaign, explaining the project to *Wyoming Eagle* Staff-Writer, Craig Watts.

I read the article, interspersing my own comments.

"LANDFILL SAID BEST SYSTEM FOR SOLID WASTE DISPOSAL."

"The most economical and environmentally sound system available to Laramie County for the disposal of solid waste is the landfill," said Peter Inniss. [Agreed.]

"Several resource recovery and energy generation systems, ranging from heat recovery incineration to material recovery plants to recycling were examined," said Inniss. [How safe are they?]

"Ecological and energy considerations," said Inniss, "may in the future make these systems extremely viable for these areas [Laramie County] especially if technological advances make the development and operation more economical." [Someday, when we know what we are talking about.]

"To use the word 'dump' when talking about a sanitary landfill is erroneous," said Inniss. "A true sanitary landfill presents no problems of vectors, visual blight or water pollution," he said.

[Right! According to the American Society of Civil Engineers: "A sanitary landfill is a method of disposing of refuse on land without creating nuisances or hazards to public health or safety by utilizing the principles of engineering to confine the refuse to the smallest practical volume, and to cover it with a layer of earth at the conclusion of each day's operation or at more frequent intervals, as may be necessary."

Whereas; a gravel pit is a hole in the earth, from which the contents have been removed, and sold or made into cement products, it is not a suitable repository for refuse, since there is no earth to be used for cover.

And Whereas; the nature of gravel and gravelly soil is porous, allowing water to filter rapidly through the gravel bed, carrying leachate material with it, to contaminate the ground-water, a gravel pit is not a suitable repository for refuse.

And Whereas; each person in the United States is estimated to consume over twenty-seven tons of gravel and by-products in highway and other construction annually; to fill all of these holes in the ground with refuse could irrevocably damage our future drinking water supply.

Further: it would be very expensive to buy enough earth for adequate daily cover.] But read on:

"Flies and other insects can be controlled through the use of biological and chemical control procedures," said Inniss. [Not on Fox Farm Road!]

He reminded people that, with the transition to the "no burning" ordinance, more than 38,000 tons of solid waste will have to be taken to the land-fill. He offered to demolish and haul away the useless ashpits for Cheyenne residents. [End of article.]

All of the publicity in the weeks that followed the announcement brought stepped-up promiscuous dumping in all of the pits, in our driveways, and more trespassers crossing our property to get to the off-road pits, regardless of signs and warnings; as if an invitation had been issued.

We held a small meeting. We reviewed our past problems that led to the protective laws, which gave us our "grandfather rights" to be safe from that pollution. My file containing a copy of the law, Judge Tidball's decree upholding it, some letters and clipping books, strengthened our resolve.

We would fight it.

On August 18, 1974, the *Wyoming Eagle* carried a double banner headline, Pat McKenna was the by-line reporter.

"REPORT FINISHED ON GRAVEL PIT LANDFILL."

McKenna's article began: "A report on the proposal of moving the city's sanitary landfill operation from west of Cheyenne to the gravel pit area southeast of the city was released Thursday amid ready-made and vocal opposition.

Three major studies were made under an Environmental Protection Agency grant of $44,500 to develop a solid waste disposal report for the county and its municipalities under the title of Project Genesis.

The final report, released last night, the Project Genesis conclusions and recommendations, will follow the previous studies — the engineering report and the environmental impact report — to city, county, state and federal officials for their study and recommendations."

The reporter quoted Inniss' acknowledgement that, "the filing of law suits is a very vivid reality and must be weighed along with other factors when considering the merits of the project."

Art Buffington, Chief of our Fire District, a veteran with much experience fighting fires in the private dumps in the gravel pits was quoted as saying, "We're gonna make Watergate look tame as far as this area is concerned."

Buffington referred to a "law passed about twenty years ago that prohibits a dump within one-half mile of a residence, stream or county road, according to Gladys Jones, also a resident of the vicinity." (Actually it was 1945.)

Inniss said that "the pits could serve Cheyenne and the surrounding area for an estimated twenty-three years." He was careful to leave a loop-hole, however. "Further study of the water problems was also recommended as a possibility exists that despite available technology ground water could be polluted with chemical leachates."

A good forty column inches was devoted to this propaganda.

The taxpayers should have gotten a water study for the pricetag of $44,500 in addition to the other pretentious "studies" prepared by VTN Wyoming, the consulting firm, in the author's opinion.

There was little in the bulky study that could not be found in the average engineering textbook. The environmental impact study was full of assumptions. Maps were erroneous, as were ownerships of the pits.

While it is possible to seal a basin or pit, a safe leachate drainage system must be provided. This is a costly process. It needs only to be done if there is no alternative place to make a sanitary landfill, as in extremely wet ground with a high water table.

Our neighborhood meeting decided that we did not have to allow garbage to be brought in. Some of us remembered what it was like in 1944-45. All we wanted was enforcement of 35-10-101.

We decided to take a petition to the County Commissioners. We worded it together, as I typed. We made arrangements to explain the law at the next meeting of the Arp Parent-Teachers' organization. The school is close to the gravel pits. The children often took shortcuts through Read's and McCard's private dumps. Parents worry. We gave McKenna a news release.

There was television coverage at the school and many people signed the petition that night. They ran out of blanks at the Union Pacific shops and used plain paper. A petition also came from the students at Laramie County Community College.

Three hundred neighbors and friends signed the petition. We took it to the County Commissioners meeting, November 12, 1974. They voted down the Genesis Plan!

Why are people so trusting of anything called a "study" paid for with government funds? Why do they not study the issues and participate in the process more fully? Who do they think "government" is? Whose money pays for these phony studies? How can we make the consulting firms liable for the validity of their plans?

As for the people of the Fox Farm Road Community, all we could do was to try to stay "on alert" and try to deter the dumpers, to watch for and report fires in the demolition pits and hang on to hope in a high wind that the State Land Use Laws would exert some authority over local governmental abuses of the environment and the rights of citizens.

Our neighbors, Francis and Florence Bennett, have had serious problems with the city-owned open dump pit north of their property on Fox Farm Road. Florence and I attended all the meetings and seminars in the process for "Land Use and Comprehensive Planning" held in our area.

In these meetings, professional people, legislators and public officials involved in the disciplines of the environment and commerce, agriculture and urban development provided expertise, while the broad cross-section of public opinion was represented in the report to the legislature.

Perhaps no other legislature had been so well briefed on an issue by its constituents. Still, special interest groups put as many rocks in the road as possible.

Sponsors of the Land Use Bill, H. B. 321, Alan Simpson, R., of Cody, and Walter Urbigkit, D., of Cheyenne, invited me to make a statement at the public hearing, February 5, 1975. In my statement, which I sent to all legislators, I tried to condense thirty years of experience as a victim of this governmental abuse, which began with unregulated gravel mining, followed by unregulated garbage dumping. (In the Enlightened Seventies, garbage is called "Solid Waste.")

Citing the infamous and costly Genesis Project as an attempt to deprive citizens of the protection we had gained under the law passed in 1945, which explicitly described the "refuse" that cannot be deposited within a half-mile of an established residence, stream or public road, I urged passage of the bill.

We asked that the laws guarantee this protection, build in enforcement, and insure that the firms and persons submitting plans are responsible for the fact and validity of the plans they present.

The lengthy bill passed and was signed into law by Governor Ed Herschler. We waited impatiently for the regulations on solid waste to be published and hearings to begin.

Finally, September 11, 1975, Florence and I attended the hearing in the Hathaway Building. We listened to disgruntled mobile-home park operators and city managers, at length. Finally the chairman announced, "Well, that about winds it up, if any of you have any other points to make, we will take it up after the break."

I stood up and asked if they would be interested in the viewpoint of a housewife? (I sensed a mild surprise.) They decided to humor me.

About four o'clock I made a short plea for passage of the regulations and strict enforcement, urging stronger regulations for the statewide problem of septic tank dumping.

Acknowledging that the average person does not willingly develop a cultural interest in solid waste, I pointed out that the people of Fox Farm Road had had the problem thrust upon them by local government. Not even the Game and Fish Department with a dead antelope on their hands should be permitted to deposit it in a neighborhood pit within 150 feet of a residence!

When the approved regulations came out, we worried that our old reliable protection of the 1945 law had not been incorporated into the new rules. We were told that they still applied. True, they were listed in: "Section 1. Authority," *Solid Waste Management, Rules and Regulations*, 1975, published by the Wyoming Department of Environmental Quality.

Since a neighborhood pit owner had been permitted to operate a "Sanitary Land Fill" by the Land Quality division as a "mine reclamation," within 600 feet of residences, we doubted that the planners and administrators had consulted the "Authority" references. We did get garbage dumping stopped there. The law, 35-10-101, should be spelled out in the regulations, and posted on the office wall.

No new gravel pits of five acres or less may be made under the Land Quality law. Too late for Fox Farm Road, most of the gravel is gone. The big operators haul it in to the plants from new pits on the Hereford Bluffs.

New regulations require contouring and sloping, terracing and reseeding, returning the mined-out land to usefulness, without the dangers of dumping. Some 10.3 acres have been reclaimed. Nature unaided has reclaimed several pits, where dumping has been kept out. Trees grow. Ducks nest.

The Enlightened Seventies drew to a close with a fine set of laws to protect the Air Quality, Land Quality, and Water Quality, with Solid Waste Management finally given the recognition it deserves in the ecology and orderly growth of Wyoming. Enforcement capabilities are being severely tested.

The Fox Farm Road experience has been a laboratory of land abuse, leading to water pollution, social problems, and finally, remedial measures to protect the environment. Much has been accomplished. Pits are being closed under careful supervision. There have been no recent fires under the new methods.

We again have reason to hope.

IT'S THE PITS

These excerpts from my journals recall the fears we have endured over the years, from fires and other nuisances in the pits: In 1971, before there were any buildings at Read's gravel pit, dumping began. It was about the time that the beautiful old Carnegie Library was demolished.

Once this dumping began, people made their contributions of refuse of all kinds. It became open season for dumping in all of the neighborhood pits. Ours was posted, "KEEP OUT." Our neighbors to the west did not allow dumping either.

Our complaints were ignored by the big company and by the county. Only the State Health Department could get any action. They would remind local officials that dumping of refuse within one-half mile of an established residence or the public highway was illegal. All of the pits in the Fox Farm Road area are within one-half mile of both homes and highway. The law, however, does not cover demolition waste, and the Health Department did not have the staff or the inclination to do more.

July 5, 1971. (At home recovering from tick fever.) Decided to pull some rhubarb. It is too dry. Won't pull properly. Two men in a faded red pickup drive onto the Read property. They empty two barrels of black oil down the face of the fill. Fools! I go to get the garden hose to water the rhubarb. On my return, I see flames leaping up, orange-red. A black cloud rolls over the neighborhood, over Anderson's house and Turk Avenue.

I went in to call the Fire Department. I was not close enough to get the license number but I know that truck. They didn't stay to watch.

Although our volunteer firemen worked late that night, they could not put the fire completely out. It smoldered and broke out again the next day. The fire department made many trips in the days that followed.

Monday, July 12: Called Fire Department, then Commissioner Vosler. I explained to him that demolition waste is a fire hazard. It attracts other dumping. Sloping and reseeding is a better way to reclaim land. An asthmatic neighbor went to the hospital on account of the smoke. Elderly folks, especially, suffered. The smoke penetrated our closed houses, in July! My lungs hurt.

The commissioner was amused that we did not want the pits to be filled. This fire continued to smolder and break out, until the snow and rains of the following spring finally put it out. There were many other fires in that pit.

THE BURIAL OF THE BARRELS

August 12, 1978, 8:45, Sunday morning: Somebody is digging a big hole with a bulldozer in McCard's pit, south of our house, in the Southwest "L". (Why Sunday morning?) Dirt piles higher, blocking our view of the hole. We breakfast and read the paper.

At 9:30 a stake truck arrives, green chassis, load of barrels, piled one layer above the stakes. It is followed by a white truck with a "cherry-picker" on it. Dirt is piled too high to see names on the trucks, if any.

A man in white coveralls, hard hat and elbow length black gloves, stands out in front of the truck on the dirt pile and directs the unloading of the barrels, which disappear into the hole. A second truck is unloaded. Dozer fires up and covers the hole.

By 11 o'clock, it is all over. Everyone leaves. What was left behind? Do we now have chemical waste, as well as methane producing refuse in that dump? What would fire do there?

August 13: Call Solid Waste Division, State Department of Environmental Quality.

THE FIRES OF APRIL

There are so many fires, large and small, in all of the pits. Grass fires, trash fires; children playing, they said. Fires singly and in series; take April 1980:

April 11, Friday: Fire in Read's pit, 6 o'clock P.M. Called 911. Then called the owner. "There's a fire in your ---- pit," I said. "I know," said the owner's wife, "the fire department just called." "Well, I called them. Get out here and take some responsibility for it." "We are on our way," she said. Soon their four-wheel-drive came into my viewfinder.

April 15, Tuesday: While I was at the grocery, about 2:45, fire at Read's again. Ray reported it. Fire soon out.

April 20, Sunday: Poured at Art Center Reception. Fire, Read's again. Same place as last time.

That evening, 7:15: Fire at McCard's pit. Fire Department left, 9 o'clock P.M.

April 24, Thursday: 11 o'clock P.M. Siren at bedtime, McCard's pit.

April 27, Sunday, 1:45 P.M.: Fire at Read's again. Same place as last time! The fire department got them to bring a dozer and cover well with dirt. (Was it spontaneous combustion? Chemicals?)

ON ALERT

We are constantly on alert, never passing the south windows without a glance toward the pits. I am usually the one who calls the fire department.

March, 1982, St. Patrick's Day: We moved into this house thirty-three years ago today. We are listening to KRAE. County Commissioner, Jack Humphrey, is on interview, discussing the recently completed Laramie County Land Use Plan. The commercial came on. I went to get some coffee. Through the back door I could see a sheet of flame and smoke. I ran to call 911. Just then I heard a siren.

I took another look. There are people out on the fill. A dozer is coming. I called KRAE. I asked if Jack Humphrey is still there? "Yes, he is." "Then tell him, if he wants to see what it is like to have a dump on fire in the neighborhood, to come on out. McCard's pit, south of Fox Farm Road is on fire again."

I put on my coat, grabbed the camera and went out to join Ray and our neighbor Jim Hammond, at the back of our lot, watching. The wind is blowing a gale.

A piece of burning debris, flying through the air, lands in the fence corner, starting another fire. Fire is burning in two other places on the fill of "demolition" waste. Someone put out the fire in the fence corner with a hand extinguisher. The radio says that the wind is up to forty miles per hour, with higher wind gusts.

In 1969 gravel pits were zoned "Industrial." The McCards acquired a mined-out pit from Henry Wilson. For a time they had a garbage route, until the neighbors got wind of it! We have seen tank dumping there, countless plastic bags and trash of all kinds. They have a permit from the Solid Waste division, Department of Environmental Quality, for "demolition waste," less than 600 feet from several residences.

Tom Bauman, operator of Radio Station KRAE drives up. We talk. I gave him background on the pits and the laws being broken, which were put in place in 1945. We are on the air, live!

The water does its work. The firemen leave about 12:30.

The owners cover with dirt all afternoon. I report the fire to the Solid Waste division, Department of Environmental Quality. An inspector came out.

March 18, Thursday, 7 o'clock A.M.: Smoke at both ends of the fill. They haul dirt and cover all day. Still working about 10 o'clock P.M.

March 19, Friday: Took pictures about 7 o'clock A.M. Light dusting of snow. Steam or smoke emanating from the face. They bring more dirt.

March 20, Saturday, 10:25 P.M.: Called 911. Sheets of flame toward the west end of the fill. I see it through Hammond's pine trees. It looks like a forest fire. Fire truck arrives quickly. It leaves at 11:15 P.M.

March 21, Sunday: I can see no smoke at McCard's dump. They are hauling dirt in the morning. They leave piles near the face, near the trouble spots.

March 23, 7 o'clock A.M.: Smell smoke. Look out and see it coming from the east end of the fill. I call McCard. They bring more dirt.

April 7, 6:10 A.M.: Dump is smoking, north face, near the original fire. Someone comes and shovels dirt on it, from the pile. Later, trucks hauling dirt, which is dumped on the fire.

April 20, 7 o'clock A.M.: Tried to get a picture of light smoke coming from east end of the fill. We could smell smoke frequently but it was not visible since last entry.

April 22, 5:30 A.M.: Fill smoking, same place. Waited until 8 o'clock A.M. Called all agencies.

April 23, 5:30 A.M.: Smoking again. (Where there is smoke?)

April 24, 5:30 A.M.: East end smoking.

April 27, 11:45: Smoke puffing out, same place, east end.

April 28, Midnight: Woke smelling smoke. Was about to call 911. Someone drove into the yard. I turn on the porch light. The driver banged on the door. He yelled, "Your yard is full of smoke, there is smoke out on the highway. I can't see where it is coming from." I thanked him and told him that it is from McCard's dump. I was just about to call the Fire Department." He left. The fire department came and worked about thirty-five minutes. The McCards worked until about 2 o'clock A.M. I don't seem to be sleeping very well lately.

April 29: Report latest event to Solid Waste, Department of Environmental Quality.

June 22, 1982: "Cease and Desist" orders were issued to Dwain McCard, at last.

September 15, 1982: A permit for "Demolition Landfill" has been reissued, allowing them to fill adjoining pits owned by the Simon/Read interests, in Clearview Tracts, according to a specific plan, requiring earth cover and a berm separating the fill from neighboring pits, where dumping is not allowed.

The work is being closely inspected by the Solid Waste Division, Department of Environment Quality.

They are apparently following the plan, although the neighborhood is skeptical as to whether other wastes can be kept out. No community should be so endangered by the operation of "demolition waste landfills," within one-half mile of our homes and schools.

We would like to see the regulations of the Wyoming Environmental Quality Department include the protection of 35-10-101, the Health and Safety Law, verbatim, in all of its explicit detail, so that no permits would be given which would violate the right of citizens to be safe in their homes from this danger to the environment. (See copy of 35-10-101 through 107, page 168.)

GENESIS

by Gladys Jones

Speak to me of GENESIS, Speak to me of EARTH,
And the new Mountains that rose from the SEA,
Greater than any Mountains, and the Waters rushed down Them
To return to the SEA,
And the Waters rushed down them in Rivers,
Tearing down the Mountains, and Grinding them to Dust.
Bearing Boulders and Stones, Bearing Gravel and Sands
To Riffles and Placers, on the New Risen LAND.
And Covering Them with new Mud and fine Soil,
Covering Them cozy as Beans in a Pod,
A Lenticular Pod.

TIME and the River left it to Sod,
And it Sodded, a Beautiful MOTHER EARTH SOD,
With its Grasses and Briers and Brushes,
And Wild, Wild Roses
And Berries and Pods,
In a Place Known Only to GOD.

MAN came one Day, came Digging, and Found the Placer
of Gravel and Sand,
He took it up and Mixed a New Mud, a Concrete, and Spread IT,
And Made Him a New Concrete Landscape, and Cities and Towns
of Concrete,
And Monuments to His Wisdom,
And Concrete Ribbons to tie His Towns Together,
And Concrete Boxes for Governments of His Towns
To Sit In, and To Lie In,
And Speak with Forked Tongue In,

And LO, when the Gravel, the Pink and Beautiful Gravel was Gone,
ALL GONE.
Gone to Build the Towns and the Ribbons to Tie Them Together,
And the Concrete Boxes for the Wheelers and Dealers,
To Wheel and Deal In, Nothing was Left,
NOTHING!
Nothing was Left but the Wounds, and the Holes in the SOD,

The Beautiful MOTHER EARTH SOD, with its Grasses and Briers
and Brushes,
And Wild, Wild Roses, and Berries and Pods,
Nothing was Left but a Hole, Nothing but a Hole in the SOD.
NOTHING!

And the Waters came up in the Hole, and the Rains came and the Willow
Welcomed the Birds.
And Boxelders and Cottonwoods Grew, and Welcomed the Birds,
And Grasses and Briers and Brushes Grew,
And Sunflowers and Thistles and Mustard Weed Grew,
And Chokecherries Grew.
And Birds came to Eat them,
And Ducks Nested
And Rested,
Together
They Healed the Wounded EARTH.

And MAN came Again, and threw Garbage, and Filth, and Trash
and Bones In,
And Broken Buildings, and Old Iron, and Cars, Tin Cans and Toys In,
And Dead Antelope, and Deer Heads Without Antlers,
And Covered the New Grasses, and Trees, and Seed Pods,
Covered Them Over.

And TIME and the WATERS, forming Acids and Gasses to Digest them,
And Homogenize Them and Reduce Them and Return Them,
To Usefulness, To Beauty,
To Heal the Wounded Land,
The Wounded MOTHER EARTH LAND,
The Gaseous, Gangrenous, Wounded Land.

But the NEW ACIDS and Gasses
Moving Within IT,
Were Poisoning the WATERS.
Poisoning and Generating Poison, and Moving
By the Power to Move and to Seek,
POISONED the WATERS and the EARTH.

SPEAK NOT TO ME OF GENESIS,

I SPEAK TO YOU OF HELL.

IT'S THE LAW

Solid Waste Management Laws

WYOMING STATUTES, 1977, Chap. 10, Crimes and Offenses, Health and Safety Laws, Article 1. 35-10-101 through 107. (See next page.)

This 1884 law, amended, recodified, renumbered as 35-462, was cited in Solid Waste Rules and Regulations, 1975. It addresses the depositing of refuse, dead animals, garbage, etc., into streams, railroad rights-of-way, etc., *or within one half-mile of ANY INHABITED RESIDENCE, or within one-half mile of ANY PUBLIC ROADWAY*, declared a nuisance detrimental to the public health and general welfare; exception; any existing municipal garbage disposal system, (1945). Requires all law enforcement officers to enforce the provision of the Act and provides penalties. (Most recent recodification, in 1977, gave this body of law the new numbering of 35-10-101 through 107.)

WYOMING ENVIRONMENTAL QUALITY ACT, 1973, establishes the department of Environmental Quality with divisions of Air Quality, Land Quality, Water Quality and Solid Waste. Enforcement and Penalties are built into the Law, *Chap. 9.1, Sections 35-502.1 through 35-502.56.* However, the requirement of *one-half mile distance from a residence or public roadway is not spelled out in the Act; 35-502.43. Solid Waste disposal requirements. This could lead to inconsistent and negligent administration.*

SOLID WASTE MANAGEMENT RULES AND REGULATIONS, 1975, citing as AUTHORITY, 35-462 (now renumbered 35-10-101 through 107) and Chap. 9.1, Sections 35-502.1 through 35-502.56. The specifics of 35-10-101 through 107 should be spelled out here also for the same reason.

PUBLIC LAW 94-580 (94th Congress) Short Title: "RESOURCE AND RECOVERY ACT," an Amendment to the Solid Waste Disposal Act, provides guidelines for Solid and Hazardous Wastes, provided some technical and financial assistance during 1978 and 1979, to States for research and demonstration plants. It authorizes, rather than requires State enforcement, however, *it prohibits future open dumping and requires open dumps to be converted to facilities which do not pose a danger to environment or to health.* Nothing in the Act may apply to any activity or substance which is subject to the *Federal Water Pollution Control Act or to the Safe Drinking Water Act.*

THE LARAMIE COUNTY LAND USE PLAN, recently adopted, cites in the Nuisance Regulations, Section 2: 35-10-101 through 107.

CHAPTER 10
Crimes and Offenses

ARTICLE 1. DISPOSAL OF GARBAGE, REFUSE, DEAD ANIMALS, ETC.

§ 35-10-101. Depositing or placing refuse matter, dead animals, garbage, etc., into rivers, ditches, railroad rights-of-way, highways, etc., prohibited; declared nuisance; exception as to municipal garbage disposal systems.

The depositing, placing, or causing to be placed or put, the carcass of any dead animal or the offal or refuse matter from any slaughterhouse, butcher shop, meat market, packing house, fish house, hog pen, stable, or any spoiled meats, spoiled fish, or any animal or vegetable matter in a putrid or decayed condition or which is liable to become putrid, decayed or offensive, or the contents of a privy vault, or any refuse or garbage, or any offensive matter or substance whatever upon or into any river, creek, bay, pond, canal, ditch, lake, stream, railroad right-of-way, public or private roadway, highway, street, alley lot, field, meadow, public place or public ground, or in any other and different locality, building, or establishment in this state so located that the said substance shall directly or indirectly cause or threaten to cause the pollution or impairment of the purity and usefulness of the waters of any spring, reservoir, stream, irrigation ditch, lake or water supply whether surface or subterranean, which are used wholly or partly as a source of public or domestic water supply, or where the same may become a source of annoyance to any person, or within one-half mile of any inhabited dwelling, or within one-half mile of any public roadway, by any person or persons, association of persons, company or corporation, incorporated city, incorporated or unincorporated town in the state of Wyoming, or the knowingly permitting of such acts by the owner, tenant, or occupant of said places, upon, into, or on said places, or the permitting of said offensive substances or other offensive substances to remain thereon or therein, shall be unlawful and is hereby declared to constitute a nuisance detrimental to the public health and general welfare of the citizens of Wyoming, provided that no present and [or] future operation of any existing municipal garbage disposal system or any extension of or changes therein, which involves substantially daily burning, and no present and [or] future operation of any now existing municipal sewage disposal system or facilities or any extension of or changes therein, shall be considered as within the scope of the foregoing provisions of this act [§§ 35-10-101, 35-10-102] or as a violation thereof but further provided that the foregoing exception concerning any existing municipal garbage disposal system, whether or not such involves substantially daily burning, shall not be applicable to or except from the scope of this act, any such system which has been commenced since prior construction in the close vicinity thereof, of occupied residential buildings or occupied business properties, ten or more in number. (Laws 1945, ch. 131, § 1; C.S. 1945, § 9-705; W.S. 1957, § 35-462.)

Cross reference. — As to nuisances generally, see §§ 6-12-101 to 6-12-109.

The police power of the state extends to the prevention and abatement of nuisances. — Wartensleben v. Willey, 415 P.2d 613 (Wyo. 1966).

And a legislative body may prescribe what shall constitute a nuisance within constitutional limits. Wartensleben v. Willey, 415 P.2d 613 (Wyo. 1966.)

It is a proper function of the legislature to define those breaches of public policy which are to be considered public nuisances within the control of equity, and it is not the province of courts to ordain such jurisdiction for themselves in contravention of the legislative declaration. Hillmer v. McConnell Bros., 414 P.2d 972 (Wyo. 1966).

A cattle feeding operation is not a nuisance per se and will not be enjoined unless the circumstances disclosing it is in fact a nuisance. Wartensleben v. Willey, 415 P.2d 613 (Wyo. 1966).

Nor a chicken or poultry business. — A chicken or poultry business is not a nuisance per se but may become a nuisance per accidents. Wartensleben v. Willey, 415 P.2d 613 (Wyo. 1966).

Nor a meat processing plant or slaughterhouse. — Neither a meat processing plant nor a slaughterhouse is a nuisance per se but may become a nuisance by reason of the character of the neighborhood in which it is situated. Wartensleben v. Willey, 415 P.2d 613 (Wyo. 1966).

Section applied to rabbit processing plant. — See Hillmer v. McConnell Bros. 414 P.2d 972 (Wyo. 1966).

Am.Jur.2d, ALR and C.J.S. references — 4 Am.Jur.2d Animals §§ 31 to 39; 56 Am.Jur.2d Municipal Corporations §§452 to 464.

Validity of statutes, etc., relating to transportation or disposal of carcasses of dead animals not slaughtered for food, 121 ALR 732.

Regulation and licensing of private garbage or rubbish removal services, 83 ALR2d 799.

Liability of owner or occupant to garbage or trash man coming on premises in course of duty, 36 ALR3d 610.

Applicability of zoning regulations to waste disposal facilities of state or local governmental entities, 59 ALR3d 1244.

62 C.J.S. Municipal Corporations § 265.

§ 35-10-102. Penalty for violation of section 35-10-101.

Any person violating the provisions of this act [§ 35-10-101] shall be guilty of a misdemeanor and upon conviction thereof shall be punished by a fine of not less than fifty ($50.00) nor more than two hundred dollars ($200) or shall be imprisoned in the county jail not to exceed six (6) months, or shall be punishable by both such fine and imprisonment. (Laws 1945, ch. 131, § 2; C.S. 1945, § 9-706; W.S. 1957, § 35-463.)

Cross reference. — As to penalty for contamination of streams or lakes by manufacturing or industrial works, see § 35-4-202.

Editor's note. — Section 3, ch. 131, Laws 1945, repealed §§ 32-709, 32-710, R.S. 1931 (§§ 1 and 3, ch. 62, Laws 1884, §§ 1020 and 1022, R.S. 1887, §1, ch. 99, Laws 1895, §§ 5114 and 5115, R.S. 1899, §§ 5965 and 5966, C.S. 1910, §§ 7254 and 7255, C.S. 1920), which contained the same subject matter as §§ 35-10-101 and 35-10-102.

Effective date. — Section 4, ch. 131, Laws 1945, makes the act effective from and after passage. Approved February 20, 1945.

§ 35-10-103. Throwing sawdust into streams.

If any person or persons who may own, run or have charge of any sawmill in this state shall throw or permit the sawdust therefrom to be thrown or placed in any manner into any river, stream, creek, bay, pond, lake, canal, ditch or other water course in this state, such person or persons shall be liable to a like penalty as is provided in section one of this act. (Laws 1884, ch. 62, § 4; R.S. 1887, § 1023; R.S. 1899, § 5116; C.S. 1910, § 5967; C.S. 1920, § 7256; R.S. 1931, § 32-711; C.S. 1945, § 9-707; W.S. 1957, § 35-464.)

Cross reference. — See cross reference to §35-10-102.

Editor's note. — The words "section one of this act," refer to § 1, ch. 62, Laws 1884. See Editor's note to § 35-10-102.

§ 35-10-104. Failure of owner to remove or bury dead animal.

It shall be the duty of the owner, or person having charge of an animal which may die in this state, to remove the carcass to a distance of not less than half a mile from the nearest human habitation, or to bury it with not less than two (2) feet of soil over it; and every person failing to so remove or bury such carcass, for more than forty-eight (48) hours, shall upon conviction, be fined in a sum not exceeding one hundred dollars ($100.00). And should such animal be the property or in charge of some person passing through this state, then any peace officer may (without warrant) detain the owner or person in charge of such animal, or of the flock or herd from which it died, as soon as such owner or person shall have shown an intention not to so bury or remove said carcass, by removing from it, or removing such flock or herd from it a distance of half a mile or more, a reasonable time, not to exceed two (2) days, until a warrant can issue upon an information duly sworn to. And the brand upon such animal may be given in proof of the ownership of the same. (Laws 1879, ch. 29, § 3; R.S. 1887, § 1005; R.S. 1899, § 5111; C.S. 1910, § 5962; C.S. 1920, § 7251; R.S. 1931, § 32-706; C.S. 1945, § 9-704; W.S. 1957, § 35-465.)

Editor's note. — The last sentence of this section was omitted from the 1899 Revised Statutes and from all subsequent compilations down to and including that of 1931. It was reinstated by the 1945 compiler.

§ 35-10-105. Placing garbage, debris, etc., on certain lands prohibited.

It is unlawful for any person to place, throw, scatter, or deposit, any garbage, debris, refuse, including abandoned or junked motor vehicles, or waste material, objects, or substances, upon any public or private property not belonging to, or under the control of, such person, or in any waters in the state. This section does not apply to any person who places, throws, scatters, or deposits any such material upon lands, premises, or property with the permission of the owner or person in control of said lands, premises, or property, nor to discharges of any materials which are now or may hereafter be subject to regulation, control or limitation by air or water quality laws. (Laws 1957, ch. 90, § 1; W.S. 1957, § 35-466; Laws 1963, ch. 27, § 1; 1973, ch. 21, § 2.)

Cross reference. — For provisions of the Wyoming Environmental Quality Act, see ch. 11 of this title.

§ 35-10-106. Same; enforcement.

It is the duty of all law enforcement officers to enforce the provisions of section 35-466 [§ 35-10-105] within their jurisdiction. (Laws 1957, ch. 90, § 2; W.S. 1957, § 35-467; Laws 1973, ch. 21, § 1.)

§ 35-10-107. Same; penalty.

Any person who violates the provisions of section 35-466 [§ 35-10-105] shall be guilty of a misdemeanor and shall be punished upon conviction by a fine of not more than one hundred dollars ($100.00) or by imprisonment in the county jail for not more than ninety (90) days, or both; provided, that if the violation is shown to have been done maliciously with intent to injure either a person, property, or any livestock, the person shall be punished by imprisonment in the county jail not more than six (6) months. In the discretion of the court, upon conviction of any person, any such fine or imprisonment may be suspended on the condition that the convicted person gather and remove from any specified public property, or specified private property, with prior permission of the owner or person in control thereof, any such material as defined in section 35-466 [§ 35-10-105] of the statutes, found thereon. (Laws 1957, ch. 90, § 3; W.S. 1957, § 35-468; Laws 1963, ch. 27, § 2; 1973, ch. 21, § 1.)

CHEYENNE, CLEAN CITY, USA?

The controversy over the transfer station issue erupted over the proposed location at a city exit on the route to the landfill. The idea of a transfer station, where packer trucks could unload their cargo into a giant compactor which would reduce the bulk to be hauled to the landfill, made sense. Supertransport trucks would then reduce the number of trips to the landfill further. The plan first appeared as a part of the Genesis Plan in 1974. Undeniably the station would save money. It would generate business income. The project, a $1.9 million gleam in the eyes of the Cheyenne City Council, with Farm Loan Board financing at stake, was highly publicized.

When the plan was unveiled, however, in the spring of 1982, the business people of Westland — Happy Jack Road soundly rejected it.

Undaunted, City Engineer Gary Grunkemeyer, announced on KRAE Radio, May 12, 1982, that the city would put the transfer station on a city-owned gravel pit, then partly filled, north of Fox Farm Road and west of the Turk Avenue residences.

When I called to explain to him why this would be illegal, he said he was unconcerned about opposition. "The idea was recommended by your own South Side businessmen," he said. "They are going to have a public meeting and we'll tell you what we are going to do."

"We will fight it," I said.

"I'll ram it down their throats," he said.

"We'll see you there," I said.

Florence Bennett and I alerted the neighborhood.

The sponsors alerted the media. Their handbills read:

"NOTICE OF PUBLIC HEARING

Subject: Proposal by the City of Cheyenne to Construct a Trash Transfer Station on East Fox Farm Road Near Turk Avenue
Place: Arp School
Date: Thursday, May 27, 1982
Time: 7:00 P.M.

Arranged and Sponsored by
YOUR SOUTH CHEYENNE IMPROVEMENT COMMITTEE
of the
GREATER CHEYENNE CHAMBER OF COMMERCE"

There was a good turnout of Fox Farm Community residents at Arp School. They listened politely to the presentation of City Engineer Gary Grunkemeyer and the panel members. John Thorpe reported on his visit to the private transfer station in Greeley, Colorado. Peter Inniss, CSSA Consultant, who had been with Model Cities in 1974 when the plan was developed explained a model of a transfer station.

According to Mike Dean, *Wyoming Eagle* reporter, the audience was saving its applause for opposition speakers, as the committee chairman, Leonard Sullivan, called on the audience for questions. There were few questions.

"Put it in Western Hills," or "We haven't got the money but we are going to try to stop it," received loud rounds of applause.

Dean also quoted Doran Lummis as saying, "the people behind the businesses on the West Side protested the proposed transfer station at 19th and Missile Drive for a reason. The city realized it would have a negative effect on their property value, and the same has to hold here."

"Do you really believe that garbage can be beautiful?" I asked, when my turn came. I reminded them of our problems with the City of Cheyenne placing a dump on Fox Farm Road in 1944 and the Health and Safety Laws that resulted from our fight at that time.

"The pollution of our well water from the garbage buried in that dump forced us to organize our Water and Sewer District. That, plus our Fire District, makes our taxes the highest rate in Laramie County.

"I say NO, NO, NO, to garbage! 'We're mad as hell and we are not going to take it anymore.' We have taken the city to court before and we will not hesitate to do it again.

"The land use laws are working. Soon this dangerous dumping will be a thing of the past. Our neighborhood will be clean and beautiful again.

"Do you want this *garbage, garbage, garbage,* brought into the neighborhood — GARBAGE! Day after day, year after year? Say 'NO' to garbage!

"Let me HEAR you say 'NO' to garbage!"

They said it loud and clear.

In answer to the barrage of publicity about the transfer station in the media, my "historical background" letter to the *Tribune*, appeared June 2, 1982. We resented the "put down" of our people by officials who said that we were "responding emotionally" against its location near residences in our neighborhood. I cautioned that increased traffic would create a dangerous situation for the school children who daily take their chances on Fox Farm Road, where traffic has tripled since the opening of the Outer Belt Road (College Drive).

We resorted to the right of petition, drafted at a neighborhood coffee.

PETITION

"WE, the undersigned, residents, property owners and concerned friends of the Fox Farm Road Community, wish to reaffirm our desire to conserve the residential character of the area, North of Fox Farm Road, South of I-80, East of the South Greeley Highway and West of Turk Avenue.

Further, we demand the abandonment of the city gravel pit in Laramie County, North of Fox Farm Road, now nearly filled. It must be covered with two feet of clean earth, in compliance with the regulations of the Wyoming State Department of Environmental Quality, reseeding upon completion.

This area should then be dedicated to public use."

When we gathered 223 signatures, Florence Bennett and I delivered copies to the County Commissioners and to the City-County Planning Commission meetings. Neighborhood delegates, Francis and Florence Bennett, Linda Pasco, Vaughn and Lorraine Ditzler, Virginia Hayward and I attended the meetings, including the hearings on the Nuisance Regulations and spoke in favor of their enforcement against private dumps and salvage operations.

The procedures of dissent and protest are time consuming and frustrating; waiting for the issue to appear on the agenda, waiting for the other shoe to drop; waiting for people to be considered as important as business.

When we finally delivered the petition to the Cheyenne City Council, Committee of the Whole; Chairman Pete Salas would not allow it to be read, cutting me off in mid-sentence. He said, "We have assigned the location of Transfer Station to a study committee, headed by Mr. Leonard Sullivan. The petition will be filed."

Councilman Marv Gertsch asked if I would be willing to serve on the committee. I accepted.

When Tom Bonds, Director of Planning, invited me to attend a meeting of the study group, I asked if I might bring State Representative Ellen Crowley, whose concern for a clean environment had involved her in waste disposal issues. She and I were the only people who were not there in some official capacity, representing various city and county boards and commissions.

After viewing a film on a transfer station operation in a large Canadian city, I asked whether the group was really interested in solving Cheyenne's solid waste problem or just in building a transfer station because the money is available? "Problems? What problems?" someone echoed.

The group met fourteen times between June 29 and November 16, 1982. Among the many facets of solid waste management environmental protection explored were private as well as municipal operation. Municipal handling seemed potentially more responsive to the public, in my view.

Marvin A. Crist of the United States Geological Survey and Dick Stockdale of the State Engineer's office discussed the soil and water realities of Laramie County. Charles Porter, Director of the Environmental Quality Department's Division of Solid Waste explained why the Cheyenne landfill did not meet the Department of Environmental Quality standards and what must be done to earn a state permit to operate a sanitary landfill. Historically, Cheyenne has yet to operate a solid waste disposal site in a safe and sanitary manner, although notices of violation have been issued from the State Attorney General's office.

Concern for the Cheyenne underground water supply was addressed by Ray Sherard of the Water Department. Test wells drilled at the landfill revealed pools of leachate had gathered under the waste deposit in 1976. The landfill had been in use since 1966. There is a strong possibility that leachate, or water percolating through the waste deposit will eventually enter the city water supply, as well as that of our downstream neighbors on the aquifer.

Grunkemeyer reported that three more wells had been drilled in 1980, two below the fill and one above the fill. "Major changes in water quality were from varying amounts of runoff," he said. New test wells being monitored in 1982 confirm the movement of leachate migration from five to fifteen feet. The "experts" do not consider this a dangerous amount, "IF" it were to enter the water supply. The question is: How much of this pollution per sip is the citizen-consumer willing to swallow?

The sandy clay which underlies the landfill is not impermeable. The unknown threat of biological, metal and chemical wastes cannot be ignored. Since there are few places in Laramie County with more suitable soil in which to inter our wastes, it is vital that meticulous operation of the landfill be enforced to minimize the accumulation of leachate.

The issue of the transfer station served to focus attention on the spectrum of Cheyenne's sanitation problems. "Six alternatives of waste management are discussed in the committee's report: transfer, baling, incineration, shredding, resource recovery and materials recovery, all are viable processes if conditions are favorable."

Maury Plambeck, Planner staffing the Waste Management Study Committee, provided resource materials, minutes and accurate summaries of the presentations and discussions, writing position papers and preparing the final report.

The Waste Management Study Report and the Transfer Station Siting Subcommittee's Report were presented to the City Council and the County Commissioners on November 22 and 23, 1982, respectively, by chairman Leonard Sullivan. The reports are available in the City-County Planning Office.

The controversy could have awakened the conscience of the community. The issues raised in 1974 are still involved and unresolved in 1983. There will be a happy ending only if and when our citizens really want to live in a clean, safe environment and are willing to participate in the solutions.

> "The most involved fact in the world
> Could have been faced when it was simple,
> The biggest problem could have been solved
> When it was small."
>
> *Lao Tze, Sixth Century B.C.*

CROW CREEK HISTORY

Crow Creek, a silver thread, running through the loom of our history, is tarnished now, and broken. The symbolism of the thread is tied to the geology, the economy and the politics of expansion in the medicine-bundle of Cheyenne's roots.

No monuments have been raised to its significance at the veritable cross-hairs of our destiny; Cheyenne's place in history, myth and legend, where the "railroad crossed the creek."

Literate and scientific men had been exploring the West. As early as 1845, four proposed routes for the transcontinental railroad were being debated. In 1853, Congress authorized the Army to make surveys of the four routes.

Jefferson Davis, Secretary of War, and trusted advisor to President Franklin Pierce, favored the southern route, via Santa Fe. However, Stephen A. Douglas, senior senator from Illinois, stole the show, according to historian Samuel Elliot Morison.

Douglas reported a bill for the organization of the Great Plains as the Territory of Nebraska. Although such bills had previously been defeated, this one was baited with the principle of "Popular Sovereignty," in which the people of the territory would vote on whether or not they would have slavery, as soon as they had a legislature. He agreed to divide the new territory into Kansas and Nebraska, adding more fuel to the slavery question. Politics and economics, plot and counterplot, were brewing backstage. Rumblings of war were growing more insistent. Everyone forgot about the railroad and the Army surveyors were ordered back to their regiments when war came.

During the war, Major General Grenville Mellen Dodge had acquired considerable experience rebuilding the destroyed railroads as the Confederate Army retreated. While on sick leave, August 1863, in Council Bluffs, he was called to New York to help Thomas C. Durant and Chief Engineer Peter Dey prepare a presentation for President Lincoln on the location of the starting point of the Union Pacific Railroad at Council Bluffs.

Wallace D. Farnham, while associate professor of history at the University of Wyoming, attempted to sort out the truth from the Dodge legend, as reported in *The Journal of American History*, Vol. LI:4, March 1965. We will accentuate the positive:

Dodge was watching for a pass for the railroad, in the late summer of 1865, while still in the Army, traveling south with his troop to Denver from Fort Laramie, along the foot of the Laramie Range, then called the Black Hills.

He wrote in his diary: "This morning I started with Pallady and Indian (guide) to examine Black Hills near Cheyenne Pass, crossed Highest Mountain, got a view of Laramie Plains and all the Passes and crossed to the Head of Crow Creek followed it down out of the Mountains and struck across

PHOTO COURTESY OF WYOMING STATE ARCHIVES, MUSEUMS AND HISTORICAL DEPARTMENT

Crow Creek Crossing, Cheyenne, Dakota Territory, fall 1867, settlement southwest of Crow Creek. Railroad grade and telegraph pole, foreground. Photographer unknown.

country to Road a few Indian signs. Indian killed two antelope Train marched 35 miles and camped at Willow Springs last 10 miles rough and Broken wrote letter to Annie." His letter to Annie told the same story, according to Farnham.

Quite a different story is told by Dodge in his later years, in *How We Built the Union Pacific.*

Mid-May, 1866, mustered out of the Army, Dodge became Chief Engineer for the Union Pacific. He sent Division Engineer James Evans back to the Laramie Mountains to make more surveys of the Crow Creek area. The gently sloping "gangplank" was found, verified and the line established. (Evans had reported, "no good passes," previously. The pass now bears his name.)

As early as 1850, Captain Howard Stansbury, on his way to survey the Great Salt Lake, had mentioned this promising route.

Although Crow Creek entered the history of the Union Pacific in 1865, it had long been known to the Indians, trappers, traders, and surveyors, by that name. In 1846, Francis Parkman and his party, using John Charles Fremont's maps, were returning from their summer with the Plains Indians. They were enroute from Fort Laramie to Bent's Fort. They crossed the hot prairie, August 11th and saw a long line of trees. They nooned on Crow Creek at a point where Carpenter is now. The creek was dry as were others in their path that summer. The route followed Crow Creek valley to the South Platte and on to the Arkansas River.

Crow Creek is a remnant of a vast prehistoric river that included the North and South Platte Rivers, and which, for millions of years had deposited material from the erosion of the mountains to build the Great Plains.

According to the United States Geological Survey: "South of Crow Creek, tertiary deposits form a gradual slope from the mountains to the plains. This slope, nicknamed "the gangplank" is utilized by the Union Pacific Railroad to gain access to the mountain uplands with the least possible grade."

"Gradients range from one hundred feet per mile on the 'gangplank' to twenty feet per mile at the eastern edge of the county."

The creek has left its mark on the geography and sociology of the county as well as upon the history of the West.

When Louis Simonin, the French mining engineer, and his party came to Cheyenne from Denver, topping the hill on the old "Denver Road," the three-month-old tent city lay before them, concentrated along Crow Creek.

Clear Creek drained the springy pastures to the southwest, meandering down to empty into Crow Creek between Sixth and Seventh Streets. Dodge House was situated beside it at Eighth and O'Neil. Possibly a hand-dug well or an oak barrel sunken into the ground at its edge provided the water supply.

J. H. Gildersleeve operated the Dodge House, or hotel, boasting thirty beds in one room. Rather than share a bed, Simonin preferred to sit in the "lounge." The next day, one of his companions, Colonel Heine, who had friends at Fort D. A. Russell, accepted an invitation, which included a tent, for their stay in Cheyenne.

While they waited for the Indian Commission to arrive, and to join the party going to a parley at Fort Laramie, Simonin studied life on the Frontier, manners and customs, and wrote about the geology as few trained observers had, at that time.

They killed time by hunting grouse, as the military and railroad hunters had already killed off most of the larger game. He called the aspens growing along the creek, "water birches."

Writing as a geologist: "Fort Russell, Dakota, under tent, 1 November," he found the thick alluvial soil "without a stone, except for siliceous gravels

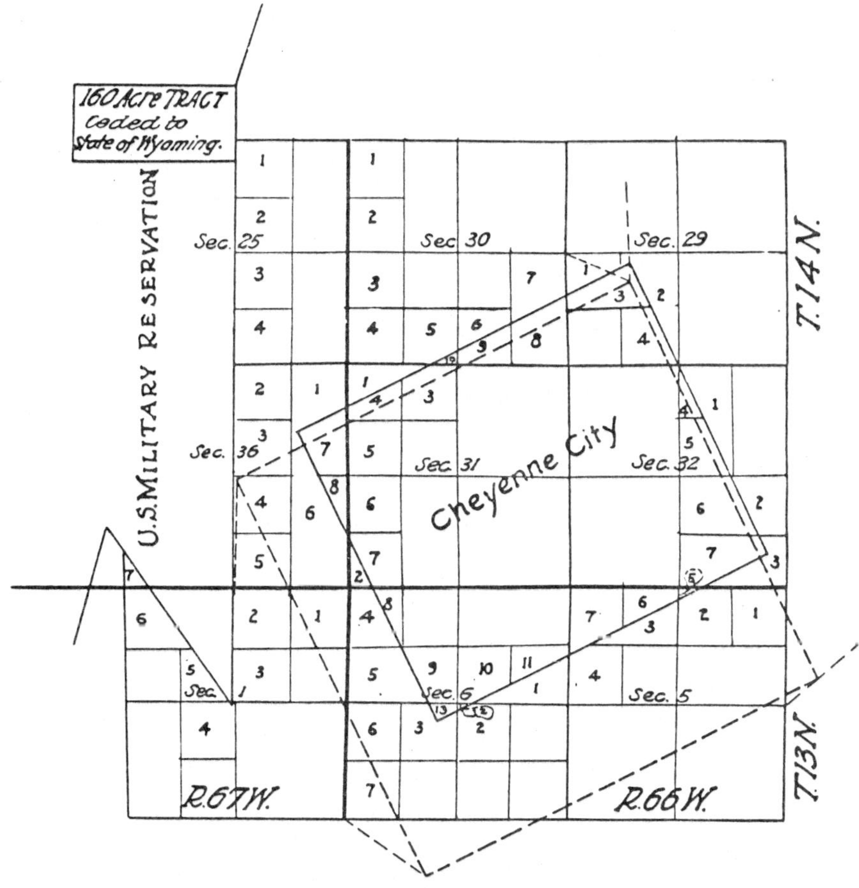

CHEYENNE ABSTRACT AND TITLE COMPANY

Diagram showing surveys of the Cheyenne townsite. Solid lines indicate the original 1870 and 1872 surveys, broken lines indicate the 1890 survey.

and round pebbles." He speculated that these "must have descended from the Rocky Mountains when they were uplifted, or when glaciers, which in former geologic ages rested upon the flanks of these high mountains, were suddenly melted." He considered them "an indication, in advance, what rocks would be found by the geologist who is headed for the great chain of the extreme west." Pebbles of rose granite, green porphyry, glossy and foliated slate and quartz of all colors, "especially the red quartz with which the beds of some streams are paved," Simonin noted in his journal.

He wrote that the only rock found in place on the prairie was the soft sandstone, "quite modern in age, whose stratifications, worked upon by the elements offered curious spectacles, resembling ruined cities."

On his way from Denver, he had probably passed "Natural Fort" on the historic road. On Crow Creek, "Initial Cliff" had once so played on the imaginations of Cheyenne children.

We are indebted to Professor Wilson O. Clough for this translation of the French engineer's journal.

Another foreign observer of the founding of Cheyenne was a young Englishman, William A. Bell, who came to observe the process of railroad construction, as a photographer. He reported that an acquaintance from Denver told him that "while he was standing on the railway platform, a long freight arrived, laden with frame houses, boards, furniture, palings, old tents, and all of the rubbish which makes up one of these mushroom cities. The guard jumped off the van and seeing some friends on the platform, called out with a flourish, 'Gentlemen, here's Julesburg.' "

Even at this early date, November 1867, pre-cut, and pre-fabricated houses were being hastily put up, moved about, ordered in any style out of catalogues, and people were settling anywhere they chose. Lots were being sold at a fast pace in July. According to some historians, the railroad made more profit from land than from the business of freight and passengers.

The surveyors of the plat of Cheyenne found that little of Crow Creek lay in Section 31 and none in Section 32. It is believed that is why they tipped the conventional grid of the survey, to include more of its meander through Sections 5 and 6, south of the tracks. They had laid out the town-site measuring one mile, each way from the 400 foot right-of-way and one mile east and west of Central Avenue. Every alternate (odd numbered section of land), in a strip ten miles wide on both sides of the railroad track had been granted to the Union Pacific by Congress.

The Union Pacific officials had really wanted to build the transcontinental road via Denver to take advantage of the new gold and mining business. The mountains presented too costly and time consuming a problem, however, and there was the competition to consider. They would have to make do with this little Crow Creek. They had to control it.

In the language of the geologist, "the area east of the mountains lies in the High Plains section of the Great Plains physiographic province. This surface has a gently rolling topography of only moderate relief and is marked by ephemeral and intermittent streams." It was a semi-arid prairie, with trees only along the streams. If there were pines on the "Denver Hill," overlooking the little creek, they soon fell to the ax.

Crow Creek was essential to man and beast whether building a railroad or a town. Here were the first tents and corrals, close to the water. There were ties to be hauled out of the hills, bridges to be built, and the railroad was approaching at the rapid pace of a mile a day.

The business section of the new towns centered around the terminal. Dodge House moved uptown, and the railroad moved on west; some settlers stayed in the bottoms, close to the creek. The oldest permanent buildings of the city may be found here.

Dodge recalled that in the winter of 1867-68, "the end of the track was at Cheyenne. During that winter there assembled a very large number of people, possibly it was the greatest gambling place ever established on the plains, it was full of desperate characters. The town of Cheyenne we had claimed, laid out, and leased the lots to the occupants, and organized the town government. There was then no title to be obtained to the town, but we treated this as all the towns, claiming it for the company laying it out into town lots and not allowing anyone to locate there without taking an agreement with us, allowing them to occupy it and agreeing to deed it to them when we got a title."

Whatever version of "Magic City" or "Hell on Wheels" legend one may choose, Dodge requested General J. D. Stevenson, commandant of Fort D. A. Russell "to use his troops to drive every citizen out of town and parley with them." The general told them that "until they were ready to comply with the orders and recognize the authority of the railroad company, they should not be allowed to go back to their property; that really, the land belonged to the United States and the railroad was occupying it under the Government's charter. This brought them to terms and we afterward had no trouble with them."

Noted in a brief history published in the first Cheyenne Business Directory; Sawtiel and Burnett, O'Neil Street, Cheyenne, Dakota Territory, February 1868:

> Nothing further of material interest transpired until the 19th, when the corps of U.P.R.R. engineers commenced staking off the town site for the city, and completed the survey on the 21st (July). People in large and small parties had arrived from Julesburg and the Cache la Poudre, and many tents were now up, which gave the place much the appearance of a fair ground. . . . A small western house was erected by one of our oldest frontiersmen, named Wm. Lorimer, on the south side of Crow Creek. This was the first wooden building put together within the city limits.

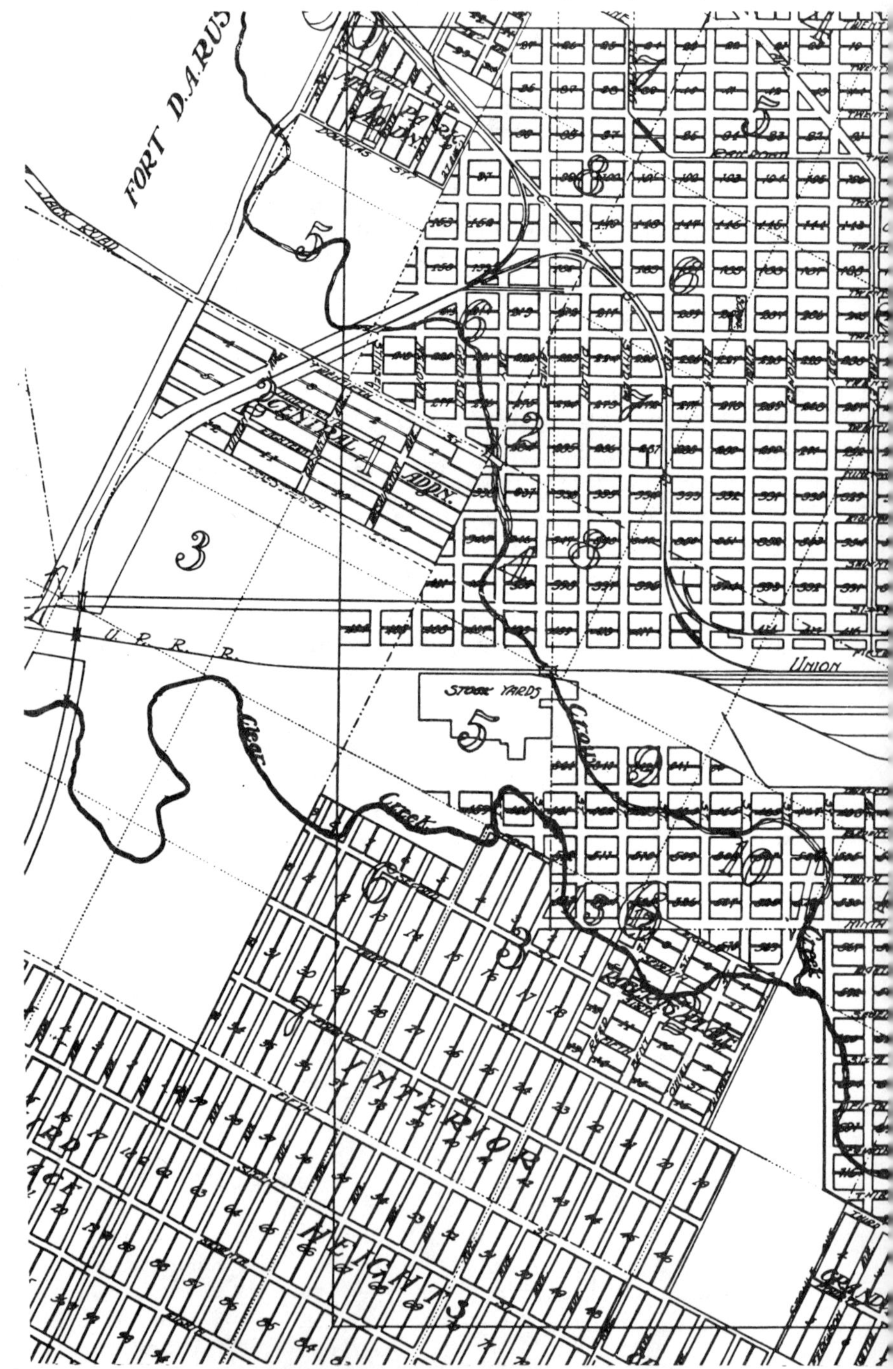

Map showing the Clear Creek and Crow Creek drainages in Cheyenne.

CEMETERY
CEMETERY
BOULEVARD
HEIGHTS
ADDN.
P. R.
P. SHOPS
SOUTH CHEYENNE
PACKING HOUSE
U. P. R. R.

According to old-timers, this log house was later moved to Eleventh and House, northwest corner, where several rooms were added, and where it remained until 1923. For some time it was the home of the Millerman family.

Could "frontiersman *Wm. Lorimer*" have been the son of *General William Larimer*, one of the founders of Denver, who was known to have been in the freighting business between Denver and Cheyenne?

"We Come and Go but the land is Always here and the people who love it and understand it are the ones who own it — for a little While."

From "*Oh Pioneers*," Willa S. Cather.

CROW CREEK TRIBUTARIES

Clear Creek, as the first adventurers and settlers knew it, was a well-fed little stream, draining the hills, boggy draws and meadows to the southwest of Crow Creek Crossing, the settlement that became Cheyenne.

Dodge House, a hotel, was situated beside it at Eighth and O'Neil in 1867. In 1950, Cole School was built at Ninth and O'Neil Avenue. The stream meandered through what is now its playground. Originally the stream emptied into Crow Creek between Sixth and Seventh Streets. In wet years and after heavy rains the water tends to follow its old course.

Springs once flowed out of Denver Hill, according to old timers. During the construction of Deming Drive this underground water caused problems. Again, when Walterschied Drive cut into the hill, nature objected.

Dry Creek embraces the city on the north and east. It was simply a "draw," dammed here and there to retain runoff water for livestock. The prairie sponge soaked up the rains and snowmelt to replenish the aquifer. Heavy rains would drain off down the ancient channel harmlessly. Today the roofs, paved driveways and streets of the new subdivisions speed the water on its way to Crow Creek, causing seasonal, intermittent flooding. Building continues in the flood plain.

South of the city, another drainage system is showing the same symptoms as Dry Creek. Will the planners and developers learn to enhance the value of streams in population centers or continue to make costly adjustments for their mistakes at taxpayers' expense?

LARAMIE COUNTY CLIMATE AND GEOLOGY

The portion of the Earth's crust that is Laramie County, Wyoming, reveals Pre-Tertiary sedimentary rocks, which may be as much as 12,000 feet thick. They are exposed only in a narrow belt along the eastern mountain front, where the formations have been upturned and faulted. Dips in the beds range from five degrees to vertical. Some beds are overturned. Horse Creek and Borie oil fields are on anticlines, and similar folds may occur elsewhere.

The extent and importance of the Laramie County oil bearing formations have not been fully explored and may have some impact on the future economy of the area.

The Ogallala Formation is the principal aquifer for Cheyenne. It consists of sand and gravels eroded from the mountains to the west. Without conformity it overlies rocks that range from the Miocene to the Pre-Cambrian ages in the beginning of geologic time. The deposit is mainly composed of quartz, quartzite, feldspar, gneiss and schist, found in lenticular beds.

The great Ogallala reservoir is affected by the climate, which is semi-arid. It is characterized by high evaporation, wide temperature range, cold winters and low precipitation. Strong winds are frequent throughout the winter and spring. Summer temperatures are relatively cool; on only eight percent of the days in an average year are the temperatures in the nineties. January is the coldest month.

The authority for these observations is a United States Geological Service paper, Number 1834, by Marlin E. Lowry and Marvin A. Crist. The authors also tell us that precipitation is the principal source of recharge to the ground-water reservoir. The 1965 report estimates that the perennial yield from the Cheyenne well field is about 1.6 billion gallons per year.

"Ground water has been developed throughout the county, but development has been intensive only in the Cheyenne municipal well field, near Cheyenne and Federal and on the Pine Bluffs lowland. The water level has been lowered as much as forty feet in the Cheyenne field and somewhat less in the Federal field," according to this study.

Since that time, Cheyenne has embarked upon extensive projects to bring water from the mountains of the Continental Divide.

According to records of permits granted by the State Engineer's office, there are approximately 2,100 privately operated wells within a five mile radius of Cheyenne. Some of these permitted wells may not, as yet, be drilled, and some are not for domestic use.

The top soil is very thin in the county, averaging from a few inches to a foot, with the exception of the flood plains, where it is much deeper. A new survey of soil and water resources of Laramie County has recently been completed by Dr. Ade Stevenson of the United States Soil Conservation Service and is soon to be released.

HIGH PLAINS HORTICULTURE

The late Dr. A. C. Hildreth, who was superintendent of the United States Horticultural Research Station at Cheyenne for thirty years, predicted a super-drouth of many years duration, during which "the gardens will go first."

"Nature played a trick on the High Plains," he said, in a *Denver Post* interview. "She gave us shrubs and grasses that would withstand the cold winters, the winds and dry summers, but no trees. The High Plains climate is most like that of west China and Mongolia, and those places are not noted for their horticulture."

Dr. Hildreth came to Cheyenne in 1929, after we had had a decade of drouth, in time to experience the high winds and dust storms of the thirties. The grass was blasted off the earth by the blowing sand and gravel. Cattle starved. Instead of moisture, upslope winds brought great clouds of dust from the plains of Kansas, Nebraska and Colorado. The street lights were required in daytime.

During his Cheyenne years, Dr. Hildreth traveled widely in the United States and abroad as a specialist and consultant. He was in charge of a research program concerned with developing rubber trees and other sources of rubber in the desert southwest, during World War II.

The Cheyenne Station did basic research into soils, fertilizers and native vegetation, but most of the work was farm oriented, concerned with feed, food and fiber. However, considerable attention was given to the development of shelterbelt trees and evergreens, some fruit trees and vegetables.

Dr. Hildreth believed that we are faced with the real possibility of dryland gardens and parks in the water-short future and "it is time to accelerate research into drouth resistant plants, shrubs and trees that can provide shade, shelter and beauty."

"Imaginative gardens are being developed using native flora, lichen-covered stones, pines and gravel. The real problem is developing drouth-resistant trees," Dr. Hildreth said. "That is a long process measured in decades rather than months or years. Legislators and budget makers were reluctant to appropriate funds for something that won't be completed during their tenure in office."

Numerous attempts have been made by national administrations to eliminate the Cheyenne Horticultural Station. Currently it has a new mission as the High Plains Grasslands Research installation concerned with cattle feeding and reclamation of the strip mines since 1973.

THE HEALING OF THE WATERS

Although the South Side people had many times tried to get the city government to empty its sewage into Crow Creek east of the city limits, no official attempt was made to clean up the creek waters with its burden of waste from Cheyenne and Fort Francis E. Warren, until the spring of 1949. The campaign for sewage treatment facilities brought out some interesting facts about the development of the life support system, the ecology, of the city.

Mayor Ben Nelson called for a bond election on April 19, to approve a $1,100,000 revenue bond for the construction of a sewage disposal plant. The announcement brought support from Governor A. G. Crane, the South Side Community League, the Izaak Walton League and health related organizations.

Governor Crane said, "We, here, in Cheyenne, stand in imminent danger of pestilence as a result of this practice, and the Izaak Walton League (of which he was a member) is tremendously interested in the approval of the bond issue when it is brought up to a vote of the people."

According to a 1928 map showing sewage outfalls, sewage entered the creek at Twenty-Second and Cribbon, at Fifteenth Street at Ames and at Evans Avenue. Another map shows an outfall at Fort Francis E. Warren.

The South Side Community League rounded up subscribers to a full page advertisement, which appeared the day before the election. It was intended to shock Cheyenne out of its complacency:

> REASONS FOR CONSTRUCTING THIS PLANT
>
> At the present time Cheyenne is dumping five and one-half gallons per day of raw sewage into Crow Creek.
>
> This raw sewage is a menace to the health of children playing in it because it may contain disease-causing organisms of typhoid fever, amoebic dysentery, diarrhea enteritis.
>
> It endangers agricultural workers using it for irrigation.
>
> Dairy cattle wading in pastures irrigated with sewage may drop fecal particles or amoebic cysts into milk. Raw sewage is offensive — its odor causes a decline in property value close to running sewage.
>
> A city which enjoys the privilege of running water should also assume its responsibility in the matter of disposing of its wastes.
>
> CONSTRUCTION OF THE PLANT
>
> The proposed plant will be located south and east of Cheyenne. It will have sufficient settling tanks, trickling filters, bacterial digestion tanks, drying beds, etc., to properly treat up to a maximum of 9 million gallons per day of sewage, or an amount to be expected from a population of 47,000 persons (predicted for 1957).
>
> This plant will cost a total of $1,100,000.
>
> This cost will be financed by Revenue Bonds.
>
> These Revenue Bonds will run for 1 to 25 years.

> Bonds will be paid by a service charge just as a water service is now paid. THIS IS NOT A PROPERTY TAX.
>
> The service charge will be computed from the average amount of water used during the four winter months (November, December, January and February.) It is a flat rate that will not vary during the year, even though a great deal of water is used during the summer. (Political advertisement.)

One of the most ardent supporters of the sewage disposal project was Dr. Paul Emerson, who had followed the project through the long legal delay clearing the right of the city to borrow money for the purpose. He addressed a number of civic organizations, regaling them with stories of Cheyenne's early attempts at creating a water supply and the schemes and follies dealing with the waters of Crow Creek. He remembered the Crow Creek of his youth as a clear and beautiful stream. It is from his manuscript for a speech before an auditorium-full of Parent-Teachers' Association convention, June 3, 1952, after the plant was functioning, that we have this condensed and edited version:

> From the first three wells in 1868, soon there was a well for nearly every house. Water could also be bought from water carts. For every house, there was an outhouse, or privy, and perhaps a cesspool. Pollution of the water began with the settlement of the town.
>
> In 1880, the Union Pacific built a small pump house with a storage tank on the east bank of Crow Creek, north of the railroad bridge. Water was pumped up Sixteenth Street, through less than a mile of pipe, to the railroad shops and the business district.
>
> The same year, the earliest ditch on record was built by the Wyoming Ditch Company to divert water from the creek through a headgate located two miles upstream from the boundary of Fort D. A. Russell [Francis E. Warren Air Force Base]. The ditch was quite small and carried water across the fort, then south a few hundred feet from Lake Absaraka, southwesterly of Lake Makhpiahlutah [Sloan's] then easterly and south to end in Lake Minnehaha.
>
> Originally, the water ran from the filter galleries at the headgate, through Lake Terry, Absaraka and Sloan's, then through the big ditch on south to town. Later a thirty-inch cypress-wood pipe by-passed the lakes because the porous soil allowed the water to soak away.
>
> Wood-lined laterals ran down Dodge, Ransom, Hill and Ferguson Streets [Warren, Central, Capitol and Carey respectively] to supply cisterns at the downtown intersections. Fire protection was the principle motivation for the delivery of water, although domestic water and irrigation of the early lawns of the town also benefitted. The laterals fed pipes under the tracks to the railroad shops. A city pump house at Twenty-Ninth and Central operated until 1919.
>
> As the infrastructure of the city continued to develop, a new pump house was built at Sixteenth Street north of the railroad bridge. Andrew S. Artist was the engineer. He and his family resided at the pump house. Filter galleries had been built for it at Twenty-Second Street and at the intake of the Wyoming Ditch.

By the year 1897, the water system and its improvements had cost about $200,000.00, including twelve miles of pipe and seventy-four fire hydrants. The cost of running the system in 1896 was $5,000.00, and the revenue amounted to over $13,000.00.

The modern water system began in 1904 with the building of the dam at Granite Springs. It served the city well until the drouth of 1933, according to Dr. Emerson, when the first city well was drilled at Ware, upstream from the first headgate. [There are now forty wells in a forty-four square mile area.]

Dr. Emerson digressed from his theme of Cheyenne's water to tell of a high-powered scheme to irrigate land by bringing a ditch around the north side of town, above the headgate. No diversion works were ever built and no land was irrigated. C. P. (Perry) Organ was the promotor of the ditch, which can still be seen here and there, about two miles north of Pershing Boulevard.

He also recounted the great controversy about how much water could be taken out of the creek for irrigation.

The records show that the first decree of the Territorial Board of Control, dated April 21, 1888, allotted the first right in the amount of 12.481 cubic feet per second [of time] to the City Ditch and Pipe Line. The record was written in long-hand and distinctly shows a period between the two and the four. However, Crow Creek water rights became a matter of early litigation and the Supreme Court ruled, in 1895, that the period was not a period, but a comma; which would have indicated a good sized river. [Miss Lulu McCormick used this story to illustrate the importance of punctuation to her eighth grade class.]

Once the pumping stations were built, water closets [flush toilets] were possible. The first sewage outfall was led into Crow Creek just below the Union Pacific bridge. [This callous act was probably the first of a long series of discriminations against the South Side and the degradation of Crow Creek. It retarded the development of what had once been considered choice real estate.]

People had not generally built close to the creek. After sewage entered the creek, its stench, especially late in summer when the water was low, kept people away. At the Hereford Ranch reservoir the concentration of sewage was so great that people could hardly bear to go near it.

Emerson who lived in the Capitol Building where his father was the janitor, recalled that there had been a typhoid epidemic in 1900 and it was found that the Cheyenne water was contaminated. (Pit privies and a high water table in central Cheyenne was the probable cause.) Milk was ladled out to order at each stop by Johnny Sloan, driver of the milk wagon. The Emersons used to let the water run for a long time to avoid taking up lead from the pipes.

The good doctor seemed to enjoy describing in great detail, the chemical and bacteriological processes that now treat the waters and return them to the stream. He had begun his talk with a Biblical quotation, "Thus saith the Lord, 'I have healed the waters, from thence there will be no more death and miscarrying.' " He urged his listeners to go and observe the healing of the waters. The Crow Creek Sewage Disposal plant is located on Rawlins Avenue between the two refineries.

A second sewage treatment plant, the Dry Creek plant, went on line in 1976. Funding for seventy percent of the cost came from an Environmental Protection Administration grant. This plant must soon be enlarged.

THE CROW CREEK FLOODS

Crow Creek rises in the Laramie Mountains, three forks, North, Middle and South, come together on the Plains, draining about 253 square miles. The area is over thirty miles long and twelve miles wide at its widest point. Each fork now has one or more dams on it to provide municipal and irrigation water.

The creek once meandered through its flood plain in wide lazy curves in Sections Five and Six in the original city of Cheyenne. It is altered from its original course, channeled, straightened, deepened, and confined by roads and levees, from I-25 to its exit near the refinery.

Its contact with man changed its role of life-giving source of water to open sewer for the fort and the city for three quarters of a century. Finally in 1951, reasonably cleaned water was returned to the stream. The creek is totally used for irrigation.

Floods recur at irregular intervals. There was an unrecorded flood in 1879 which may have caused many people to leave the bottoms. Much, however, was written about the 1904 flood.

The 1904 flood began with a cloudburst in the vicinity of Silver Crown, on the evening of May 20, approximately twelve miles upstream from Cheyenne. According to a yellowed clipping given to me by Floyd Artist, "a wall of water came down Crow Creek carrying everything in its path before it, including livestock, buildings, fences and bridges. The Granite Springs dam had recently been completed and there were many rumors that it had given way."

> The Union Pacific bridge over Crow Creek was a pile bridge and the debris that washed against it formed a dam, which caused the water to back up as far as 19th Street and flooded all of the homes in the bottoms.
>
> The house belonging to C. E. McGarvey located near 16th and Snyder was washed against the Snyder underpass and dammed up the only remaining outlet for the water. Another house belonging to Sam Brown located between Dillon and Ames, floated to 16th and Snyder, where it finally came to rest. In order to permit the water to get through the underpass, the Union Pacific used a wrecking crane to lift the McGarvey house over the right-of-way to the south side of the tracks.

> The pioneer Artist family lived in the pump house. Jessie and May Artist and Amy Parshall, (Mrs. Whittington, Mrs. Wolcott and Mrs. Ohnhaus) were rescued after the water receded. They had to stand on the kitchen table to keep their heads above water.
>
> The flood caused the death of two Clayton children whose bodies were found in the morning following the flood. They were drowned in their bed in a house at 15th and Snyder. (From the *Rotary Club Bulletin.*)

While it may not have been the same house, an elderly woman was drowned in a small house on the bank of the creek beside the same underpass in the flood of June 2, 1929. It is believed that she could not hear the warning to evacuate.

The spectacular floods of 1904 and 1929 were not gauged but computed from measurements of the flood's high water marks, according to reports of the United States Geological Survey.

The 1904 flood was computed to be 8,500 cubic feet per second and the 1929 flood reached 8,200 cubic feet per second of time. The next highest amount was 395 cubic feet per second in 1955.

The 1929 flood was due to not unusually heavy showers that occurred near the headwaters where ground was already saturated and tributaries were full from heavy snows that had fallen in April.

The highest record rainfall, however, was 4.78 inches in a three hour period at Cheyenne. If spread over the entire basin it may have produced an "Intermediate Regional Flood," sometimes called a "Fifty Year Flood." There was no record of widespread flooding in this instance.

An Intermediate Regional Flood would top all of the bridges and bridge approaches, except Interstate 25, the I-180 Connector (Central Avenue) and the railroad bridges.

The "One Hundred Year Flood," or Statistical Flood, is the maximum flood event in any one hundred years. There could be two hundred years without a One Hundred Year Flood, or a One Hundred Year Flood two years in a row. It is the one-percent chance of a flood of magnitude occurring every year.

A flood of the magnitude of the 1904 or the 1929 floods would find more buildings and other obstructions in the flood plain. Ironically, more businesses have been allowed to enter the flood plain since the great Crow Creek beautification campaign was launched by Model Cities in 1971. The flood hazard was highly touted as a reason for immediate concern.

A city zoning ordinance was enacted to "prevent further building in the established flood area." The city also made available flood insurance, under a federal program which could be obtained through private insurers at a nominal fee.

The "dangerous" creek seen as a source of federal funds in 1971 had been straightened from its original course through the flood plain in the late thirties. It had become a deep ditch, partially rip-rapped with rock, averaging

9.5 feet in depth, having a top of 125 feet in width. The depth downstream, as it meanders in a more or less natural state through a 1,000 foot flood plain (Lummis meadow) is 3.5 feet, according to statistics quoted in the 1971 Crow Creek Feasibility Study, produced by Model Cities.

The planners estimated that an Intermediate Regional Flood would spread out to 600 feet in width. As it would come into contact with roads, bridges and culverts, a flood crest of an additional five feet could probably rise.

After the flood of 1929 there was a good deal of public discussion about keeping the creek's passageway through the city as free as possible of buildings and other obstructions. Even as the town lined up above the high water mark watching the flood, many said that it was "a good thing that there were so few buildings in its path."

Two Cheyenne businessmen, William C. Deming and George Brimmer retained at their own expense, the noted designer of the Denver public parks, S. R. DeBoer, to create plans for a scenic drive which would emphasize the assets of the creek as well as eliminate the hazards.

The creek is the exposed water table. Due to irrigation and the "draw down" by the city well field, the flow of the creek varies from a high spring runoff to a mere trickle in many places by the end of the summer. The 1971 plan depended upon a dam or series of dams to insure a constant "in-stream" flow for which there were no water rights available.

Cheyenne's early settlers as well as the newcomers have made many mistakes in dealing with Crow Creek. We should try to understand that Nature will continue its cycles of drouth and flood in the high plains and develop the stream's potential for safe and beautiful open space, as well as beneficial use.

THE DEMING DREAM

William C. Deming, publisher of the Wyoming State Tribune and his friend, George Brimmer, prominent Cheyenne attorney, saw Crow Creek as an asset to Cheyenne and the focal point of a proposed scenic drive or parkway. Deming described it in his will, made in 1947.

> EXCERPT FROM THE WILL OF WILLIAM C. DEMING, Filed May 6, 1949; Signed June 20, 1947. . . . . ITEM EIGHTEEN. I hereby give, devise and bequeath to the City of Cheyenne, Wyoming, the sum of Ten Thousand ($10,000.00) Dollars to be used primarily for the extension and construction and secondarily for the landscaping of Deming Drive along Crow Creek extending from Lincoln Highway northerly to Hynds Boulevard under the plans and supervision of competent engineers and landscape architects, said bequest to be administered by the Board of Park Commissioners of the City of Cheyenne or if there be none duly authorized and acting then by and with the consent of the Mayor of Cheyenne, the

> President of the Cheyenne Chamber of Commerce and the Judge of the First Judicial District of Wyoming; provided, however, that this devise shall be null and void unless the link in said Deming Drive extending from the Lincoln Highway southeasterly to the Denver Highway is being maintained at the time of my death. It is my hope that the Deming Drive will be extended within a reasonable time across the Denver Highway though intervening land to and through the Hereford Ranch, to a point on the Lincoln Highway to or near Archer east of Cheyenne, thus making an attractive suburban drive, and to Hynds Boulevard along Crow Creek through the former Maude Brown property. If needed $1,000.00 of the above sum may be used to purchase rights of way.

Cheyenne's treatment of the creek is a disgrace to our history. In addition to being an open sewer for many years, the banks and flood plain north of Sixteenth Street had been used by the city as an unsightly, odorous open dump as late as 1944. (This statement was verified by Street and Alley Commissioner Gus Fleischli in the case of the Fox Farm Road people vs. the City of Cheyenne.) The deep, waterfilled barrow pits on Nineteenth Street also had been filled with garbage and refuse.

Deming and Brimmer presented a copy of the DeBoer parkway plans to the City of Cheyenne. Eventually the city had gone along with the plan to the extent of building a combination road and levee as a part of the Works Progress Administration project and naming the road Deming Drive in his honor. A new underpass on Ames Avenue was constructed and the old Roman-arched Snyder Avenue underpass of cut stone matching the depot, was finally buried as the railroad yards were filled in and enlarged.

Truck traffic to the refinery increased on Deming Drive. The South Side Community League was vigilant to keep the name from becoming "the truck route."

In 1949, the campaign for the sewage disposal plant began. Although sewage still ran in the creek, the South Side Community League went ahead with plans for a park along Crow Creek.

We now turn the civic clock back to the following excerpt from City Council proceedings, (Official Abstract) Legal Notice in the *Wyoming Eagle* :

"February 14, 1950. Monday 13, 1950, being a legal holiday, the City Council met in regular session February 14, 1950, convening in the Council Chambers at 9:30 o'clock, a.m. with all members present. . . .

Several members of the South Side Community League were present at the Council Meeting. A portion of Block 530 which is bounded on the North by Tenth Street, on the South by Ninth Street, on the East by Carey Avenue, and on the West by Pioneer Avenue, near Crow Creek is city owned. Mrs. Raymond R. Jones addressed the Council and stated that said League desired permission to develop the City's portion of this block for a park. The request was granted by unanimous vote of the Council."

(The City Council was composed of Mayor Ben F. Nelson, Parks and Finance Commissioner Ed Gowdy and Street and Alley Commissioner Art Trout.)

No one in the county assessor's office told us, when we were looking for city owned land on the creek for our park, that the Deming 1930 gift of Block 529 lay directly across the creek from our parcel. A slice of Block 529 had already been used for Deming Drive and the new Crow Creek channel.

On March 8th, 1950, an outlet for water was installed in South Side Community Park. When the trees from old City Park had been relocated to our new park, we could not agree on a name. Some favored calling it Deming Park, others preferred Washington Park to complement our Lincoln Park. I thought South Side Community Park was more representative of the volunteers who had worked on the tree planting and other landscaping work.

Several years later, Mayor Val Christensen called me to ask if we would like to have some playground equipment for the park. "Fine," I said, "but I am no longer the park chairman. Let me give you the number of our new president, Mr. Wallerstedt."

"I just wanted you to know there are strings attached," said the Mayor.

"There always are," I said.

"They want to name it Optimists' Park, if they do it," continued the Mayor.

"Couldn't they just give it to the South Side Community Park?" I asked.

The Mayor reminded me that the park had not been officially named.

Although South Side Community League officers objected, the park was named Optimist Park for the donors of a set of backyard swings which somehow lasted until the government funds remodeled the park and paid for an expensive climbing tower. Our original trees continue to flourish and the hackberry trees still bloom in May.

When the extension of the drive north of Sixteenth Street was made, it was not designated as a continuation of Deming Drive, although Deming had left $10,000 for the project in his will. They named it for the missile which had brought short term prosperity in its wake in 1958. The drive was built with state and federal funds. How soon they forget.

Our saga of Crow Creek and the Deming dream would not be complete without recalling the fervor of the "ecology decade." In 1970 a team of interested engineers and specialists from government agencies made a field survey of Crow Creek and found that sources of pollution were due to returned used water from the railroad, the refinery, the City of Cheyenne and a motel. Numerous substances from fecal coloform and nitrates in the effluent from the city treatment plant, a trailer court and oil from storm drainage sewers to chemicals and litter were found.

Boy Scouts and ordinary citizens got out in the mud and pulled tons of trash from the creek. The League of Women Voters held public meetings to discuss and promote the plan. CEECC, pronounced "seek," a Committee for Environmental Enhancement of Crow Creek was formed to coordinate expert and citizen efforts. The city made flood insurance available through a federal program which could be obtained through private insurers at a nominal fee.

"It's not much of a creek, but it's the only creek we have, and as such a matter of concern to people, no matter in what portion of the city they live," wrote Kirk Knox in his column, "Knocking 'Round," *SunDAY Magazine*, March 28, 1971.

Knox had been a member of the League of Women Voters' public discussion panel. The question he raised was whether or not it was wise to spend $17,000 or a substantial portion of it just for planning. He reported that Ed Francis, a rancher west of Cheyenne, proposed spending the entire $20,000 directly on Crow Creek improvement, instead of the planning expenditure. Francis pointed out that it may not be necessary to buy the study; services are already available at three levels of governmental agencies already on the payroll.

"One hears, 'This is the way federal projects work. You have a planning study and then you go back and ask for monies with which to implement it.' That generally is true," wrote Knox. "It may not always be the best way to approach a matter."

Knox thought that this could be one instance where interested lay people had a better idea. He cited the example of one concerned citizen, William C. Deming, a former publisher of the *Tribune*, "whose intentions somehow became sidetracked. He willed $10,000 to the city for the improvement of Crow Creek. That sum, with accrued interest now has brought it to $15,121 still reposes in a local depository."

"The present City Council is in no way to blame for that," he wrote, "or its predecessor, or even the one before that. But somewhere along the line was a council which should have put the money to wise use to do whatever that amount would then have done to make Crow Creek better."

"Maybe, in some minor way, that proves that plans are nice, but accomplishment is a lot better." *Supplement Sunday, Wyoming Tribune-Eagle*, March 28, 1971.

The City Engineer's office signed a contract with the Model Cities Program for $20,000 to be used for Crow Creek. The plans by the firm of Ware, Lewis and Eaton; architects, engineers and designers, were reminiscent of the DeBoer plans with small parks, plantings and recreational areas along the course of the creek through the city. There is no evidence that the DeBoer plans were consulted. In fact, they cannot be found.

Sunset Park on the east bank of Crow Creek, north of Sixteenth Street had recently been improved so the City Council was of the opinion that the conditions of the Deming will had been met. The costly Crow Creek

Feasibility Study was never implemented, although there was a weed program with young people cleaning the creek bed. Public interest waned.

Things are back to normal. Beer cases are tossed into the creek, chemicals spill and drain into the weedy bank. High water washes out crossings and more businesses are planned for the flood plain.

The best laid plans of mice and men are left to gather dust in some obscure storage bin until they are carted off to make room for more plans. "Men may come and men may go," but Crow Creek will be here when we are gone.

EARLY INHABITANTS

Although there were no parks on the South Side before the twenties, the generations of Cheyenne children had their own enchanted place to play at Initial Cliff on the south side of Crow Creek. The soft sandstone could be dug into for "caves," handholds for climbing, and adventure on their very own mountain. They found arrowheads and imagined Indians sneaking up on their forts and treehouses.

Anna Ekstrom McBee and Geraldine Galloway Kirkbride treasured arrowheads found here as children. Mrs. Kirkbride also found them in her garden, when she lived on the hill above the cliff and the creek. The Hayward children, James and Edward, too, found artifacts in the late forties and fifties around their home nearby.

Artifacts of red jasper, agate, flint and schist, as well as prized black obsidian have been found in the area. Obsidian, the volcanic glass, was so desireable that it found its way, through trade, as far as the Ohio burial mounds. Ernest Logan's interest in artifacts as a boy led him to operate an Indian and Curio store on Capitol Avenue from 1892 to 1932.

In the fifties, a delegation of South Siders pleaded with a concrete block operator not to deface the cliff with his proposed new plant. He built it somewhere else. They merely postponed its destruction.

A contractor, cleaning cinders out of the railroad yards, disposed of them down the "Devil's Slide." Highway construction and motorcyclists took further toll of the little cliff. A tourist attraction, "Hell on Wheels" was situated at its base for a time. There are those who believe the cliff could still be reclaimed and beautiful again.

The Indians of history came upon the Great Plains from the north and east in the mid-1700s. At that time few of them had horses. They raided the Shoshoni tribes who had brought horses with them from the Great Basin. Horse stealing was a matter of survival and status.

According to Virginia Trenholm's account of the Arapahoe migration to the Great Plains, those who remained behind, said that their people had taken the "Buffalo Road."

The Crow, Cheyenne, Arapahoe, Grós Ventre and Ogallala Sioux moved freely over the plains until the migrations of the white man, the coming of the Great Father's soldiers, the telegraph and the railroad.

Interstate 80 runs its course through Cheyenne on the bluff, called "Denver Hill," above Crow Creek and Initial Cliff. New regulations require that prehistoric sites, encountered in laying out new highways be investigated, evaluated and recorded or preserved, before construction can begin.

Two pre-historic sites were found on the Lummis ranch, traversed by this route, southeast of Cheyenne. The first one to be excavated by the Cheyenne Chapter of the Wyoming Archeological Society was in the east-bound lane, about a half-mile east of Avenue C (South Morrie) underpass.

This site was found to be contemporary with the middle occupation level of the second site. How much pre-historical material was lost when the topsoil was stripped is unknown. In the near hillside, one-and-a-half-foot boulders can be found. One can speculate that the creek ran at a much higher level in that archaic time.

Dr. George C. Frison, who instructed the group in the procedures of the dig, estimated the pottery fragments found in the most recent level to be from circa 750 - 1250 A.D. Three lower levels are judged to be from the Middle Prehistoric period before the bow, arrow and pottery were in use. This site is located at a point under the College Drive overpass in the westbound lane of Interstate 80.

An account of the archeological dig, which first appeared in *The Highwayman*, a publication of the Wyoming Highway Department, concluded that these people, whose grinding stones were found, in spite of their primarily vegetarian diet of roots and seeds, were not farmers. They used the "atlatl," a throwing stick with a projectile point, to bring down game. After 500 A.D. the bow and arrow made the Late Pre-Historic people more efficient hunters.

John P. Albanese, a Casper, Wyoming, geologist, said, "Archeological sites as extensive as the one in Cheyenne are fast disappearing due to modern impact and development. It is unfortunate that no serious attempts are being made to preserve some of them for posterity. People living several hundred years from now will look back and wonder why we were so thoughtless."

Many of the sites throughout the Great Plains indicate that these people probably practiced a sort of cyclical nomadism of small groups, or perhaps, an extended family of a dozen to a score; seasonally returning, intermittently, to previous campsites. These forager people used grinding stones to prepare the seeds and grains for food. They followed the harvest to higher elevations where they gathered piñon, returning to the plains to winter.

The mystery is what happened to the plains people between the Late Pre-Historic period and the coming of the new Indians? Perhaps local archeological searches will complete the story of early man on the Great Plains and our own High Plains.

I hold a small, translucent, agate arrow-point in my hand, a tiny, polished sculpture made by a primitive man. It is a sharp, well-balanced, lethal missile.

Who will find our artifacts?

EARLY INHABITANTS OF CROW CREEK VALLEY USED THESE TOOLS

The two radiocarbon dates from the Lummis site are as follows:

Date	**Lab No.**
1080 ± 180 (A.D. 870)	RL-453
1130 ± 110 (A.D. 820)	RL-472

In association with these radiocarbon samples were several pottery sherds that may be of Woodland origin. The diagnostic points are small and corner notched (see Fig. 1). An earlier component is undated but is probably Late Archaic in age or between 1500 and about 2000 years ago. The projectile points here are larger and of different style (see Fig. 1). Common also at the site were grinding stone materials suggesting plant food use.

Fig. 1. Lummis site. Woodland.

Fig. 2. Lummis site. Late Archaic.

PHOTOS COURTESY OF DR. GEORGE C. FRISON, HEAD OF DEPT. OF ANTHROPOLOGY, UNIV. OF WYOMING

Fig. 2. Lummis site. Flat grinder and mano stone.

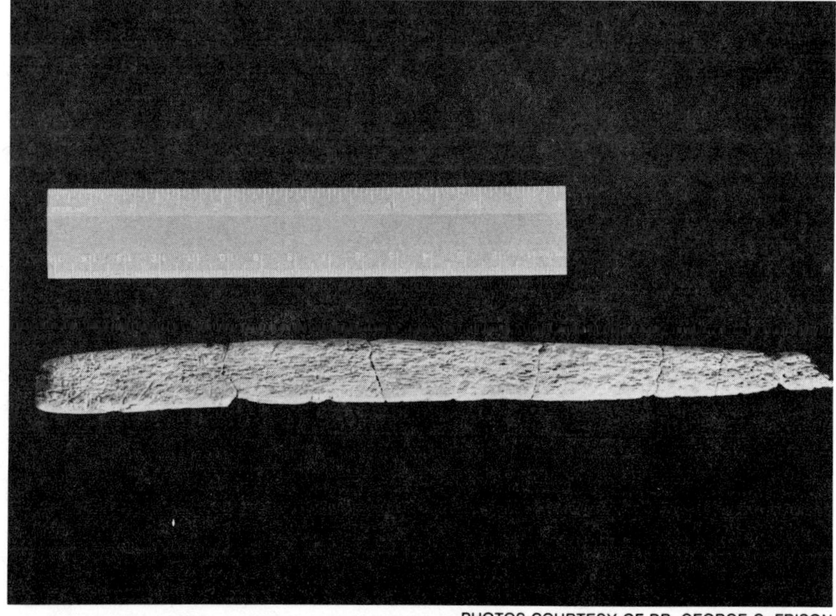

PHOTOS COURTESY OF DR. GEORGE C. FRISON

Fig. 4. Lummis site. Unidentified bone object.

Fig. 5. Lummis site. Mano stones.

PHOTOS COURTESY OF DR. GEORGE C. FRISON

Fig. 6. Lummis site. Ceramic sherds.

TO CROW CREEK

by Gladys Jones

Creek that once ran thick with boulders
Grinding dust to make a prairie,
Hardly wets a bird's tongue singing.

Snows were deep upon your mountains,
Then, your song rose to the heavens,
Then your trout leaped high and higher.

Then your iris sparkled dewy,
And you lingered by your mosses,
Blessing the rose and columbine.

Now your willows weep with oil slick,
Now your sedges and your grasses
Drink a potion from the sludges.

Drink a potion to your killer,
Drink to man (a potion fatal)
For he who kills you, kills himself.

BIBLIOGRAPHY

BOOKS AND PAMPHLETS:

By-Laws of the Railway Employees Building and Loan Association, Cheyenne, 1901.

Centennial Historic Committee; *Magic City of the Plains*, Cheyenne, 1967.

Cazier, Lola. *Surveys and Surveyors of the Public Domain, 1785 - 1975*, United States Bureau of Land Management, Department of Interior, United States Government Printing Office.

Compilation of Records of Surface Waters of the United States, Geological Survey Water Supply Paper #1310 and #1730.

Crist, Marvin A. and Marlin E. Lowry. *Ground Water Resources of Laramie County*, Geological Survey Water Supply Paper #1834, 1965.

Dodge, Grenville Mellen. *How We Built the Union Pacific Railway*, Monarch Press, Council Bluffs; reprint, Old Army Press, Ft. Collins.

Faculty of the University of Wyoming. *In Memoriam: Grace Raymond Hebard*, 1936.

Irwin, Marie H. *Wyoming Blue Book*, Vols. I & II, Wyoming State Archives, Museums and Historical Department, Cheyenne, 1974. Edited by Virginia Trenholm. *Wyoming Blue Book*, Vol. III, Virginia Trenholm, Wyoming State Archives, Museums and Historical Department, Cheyenne, 1974.

Larson, T. A. *History of Wyoming*, University of Nebraska Press, Lincoln, 1965.

McGovern, George and Guttridge, Leonard. *Colorado Coalfield War*, Houghton-Mifflin, Boston.

Neimuth, Gregory G. *Laramie County Community College, The First Ten Years*, 1978.

Polk, R. L. *City of Cheyenne Directory, 1922*, Kansas City.

Reps, John W. *Cities of the American West*, Princeton, 1978, Princeton University Press.

Sawtiel and Burnett. *First Cheyenne Directory*, 1867.

Simonin, Louis L. *The Rocky Mountain West*, Translated and Anotated by Wilson O. Clough, University of Nebraska Press, Lincoln, 1961.

Wade, Mason; Editor. *The Journals of Francis Parkman, Vol. II*, Eyre Spottiswoode, London.

Wedel, Waldo. *Prehistoric Man on the Great Plains*, University of Oklahoma Press, Norman, 1961.

GOVERNMENT REPORTS, DOCUMENTS; PEOPLE AND PLANNING:

Agricultural Statistics, Wyoming, United States Department of Agriculture, 1923-1928.

Annual Reports, Comptroller of the Currency, United States Treasury Department, United States Government Printing Office.

Annual Reports, School District Number One, Cheyenne, Wyoming, 1919-1928.

Census, 1980, Tape STFIA, Printout, Cheyenne Division, Bureau of the Census. *Statistical Abstract of the United States, National Data Book and Guide to Sources*, United States Department of Commerce, Bureau of the Census, 1879-1970, United States Government Printing Office.

Cheyenne Area Development Plan, Cheyenne-Laramie County Regional Planning Office, 1982.

Design Team Report, Cheyenne Interstate Spur, I-180, Wyoming State Highway Department.

Draft, Laramie County Comprehensive Land Use Plan, Laramie County Planning Advisory Committee, Cheyenne-Laramie County Regional Planning Office, 1981.

South Side Area Study, Cheyenne-Laramie County Regional Planning Office, 1981.

Statewide Land Use Planning Program for Wyoming, Vols. I & II, Wyoming Conservation and Land Use Study Commission, 1974.

GOVERNMENT REPORTS, DOCUMENTS; ENVIRONMENT:

Crow Creek, Vol. II, United States Army Corps of Engineers, Cheyenne, Wyoming, 1970.

Crow Creek Feasibility Study, Ware, Lewis and Eaton, Cheyenne, Wyoming 1971.

Letter re: Crow Creek Feasibility Study, Floyd A. Bishop, State Engineer to Peter L. Inniss, Urban Designer and Environmental Planner, Department of Model Cities, August 24, 1971.

Department of Environmental Quality Rules and Regulations, 1982, Land Quality Division, Wyoming.

Engineering Report, VTN, Wyoming, S. Dennis Dawson, October 1, 1974. (Genesis Project)

Genesis Project, The, Regional Solid Waste Management Plan, Grant L008045, 1974.

South Cheyenne Gravel Pits Genesis Project, Environmental Impact Report, Peter L. Inniss, September, 1974, Cheyenne, Wyoming.

Public Law 94-580, *Resource and Recovery Act of 1976, Amendment to Solid Waste Disposal Act*. United States Government Printing Office, Washington, D.C.

Report: *Solid Waste Management Study*, Cheyenne-Laramie County Regional Planning Office, Cheyenne, Wyoming, 1982.

Solid Waste Rules and Regulations, 1975, Wyoming Department of Environmental Quality, Cheyenne, Wyoming.

Wyoming Environmental Quality Act, 1973, Chap. 9.1, Sec. 35-502.1 — 35-502.56.

Wyoming Public Health and Safety Law, Sec. 35-10-101 through 35-10-107, 1945.

Water Rights Compilation; Crow Creek, Office of Wyoming State Engineer, Cheyenne, Wyoming.

201 Waste Water Study, Cheyenne-Laramie County Regional Planning Office, Cheyenne, Wyoming.

DOCUMENTS:

J. W. Snyder. *Report of the Wyoming State Treasurer*, November 30, 1924.

Water Right Number 34, Office of the Wyoming State Engineer, Cheyenne, Wyoming.

Letter: Blue Cross & Blue Shield to Members of the South Side Community League, October 2, 1952.

MANUSCRIPTS:

Cheyenne Refinery, Husky Oil Company, Cody, Wyoming, 1982.

Lewis and Lu Wanda Ashe. *Cheyenne City Records*, Works Progress Administration Manuscript #233, Wyoming State Archives, Museums and Historical Department.

Emerson, Dr. Paul V. *Paper on the Disposal of Sewage*, Cheyenne, Wyoming, June 3, 1952.

William J. McInerney. "History Notes, Downtown Parking Lot," Unpublished Manuscript, 1975.

PERIODICALS:

Buckley, James; Editor. *Wyoming Weekly Labor Journal*, Bound copies, 1922-23, AFL-CIO office, Cheyenne, Wyoming.

Farnham, Wallace D. "Grenville Dodge and the Union Pacific, A Study in Historic Legends," *Journal of American History,* Vol. LI:4, March, 1965.

Fischer, David Hackett. "Chronic Inflation: The Long View," *Journal of the Institute of Socioeconomic Studies*, Vol. V: Number 3, Autumn 1980.

"History of Ft. F. E. Warren," *Annals of Wyoming*, Vol. 18, No. 1, January, 1946, Wyoming State Archives, Museums and Historical Department.

Huntoon, Peter W. "The National Bank Failures in Wyoming," *Annals of Wyoming*, Vol. 54, No. 2, Fall 1982, Wyoming State Archives, Museums and Historical Department.

MICROFILM:

WYOMING STATE ARCHIVES, MUSEUMS AND HISTORICAL DEPARTMENT

City Council Minutes, # MAH 989; September 5, 1923 to December 3, 1940, City Clerk and Treasurer of Cheyenne.

Cheyenne Daily Leader, 1919 to 1921; March 1, 1922 to January 3, 1922, (weather).

Wyoming State Tribune — Cheyenne State Leader, 1921-1929, "Bank Accounting," February 20-21, 1926.

Wyoming State Tribune, 1930-1959.

Wyoming Eagle, 1944-1959.

CLIPPING BOOKS:

Author, 1944 — present.

INTERVIEWS:

Shirley Wittler, State Treasurer, September, 1981.

Dwight Bonham, State Examiner, August 29, 1981.

Lowell Burns, Director, United States Department of Commerce, 1981.

MAPS:

1. 1910, R. L. Polk, *Cheyenne City Directory Map*, (showing Clear Creek)
2. 1919, R. L. Polk, *Jones Map of Cheyenne*, (showing subdivisions and Clear Creek)
3. 1926, *No Name Ditch*, Division Engineer's Office, Union Pacific Railroad, Cheyenne, Wyoming.
4. November, 1870, *Surveys of Cheyenne and U.S. Military Reservation*, United States Surveyor General's Office, signed by Clyde W. Atherly, E. Johnson Abstract.
5. a,b,c, *Sewage Outfalls on Crow Creek*, 1928.
6. a,b, *Crow Creek Parkway Improvements*, CWA Program, Cheyenne, Wyoming, (showing present channel), April 1, 1934.
7. a,b,c,d, *Crow Creek Valley Improvement*, Creek Channel, Archives, 688.
8. *Ft. Francis E. Warren Military Reservation Survey*, Section No. 1, *Proposed Crow Creek Drive*, (showing outfall), July 3, 1935.
9. February 1938, *Showing Ownership of Property, from Union Pacific Bridge to Tenth Street.*
10. Marlin E. Lowry, *Geologic Map of Laramie County*, Plate 1, Water Supply Paper #1834, United States Department of Interior, Geologic Survey, 1965.

MAPS, CONTINUED:

11. Marvin A. Crist, *Hydrologic Map of Laramie County*, Plate 2, Water Supply Paper #1834, United States Department of the Interior.
12. *Land Use Management Maps*, Draft, *Laramie County Land Use Plan*, Cheyenne-Laramie County Regional Planning Office, Cheyenne, Wyoming, November 1981.
13. *Desired Land Use Maps, Cheyenne Area Development Plan*, Cheyenne-Laramie County Regional Planning Office, Cheyenne, Wyoming, 1982.
14. *South Side Area Study*, Cheyenne-Laramie County Regional Planning Office, Cheyenne, Wyoming, December 28, 1981.
15. *Cheyenne Irrigated Gardens*, October 1923, T. H. Baldwin, Engineer.
16. *Clearview Tracts*, February 1931, T. H. Baldwin, Engineer.
17. *City of Cheyenne and Adjacent Additions*, 1942, copyright W. C. Hoskins.

INDEX